# TANTRIC ART OF ORISSA

# TANTRIC ART OF ORISSA

# TANTRIC ART OF ORISSA

By
**Jitamitra Prasad Singh Deo**

KALPAZ

ISBN : 978-81-783-5041-7

First Published, 2018

*Published by*

Kalpaz Publications
C-30, Satyawati Nagar,
Delhi – 110052
Ph.: 011-47034999, 9811692060
www.kalpazpublications.com
E-mail: kalpaz@hotmail.com

*Printed at:* G. Print Process, Delhi

*Dedicated at the sacred feet of the Great Mother Maa Kāli*

Author

# Contents

# Abbreviations

| | |
|---|---|
| E.I. | *Epigraphia Indica* |
| O.H.R.J. | *The Orissa Historical Research Journal* |

# Preface

Tāntric tradition of India has a long history and is commonly much misunderstood. Its literatures and traditions are vast. Much have been destroyed, but among the surviving literatures, "Mahānirvana Tantra," is the most important of all the Tantras, that are to be found now. In the present form, its text is not much earlier than the 18th century A.D. and it is full with Vedantic elements, but there are reasons to show that the text had an older form. As the name of text shows, its earlier versons were utilised by the Buddhists. Subsequently Vedantic ideas were introduced or interpolated and fashioned in such a way that it appeals the Vedic alias Hindu taste.

According to Mahānirvana Tantra, the twice-born, vitiated by the impurities of Kali, will not make any distinction between what is holy and unholy. So, they will not acquire Salvation through works laid down in the Vedas. Under these circumstance Sruitis and Saṁhitas will not lead to the Well-being of Mankind. I tell you truly, O dear, there is no other road in Kali but Agama. I have described in the Vedas, Smritis and Purāṇas that in the Kali-Yuga the worshippers will worship the Deities through Tāntric rites.

Further in Chapter VIII, Sloka 98, of Mahānirvana Tantra, Tirṭhas alias Holy sites of the Kali Yuga are mentioned and stated that the river Gaṅges and the Mahāṇadi are the residence of the Spiritual guide and the celebrated Shrines, these are the Tirṭhas or the Holy places of pilgrimage in the Kali Yuga. Literarily Mahāṇadi means a great river. Here it refers to a river of that name falling into the Bay of Bengal. The enumeration of these rivers show that the cultivation of the Tantras were chiefly confined in present day Orissa and Bengal provinces of India.

The river valleys are the net product of the action of rivers. The major river valleys of Orissa are associated with the Brahmani, the Mahāṇadi and the Vamsadhara. Mahāṇadi is the most major river which present an undulating topography. Mahāṇadi river starts from hilly area of Sihawa in the south-east of Raipur district in Madhya Pradesh and flows through Orissa to meet Bay of Bengal at Paradeep. It forms the main water source and in rainy season, the stream varies in breadth from one to two miles. Its bed is rich in precious stones.

This Mahāṇadi river is known as Citrotpalā also, which is a name given to a portion of the Mahāṇadi between two holy places Śrī Rajiblochan Kshetra (i.e. modern Rajim in Raipur district) and Subarnapura (i.e. Sonepur) in Orissa. This river is mentioned as Citrotpalā in the Mahābhārata, Mārkaṇḍeya purāṇa, Brahmāṇda purāṇa, Kūrma purāṇa, Vāmana purāṇa and Padma purāṇa. There is description of Mahāṇadi in Skanda purāṇa also. A reference of Mahāṇadi is found in Ptolemy's work of 2nd century A.D.

In Proto-historic period State formation took place in this Mahāṇadi river valley. Utkala state occupied the coastal northern portion of this river, in the coastal southern portion; Kaliṅga state developed and the whole upper Mahāṇadi valley comprised the Kōśala state, which came to be known as South Kōśala by Scholars, only to differentiate it with North Kōśala. The history and culture of the whole Mahāṇadi valley is very ancient, where much refinement of Tantra took place. Though the Yoga of Sexual transformation had Vedic origin, it was forgotten and re-discovered through Hatha Yoga practice of V A J R O L I and developed by the Yogis of Mattamayura Śaivism and Yogi Matseyendranāth, who was born in Chandbali – Dhamra area of coastal Orissa. Yogi Matseyendranāth was the founder father of Nāthism and Yogini Cult in India. So, it can be claimed that Orissa has gifted much to the development of Tāntricism. There was movement of Mattamayura Śaivism, which was Tāntric Śaivism throughout the length and breadth of Mahāṇadi river valley.

Temple architecture in Orissa developed with Tāntric influence and therefore the most Sensuous erotic figures, sculptures and arts are found in Orissa and Khajuraho in Madhya Pradesh, where the human body vibrates with tremendous nest and desire. The summom-bonum of desire is Salvation, Nirvana or Mukti as variously called or known. Vajroli practice of Tantra leads an individual from Sex to Super-consciousness or Samadhi.

This aspect of Sexual transformation is not popularly known and people abuse the erotic arts without knowing its significance. Therefore the author's friend, philosopher and guide Śrī Nrusingha Prasad Tripathi asked the author to write a book named *Tāntric Art of Orissa*, for which he was bear – a –hand in giving all assistance to the author. Therefore the author is much indebted to him. The author is thankful to Śrī

Sadananda Agrawal of Menda, for doing the diacritical correction of the manuscript. The author expresses gratitude to authors and Scholars from whose works, extensive materials have been used, for writing this Book and is thankful to ....... for taking up the publication of this writing.

The author's wife Smt. Rajshree Devi needs reverence, because without her co-operation, this study couldn't have seen its completion.

*Khariar*
*2001*

**JITAMITRA PRASAD SINGH DEO**

# Introduction

Orissa consists portions of three ancient regions of Kaliṅga, Utkala and South Kōśala. In course of centuries due to Cultural, Social, Political and Economic factors these areas came together and formed the Province of Orissa in India. Orissa is and has been the seat of Tāntric culture, art and philosophy at all times. The type of Vaiṣṇavism that is prevalent in Orissa is inbedded in the highest form of the Tāntric way of life and thought, namely the much misunderstood and much abused "Kaulācāra," of a carefully thought-out way of life for the adept, who has achieved a balanced equilibrium of the conflicts facing man in the multifarious departments of existence and behaviour.

The Tāntric method of Sādhanā was in existence in essence from very ancient times and was in vogue widely in all parts of India and its doctrines and percepts even gained circulation beyond the Seas and behind the frontiers. This will be evident from the fact that the old Tantras divide Tāntric World into three main regions viz: Viṣṇukrānta (a region extending from the Vindhyas upto Chattla), Asvakranta (a region extending from the Vindhyas to Mahācina and Nepal) and Rathakrānta (from the Vindhyas to the great ocean including Kamboja and Java).

More detailed description of the countries where Tantras spread is obtainable from some Tāntric texts which fix the zones according to two different Tāntric modes Kādi and Hādi, which are known as Prakāśa and Vimarśa aspects of Śākti.

The Countries where the Kādi mode of Tantra gained popularity were: Aṅga, Vaṅga, Kaliṅga, Kerala, Kaśmtra, Kāmarūpa, Mahārāṣṭra, Saurāṣṭra, Dravida, Tailiṅga, Malayādri, Karṇāṭa, Avanti, Vaidarbha, Ābhira, Mālavā, Caula, Cula, Kamboja, Videha, Bahlika, Kirāta, Kaikaṭa, Airuka, Bhota, Cina, Mahacina, Nepal, Silahatta, Gauḍa, Kōśala, Magadha, Snotkala, Kuntala, Hūna, Kōnkana, Kekaya, Sūrasena, Kaurava Siṁbala, Pulinda, Kaccha, Madra, Sauvira, Lāṭa, Barbara, Matsya and Sindhu.

The Countries in which Hādi mode was in vogue were: Aṅga, Vaṅga, Kaliṅga, Sauviraka, Kaśmira, Kamboja, Saurāṣṭra, Magadha, Mahārāṣṭra, Mālavā, Nepal, Kerala, Cola, Cala, Gauḍa, Malaya, Siṁhala,

Vonka, Vido, Vyonda, Karṇāṭa, Lāṭa, Malata, Panata, Andhaka, Pulindaka, Hūna, Kaura, Gāndhāra, Vidarbha, Videha, Bahlika, Barbara, Kekaya, Kōśala, Kuntala, Kirāta, Sūrasena, Sevdra, Banata, Tonkana, Kankana, Matsya, Madra, Maida, Saindhava, Parsvakika, Dyorjala, Yavana, Jala, Jalandhara, Salva and Sindhu.

In these two lists of two zones of Tāntric modes Kādi and Hādi, Kaliṅga and Kōśala are found. Kaliṅga is well known, but Kōśala, mentioned in these zones, definitely identifies South Kōśala because North Kōśala (i.e. Ayodhya) by 5th century B.C. had divided itself into many Gaṇa States like Sākya Gaṇa, Koliya Gaṇa, Moriya Gaṇa and Malla Gaṇa. As by 5th or 6th century A.D. Tantra as a distinctive philosophical or religious concept came into practice in India, the Kōśala mentioned in the above two lists definitely identify South Kōśala State of ancient and medieval India, comprising the upper Mahāṇadi valley.

Jājpur, Bhubaneswar and Puri were important centres of Tāntric Cult in Orissa. Purușhottam Puri still continues and will continue as a Great Tāntric piṭha for ever, as dealt in this work. Jājpur, situated on the bank of river Vaitaraṇi was an old and prominent seat of Tāntric Cult. Its history is traceable since the days of the Mahābhārata when it was a sacred place of pilgrimage. This site is known as Nāvi Gaya in Viṣṇu purāṇa. Kapila Saṁhita and Brahma purāṇa speak about the sanctity of this place. The presiding Deity of this place is Virajā, which is mentioned as one of the Śākti siddha piṭha (centre) in Kubjika tantra, Jnānārṇava tantra, Brahma Nila tantra, Aṣṭādaśa pīṭhas of Saṅkarācārya and Piṭhanirnaya. Jājpur is famous as Virajā Kṣetra (site).

The Religious history of Orissa is cosmopolitan in thought, practice and action. The Pañcadevatās like Śākti, Śiva, Sūrya, Gaṇapati and Viṣṇu are worshipped in their five pīṭhas in Jājpur, Bhubaneswar, Koṇārka, Mahāvināyaka (Chandikhola) and Puri. In spite of varieties of Gods and Goddess, Śākti worship continued in its Tāntric form and is still continuing in Orissa. So, Tāntric worship and Tāntric Art flourished in Orissa from about 6th/7th century A.D and is still continuing. Tāntrism, which became a determining religious force in early medieval period brought about a renaissance in art, architecture, culture and introduced new Gods and Goddesses with different iconographic features. The best form of art in Orissa are Tāntric Art.

Bhubaneswar is known as Ekāmra Kheṭra in Ekāmra purāṇa, Ekāmra Candrikā, Kapila Saṁhita, Tirṭha Cintāmaṇi of Vacaspati Misra and Svarnādri Mahodaya. It is mentioned as Śākti pīṭha in Nāmostottarasata and Brahma Nila Tantra. Tāntric relics, sculptures and temples are plenty at Bhubaneswar.

Many Tāntric texts like Devi purāṇa, Kalika purāṇa, Devi Bhāgabat and Tantra Cuḍāmaṇi mention of Puruṣottama Kseṭra (site) as Pithasthāna of Vimalā, i.e. modern Puri. In this pīṭha of Śāktas, Vimalā was installed as Kṣetraśākti. Even the holy traid, in the temple of Jagannātha are worshipped in Tāntric, Purāṇic and Vaiṣṇavite form till today. Bhāgavata purāṇa (Ch. XI, 27/7) mentions that the best way of worshipping the Lord is the mixed form of worship, both Vedic and Tāntric. The Bhāgavata further notes that those who are desirous of attaining Mokṣa should worship the Lord in both ways, Vedic and Tāntric. It is therefore clear that the mixed worship conducted in Jagannātha temple of Puri is based on authoritive text.

Hevajra Tantra, which is a Buddhist Tantra (composed around 690 A.D.), mentions about four Tāntric piṭhas: Jalandhara, Uḍḍiyāna (Oḍḍiyāna), Pūrṇagiri and Kāmarūpa. In the same work in place of Oḍḍiyāna, the word Uḍra is mentioned where Jagannātha has been described as Bhairava and Katyāyini as Bhairavi.

Jalandhara is situated on the highway connecting Tibet with India, Kāmarūpa is in Assam, otherwise known as Prāgjyotiṣpur. Pūrṇagiri has not yet been identified. Regarding the identification of Uḍḍiyāna (Oḍḍiyāna), lot of controversy are continuing among Scholars. Some identify Uḍḍiyāna (Oḍḍiyāna) with Swat river valley, while others identify with Orissa, where Oḍra as a geographical unit once existed (vide : Sahu, N.K. *Utkal University of Orissa*, Vol. I, 1964). Oḍra was a Viṣaya (district) in the Uttara Tosāli, located in the Yamagarttamaṇḍala, which comprised the areas of Dhenkanal and Talcher. In Copper plate grants of Tuṅga Kings and Somavaṁśī Kings Orḍa and Oḍra names are found. Bṛhan – nilla – tantra also declares that Bhairavi (consort of Jagannātha – Bhairava) is the Goddess of Uḍḍiyāna. In a later Tāntric text like "Śākti Saṅgama Tantra," the compilation of which may be fixed at circa. 7th century A.D. and which is now preserved in the library of the R.A.S.B. (No. 323) in fragments, the second part being Satpanchāsat-desa Vibhāga (G. 9680, foll. 1 B – 3 B) contains the names of Kaliṅga and Utkala. Samohana tantra which was composed before 1450 A.D. mentions names of Kāliṅga, as well as Utkala. Other Tāntric texts also refer to the regions as well as to the celebrated deity Jagannātha.

For a long period it was regarded in Orissa that Jagannātha has been referred to for the first time in "Jnānasiddhi," of Indrabhuti, written in c. 717 A.D. It is a wrong statement or opinion, because, it is known that the title "Jagannātha" has been used in Sanskrit literature "Devi Māhātmya," composed in late Gupta period i.e. 5th century A.D. and added as an integral part of the Mārkaṇdeya purāṇa. The title "Jagannātha

(Lord of the World) itself was unspecific. It was applied for Buddha, for Śiva, for Mahāvira and for Viṣṇu. Its uncompounded varient Jagato – nātha was similarly used for each of these Deities, like "Lokanātha," "Lokeśvara," and "Visvanātha". In Padma purāṇa, Maheśa has been addressed as Jagannātha. Adi Śaṅkarācārya addresses Śiva as "Jagannātha," in his composition "Śiva Bhujangam." Therefore, it is definite that till the composition of "Śiva Bhujangam," Jagannātha was not yet installed as a Deity and the word "Jagannātha," was used for addressing Viṣṇu, Śiva, Gautam Buddha and Mahāvira. In recent years, it has been proved that Śaṅkarācārya during his digvijaya established or recognised one of the icon of Buddha, signifying non-violence and established as "Puruṣottama – Jagannātha Deity," in 9th century A.D. at Puruṣottama Kṣetra Puri.

Rudrayāmala Tantra and Kulārnva Tantra mention about Uḍḍiyāna (Oḍḍiyāna alias Uḍḍiyāna) pīṭha, Kabjikā Tantra names Virajā and Uḍḍiyāna pīṭhas. Jñānarṇava tantra recognises Ekāmra (Bhubaneswar), Virajā, Uḍḍisa (from Prakrit Uḍḍavisa, Oddaisa – Sanskrit Oḍraviṣaya, i.e. Orissa), Jaleśvara (a town in Balasore district) and Oḍḍyāna as pīṭhas. Kālika purāṇa, which was composed within 10th-11th century A.D. and is taken as an authority on Hindu Tantra mentions that first Tāntric pīṭha in India was Uḍḍiyāna where Jagannātha as God and Kātyāyani as Goddess are worshipped. All these facts definitely prove that Uḍḍiyāna signifies modern Orissa, because Lord Puruṣottama – Jagannātha is the presiding Deity of Orissa, whose esoteric worship is associated with Vimala, which proclaims allegiance to Śiva as Bhairava and carried out with Tāntric formulae and formalities till today. So, Orissa is not the land of sentimental Vaṣṇavite effervescence only.

From the name "Uḍḍiśā," signifies the land appertaining to Śiva with epithet of Uḍḍiśā or the flying Deity. This title of the God is given in the "Vaijayanti – Kośa". Uḍḍiśā and Kriyoḍḍiśā Tantras are well known.

It is interesting in the information furnished by the Dakṣiṇācāra – tantrarāja," that Gauḍa, Kerala and Kaśmira (with Kālika, Tripurā and Tārā as Goddesss, respectively, according to a later account) are the homes of the purer (Dakṣiṇācāra) Sects. Elsewhere (Brihat – Gautamīya Tantra) it is stated that, of Gurus, those coming from the west are the best, those from the south are middling, those from Gauḍa and Kāmarūpa are inferior to the preceding, and those from Kāliṅga are the worst. An amplified description in "Jābāla" (quoted by Vidyādharācārya) puts the Gurus from Madhyadeśa (Aryāvarta), Kurukṣetra, Lāṭa (Naṭa), Koṅkaṇa, Antarvedi Pratiṣthāna and Avanti at the top, those from Gauḍa, Salva, Sūra (?), Magadha, Kerala, Kōśala and Daśārna in the middle, and those hailing from Karṇāṭa and the banks of the Narmadā, the Revā and Kachcha, the Kālindas, the Kambalas (or Kalambas) and the Kambojas (probably in Assam) at the bottom of the scale. The "Kulālikāmnāya," mentions five celebrated seats of Tāntric cult in different parts of the Country, namely Oḍiyāna, Jāla (Jālandhara), Pūrṇa (- giri), Matanga (Śriśaila) and Kāmākhya, in the "Sādhanāmāla," the four celebrated Tāntric pīṭhas are Kāmākhya, Sirihaṭṭa (with Arbuda or Jalandhara replacing Sirihaṭṭa in some texts), Pūrṇagiri and Uḍḍiyāna.

As already observed Uḍḍiyāna is identified with Mahāṇadi river valley because the earliest Nataraja image of India with ūrdhvaliṅga (penis erectus), is found at Śripur and the second oldest at Asanapat, practicing Uḍḍiyāna bandha. In Hatha Yoga, Uḍḍiyāna bandha (abdominal retraction lock) means to "to rise up" or "fly". In the practice of Uḍḍiyāna bandha the abdominal organs are pulled up and in creating a natural upward flow of energy, therefore it is often translated as the Stomach lift. These areas for Tāntric Gurus of different grades of excellence and these Tāntric centes, throw an interesting light on the diffusion of the creed and the probable place of its origin. From about the tenth century A.D. a composite Tantra, drawing materials from Brāhmanic, Buddhistic and Nāthist circles, grew up, and some Deities, Adepts, Cults and practices became common to all of them, though the traditions did not always tally among the different communities and localities.

Among the composite Tantra, Jagannātha Cult sprang up within 9th-10th century A.D. and has become very popular.

With this background of Tantra, this Book name *Tāntric Art of Orissa*, is written, because the study of Tantra in Orissa province of India, is still in its infancy.

Definition of Tantra is given in Chapter – I. Sexual transformation is dealt in Chapter – II, which is known as lefthand path or Vāma mārga in Tantra. The science of Tantra has two main branches, which are known as Vāma mārga and Dakṣiṇa mārga. Vāma mārga is the left path which combines sexual life with yoga practices in order to explode the dormant energy centers. Dakṣiṇa mārga is the right path of yoga practices without sexual enactment. In Chapter – III, the historical prospective of Evolution of Tantra in Orissa is narrated. Nāthism is claimed to have been originated in Orissa.

An opinion of Krishna Chandra Panigrahi, in *History of Orissa*, 1981, p. 312, may be quoted here: "During the Bhauma period tracts Maṇdalas, Maṇtras and Japas were widely in use and their prevalence is attested to by the inscriptions on the Buddhist images to be found at Ratnagiri, Udayagiri and Lalitagiri in the Cuttack district: Jājpur and Khadipada in the Bhadrak sub-division (new district). The Khadipada image inscription records the name of the sage Raghula who is said to have been proficient in Maṇḍalas. Though the latter Bhauma rulers became Brāhmanical Hindus, they continued to believe along with the People of Orissa in the efficacy of the Tāntric practices. The next ruling dynasty the Somavaṁśīs, did not favour the Tāntric practices. They were the followers of Śaivism and from the beginning of their rule Śaivism had a period of ascendancy in Orissa. They appear to have discovered Tāntric practices. In the Bhakti Bhāgavata, "of Kavi Ḍiṇḍima Jīvadeva, it is stated that the famous Brāhmin Bhavadeva, who was the family priest of Udyotakeśari and who was also honoured by the family of Someśvara, lifted the World when it was being submerged in the ocean of the Tantras. The Somavaṁśī Kings performed Aśvamedha Yajña at Jajpur, invited the Brāhmins proficient in sacrifices, from outside and built numerous Brāhmanical temples of which the temples of Jagannātha at Puri and of the Liṅgarāja at Bhubaneswar were most prominent."

This view of learned Scholar that "Somavaṁśīs, did not favour the Tāntric practices, "can't be accepted. As dealt in Chapter III of this work, Tāntricism was in full swing during Somavaṁśī period and it was the period of Religious eclecticism. There was a Religious revolution in Mahānadi valley in 10th century A.D. and finally, the instalment of Jagannātha as the presiding Deity of Puruṣottama Ketra, i.e., Puri, by Somavaṁśī King Yayāti – I, immortalised Jagannātha as Puruṣottama – Jagannātha. Lord Jagannātha is worshiped by Tāntric rituals and no power on earth can stop it.

By taking one instance of the literature "Bhakti Bhāgavata," of Kavi Ḍiṇḍima Jivadeva, K.C. Panigrahi has given this opinion, which seems to be very nary observation. The statement of Kavi Ḍiṇḍima Jivadeva shows that he was a follower of Bhakti Vaiṣṇav path and didn't like Tāntric practices. Most probably the most popular and famous words "Vimalā Bhairavi yatra Jagannāthastubharivaḥ," of Tantra Cūḍāmaṇi was not yet composed, when Kavi Ḍiṇḍima Jīvadeva wrote "Bhakti Bhāgavata".

With the purview of Tantra, gradually Buddhism was observed into Jagannātha Cult and this revitalizing of Vedic culture took place in Orissa province.

Chapter – IV deals with Tāntric Art of Orissa, which is very much misunderstood.

In Chapter – V, it has been dealt that the Yoga of Sexual transformation yoga was re-discovered in Mahāṇadi river valley, i.e., Orissa province and it is the land of KĀMAKALĀ.

CHAPTER I

# Definition of Tantra

The Sanskrit word 'TANTRA', is derived in the 'Kāśikā-vṛitti' from the root 'Tan,' to spread. The evolution of human knowledge has spread through imitative, repetitive, derivative, educative and intuitive knowledges. Through intuitive TOGIC process Mankind has achieved different Samādhis, which are generally known as Sabikslpa Samādhi and Nirvikalpa Samādhi. By spreading or progressing through Tantra practice, one can achieve Nirvikalpa Samādhi, which is the Summom Bonum of human achievement (Vide : Appendix – I).

Tantra is a branch of knowledge which offers a systematic and scientific method by which high Spiritual powers can be achieved in human life for realisation of the Self that leads one to the path of Salvation.

The exact origin of Tantra is lost in mysterious antiquity. The chief peculiarity of the Tantras is the prominence they give to the Female energy of the Deity. Śākti (KĀLI) of the Śākti cult is the Mother or the Supreme Being. Similarly, Śiva of the Śiva Cult is the father or the Supreme Being. The Tantras attempt to blend these two concepts, the motherhood and the fatherhood of God.

The earliest antiquity of Śākti are the Ring – stones of Stone age. They can be taken as Cakra and Yantra of the Śāktas in historical period.

In proto-historic period Yonis and Liṅgas are found. One stone YONI has been discovered at Maraguda valley, situated in Nuapada district of Orissa, in 1982. The YONI is chiseled on quartzite stone and is of ferruginous colour. It measures 23 cm. in circumference. Another YONI is discovered from Soseng village, situated on the Sunabeda plateau of Nuapada district. Because of human vandalism, the central portion of the YONI is damaged. These findings have similarity with objects discovered at Mohenjodaro, which have their upper and lower surfaces undulating, while in some others the lower surface is flat, but the upper one takes a quartre – foil form. The YONI is the female organ of generation symbolizing motherhood and fecundity. The worship of the Liṅga of the great God Śiva originated from the conception of the God as the father or procreator. But in the matter of the procreation of beings the YONI (pudendum muliebre) of the Mother Goddess should naturally be regarded as much important as the Liṅga of the father God. Both the father God and the mother Goddess were worshipped by the ancient people of India.

The worship of YONI of the Divine Mother is referred as certain Tirṭhas, containing YONI tanks and YONI mountains in the Mahābhārata, but the worship of YONI is also prescribed in the late medieval Tantra works like "YONI TANTRA," "BṚHADDHARMA" and others. YONI is still worshipped as "DUARSANI," near Boden in Nuapada district and Sindhekela in Balangir district of Orissa.

Vedic background is also found in Tantra. Aspects of Macro-micro cosmic symbolism are found in Rig-veda. The Agnicayana, Rājasūya and Vājapeya rites are mentioned in Śatapatha Brāhmana of Rig-veda. The Agnicayana is still kept alive by the Nambudiri Brāhmins of Kerala and was performed in 1975. The entire ritual was filmed and recorded under the directions of Prof. J.F. Staal, whose illustrated two volumes, "AGNI", provide complete account on all aspects of the 1975 performance of the Agnicayana (the Fire-Altar) ritual.

According to Tantra, every human being is a Temple of God. The Tantric maxim that the body is the epitome of the Universe is the basis of Indian medical science, it rests on the assumption that the elements forming the body cannot be dissociated from environmental elements and that by applying the laws which govern the latter, the former may be brought to order. The happy union between science and art that is patent in the symbolic imagery of the Vedas and the Tantras can never hope to be replaced by the dry exact language of philosophic reasoning, which is like a huge chain forged to bind the World, but which inevitably ends in enmeshing its creator itself.

In philosophy of Tantra, Human being is Divine and only the Divine can worship the Divine or realise the Divine. Tantra emphasies the Motherhood of God. The Eternal and Infinite Brāhman is both the Mother and the Father of the Universe. Tantra holds up the Supreme Deity as the Eternal Mother. God's love for the creation is like Mother's love, deep and pure.

God and the Universe are inseparable. They are one and the same. The Creation is the Divine manifestation. Matter and energy are inseparable and they are also Divine manifestations. The Divine energy constitutes the principal element in religious worship, which is the life-spirit of religion.

Tantras give prominence to the worship of Śākti. It is through the manifestation of the Divine energy in the Universe that the existence of God can be realised. This Energy is Śākti of Tantras. This Cosmic Energy which has created the Universe, governs, upholds and sustains it.

In philosophical terminology Śākti is the kinetic energy of Brahma, while Śiva represents the static aspect of Brahma. It is like heat and fire. The one is inseparable from the other. Goddess Śākti is the fullest conception of Brahma, in all the aspects such as Creator, Preserver and Destroyer of the Universe, with the three *gunas* (qualities) of Sattva, Raja and Tama.

God revealed the Tāntric scripture for the good of humanity through intuition, so that the entire life and energies of mankind might not be taxed in a chaotic state of competitive transformation of the World where poverty and tension of all kinds were harnessed to welcome disease and reduce expectation of life to a quarter of what it should be in sane and normal circumstances.

The Tantras represent the essence of Vedic mysticism in a nutshell, because they concern themselves with the implied portion of the Veda, which was devoted to the esoteric methods of contacting occult powers, assumed by its external literatures, that was developed to act as aids to the memory at a time when ramifications and complexity of ritual began to increase in this field of religious observance. These methods were usually handed down from Master to pupil directly to preserve the continuity of the tradition of the particular branch of the Veda to which they were peculiar and only faint hints about this and the secret doctrines they contained, can be found in the Upanisad texts.

As to the antiquity of the Tantras, they are older than the two Hindu epics, the Rāmāyaṇa and Mahābhārata. In the Rāmāyaṇa of Vālmiki (1/22/15 – 18) there is an episode that Viśāmitra taught the two secret and mystic sciences called "balā," and "atibalā," to Rāma and Lakṣmaṇa. The process of attainment of these two esotoric sciences have been dealt in the Tantra. Similarly Tāntrik terminology and ritualism have been expressly mentioned in Mahābhārata of Vyāsadeva.

Tantras are practical Śāstras and they recognize no distinction of Caste, Creed, Colour or Sex. The sacred scriptures were revealed in the shape of dialogue between Śiva and Pārvati, for the welfare of the people of the fourth cycle of human ages (Kaliyuga), according to "Kulārnava tantra." There are two main classes of the Tantra literatures viz: Āgama and Nigama. While in the Āgama, Pārvati is the enquirer and Lord Śiva is the answerer; in the Nigama, it is just the reverse.

The ipsissima varba of the allegorical utterances of the Tantra śāstra may be quoted for its confirmation. "The Vedas, the Śāstras and the Purāṇas are like a public woman, but the doctrine revealed by Śambhu i.e. the Tantra remains veiled like a chaste house wife." The obvious import of it is that under no circumstances the secret doctrines of the Tantra should be disclosed to the laities.

### Kuṇḍalini

According to Tantra the evolution of the Universe, in the form of a mysterious but very beautiful lotus, expanding to the vitalizing rays of Heaven and having its roots in the depths of the all-pervading waters of all-potentiality, where the Supreme Lord reigns as the mighty serpent of the fundamental abyss with his fiery consort, the subtle manifestation of the Śākti, in Her residual aspect. This symbolism reflects in the microcosm of the mystic meditator and is expressed as the Serpentine energy resting in the fundamental centre, contemplated as a red four-petalled lotus. The symbolism of the lotus, is 'motif' adopted by the 'Kuṇḍalini Mantra Yoga,' the vital centre with the spinal chord.

A human body is an epitome of the cosmic body of 'Puruṣa.' It is an aggregate of innumerable nucleal cells. The finest and subtlest cells constitute the grey matter of the brain and the spinal channel. This grey matter is the vehicle for the flow of vital energy. As energy remains static in the cerebrum with one thousand dynamic potency, the cerebrum is called 'Sahasrara Padma,' (lotus with one thousand petals).

In the "Mahānirvāṇa Tantra," and "Sat – chakra – nirupana," the two famous Hindu tāntric texts the Yogic body model is taught to have six cakras (Centres) or lotuses beginning at the base of the spine and ending in the brain, while some other texts speak of twelve such cakras (Centres). The Buddhist tāntric tradition usually assumes four cakras (Centres) in the Yogic body. Tantra incorporate the Yoga method of Patanjali and the Mantra element of the Atharva Veda.

### Bhāvas

According to Tantras, human beings are divided into three "Bhāvas," or attitudes of Tāntric mysticism. The three attitudes consist of the *Paśu-bhāva*, or the animal attitude in the practice of ritual life, the *Vīra-bhāva*, or the heroic attitude in the pursuit of observance leading to enlightenment and the *Divya-bhāva*, or the Divine attitude towards life, regulated or being regulated for attunement with the Infinite. Thus classified by the observant Preceptor, according to taste, upbringing and Spiritual development, for both Veda and especially the Tantras take great pains to provide the means for the Spiritual uplift of human beings in all classes, categories and stages of advancement, the initiated seeker proceeds along the mysterious path leading to the Gods. The "Paśu," attitude connotes the way of life according to the traditions associated with the Veda and its various restrictions and injunctions. Just as an animal is tied to keep it under control and direct its motions along lines, beneficial to itself and its surroundings, the mystic to be, is kept restricted by various injunctions and observances for Self-discipline, essential for the channelization of powerful instincts and ritual purity, leading to a healthy moral outlook, according to the accepted standards of the community. The "Vīra," attitude signifies the typical attitude of the Hero, who goes out to meet his opponent face to face, instead of shirking the dangerous issue and who loves a good struggles; distinguished by skill and courage. The inclination to passion and indulgence in human beings is faced clearly and squarely here and the conquest of evil is decided by going out to meet it. The initiates of this mode of communion drink deeply of the poisonous cup of the World, as the ugly facts of life are considered to be the necessary gifts of the same power, that grants immortality to Souls dedicated whole-heartedly to Divinity. Fortified in Self dedication to the cause of life and death, the challenge put forth by the heroic pilgrim, as one places one's foot on the path, sharp like a razor, that passes over the ravine of eternal damnation, is as a match against the strength, concupiscence can muster against him, knowing full well that one false step is bound to hurl him down to the regions of boundless misery. One has this consolation, however, that if that individual succeeds in balancing the forces to succeed in negotiating this short cut leading to the realms of light, one is sure to win that golden armour as one's prize, which the adamantine bolt of the King of Heaven even, cannot penetrate. The Divya attitude consists of the complete and uninterrupted absorption of the Soul, chastened into the purity of crystal, in the object of Divine adoration, without giving anytime or opportunity for baser thought and action. Seeing the great Lord in all thought, speech and action, the Divine mystic proceeds through life in the World without being affected by it in any way. This is the highest form of life an initiate wishing to become an inspired mystic can adopt and it is unanimously recommended by all the Tantras. All these three attitudes, recommended for mystics of different temperament, it must be understood, form self-contained systems as well as being cumulative, so that an initiate can either adopt one of these attitudes and remain in it till the attainment of the final fruits of his efforts or can go through all the three stages, ending up with the adoption of the Divine attitude for the final efflorescence of one's inner realisation. Even here the similarity to the three modes of life in the Vedic period is too obvious to escape notice.

## Seven Classes

The Tantras have divided the worshippers mainly into seven classes: Vedācāra, Vaiṣṇavācāra, Śaivācāra, Dakṣiṇācāra, Vāmācāra, Siddhāntācāra and Kaulācāra.

The seven 'Acāras,' or 'Types of observance and behaviour fall within the three 'Bhavas', narrated above. They are known as "Vedācāra", or the rules of conduct prescribed in the Vedas and the traditional injunctions of those who have followed its discipline and gained insight from it in the past, "Vaiṣṇavācāra", or the observance based on the notion of God as pervading everything and the subsequent sense of affection that follows for one's fellow people plus a sense of humanity and devotion to the Lord, manifest as "Viṣṇu", "Śaivācāra", or the conduct based on the conviction of the great Lord being the source of all auspiciousness, cannotes the practice of celebacy, strict non-violence to all creatures, purity of word, deed and thought and the attainment of the grace of Lord Paśupati, the Preceptor of the Universe, bound like an animal in the chain of instinct through Yoga communion and constant meditation, "Dakṣiṇācāra"; or the observances connected with the worship of the Supreme Goddess Durgā or "Dakṣiṇa", or the embodied sacrificial fee (regarded as the wife of Rudra called 'Mṛḍa', the name of which the sacrificial flame is invoked to make the sacrifice complete), without whose favour all rites and sacrifices are devoid of fruitfulness, commonly known as the right hand path, involving purity in all thought and action and meditation accompanied by "japa" of the sacred Word revealed by the Preceptor, after partaking of the remainder of the consecrated "Vijayā" (cannabis sativa) offered as a libation to the Goddess after sunset, "Vamācāra", or the conduct involved in the worship of the Supreme Goddess or Her manifestations as "Vāmā", (the Energy or Consort of Śiva-Vāmadeva, the northern countenance of the five-faced Deity), who is no other than Viṣṇu in the form of "Mohinī", - the Enchantress, popularly known as the left hand path because of the use of the left hand in its ritual, where in consecrated wine, meat, fish, cakes, the assistance of the Wife of the worshipper as the living reflection are the necessary ingredients of worship, demanding great strength of will and disattachment from the sacrificer, "Siddhantācāra", or the practice of the great principle consisting of internal purity, quietism and mystical absorption in Durgā, the Divine Mother of all, in which the initiate assumes the attributes of "Bhairava", and roams about the World at will as his house and lastly "Kaulācāra", the observance of the "Kula --Yogī", who communes perpetually with "Kula-Kuṇḍalini Mahāśakti", presiding over the fundamental Earth – centre of being, whose one aim is union with Heaven once. She is aroused, and who (the Kula-Yogī) is the embodiment of the great Mystery that is immanent in existence as none can tell to what Sect or what rite this type of mystic practices. The Kula-Yogī remains externally like an ordinary man of the World apparently enjoying the boons this World has to give but really one offers up everything to the flaming energy of the Lord who courses as vitality within his being and as such leads the existence of the proverbial lotus leaf which although immersed in water is not touched by it. The first three or these "Ācāras", belong to the followers of the "Paśu", attitude, while "Dakṣiṇācāra", and "Vāmācāra", fall within the "Vīra", or heroic category. "Siddhāntācāra", is a type of "Divya", attitude while "Kaulācāra", lies both within and outside all the "Bhāvas". It should be remembered that like the "Bhāvas," the "Ācāras", may be adopted singly or successively.

As the "Dakṣiṇācāra", and the "Vamācāra", are the two most common practices attributed to Tāntric mysticism a few words on the "Śāstric" origins of these paths of mystic ritual may be mentioned. The five-faced Lord, "Śiva-Pañcānana" has different names for each of His faces, which is turned towards a specific direction. The northern face is called "Vāmadeva", and is composed of ruddy lustre, being the manifestation of the Lord as Viṣṇu, the face turned towards the south is called "Aghora", and is made up of glory coloured deep blue like storm-cloud. This is the aspect of the Lord as Rudra. The western face of the great God is of white lustre and is called "Sadyojāta", being the embodiment of Brahmā, the creator of the Universe. The eastern countenance is known as "Tatpuruṣa", and is made up of golden light. It is the manifestation of Maheśvara as Īśvara. The face facing upwards is composed of rainbow-coloured pearly glory and is called "Īśāna", and is the embodiment of the incorporeal Śiva Himself, who is of the essence of all Deity. The "Mantras," used in the worship of each of these countanences are contained in the Taittīya Araṇyaka of the dark Yajurveda and begin with the names "Sadyojāta", the spontaneously born; "Vāmadeva", the beautiful or crooked Deity, "Aghora", the non-terrific or exceedingly terrific Deity; "Tatpurṣa", that supreme Male, who existed before Time and "Īśāna", the Supreme Lord of all creature and knowledge. It is interesting also to remember that the eastern countenance of the Lord is the embodiment of Sāmaveda, while the southern typifying Atharvaveda. The western and northern faces are Rigveda and Yajurveda incarnate respectively. The upper most countenance – Īśana, is the embodiment of the ineffable Omkara.

Northern and southern faces of the Great God, called "Vāmadeva", and "Aghora", respectively, through which the secret doctrines state that the Scriptures belonging to the "Vamācāra", and the "Dakṣinācāra", were revealed. The "Vāmācāra", is ascribed to the Divine Vāmadeva, who is no other than the Lord as Viṣṇu, the beautiful as well as the crooked God. Please note the popular adage in Sanskrit in this connection, "Devānāṁ Keśavo Dhūrtta." It is important to remember that the first Precepters of these doctrines; in the form of the "Vāmakrama" and the "Cinakrama" are reputed to be the Sages "Dattātreya", and "Buddha", both of whom are considered to be the incarnation of Viṣṇu. The "Daksiṇạcāra", said to originate from the countenance of the Lord called "Aghora", facing south, i.e. the "Dakṣiṇa", direction, is also interesting. This face is the embodiment of the Lord as Rudra and the name "Aghora", is particularly instructive in this respect as it brings out in one epithet the dual attributes of that God (Rudra). "Aghora", is interpreted both as "no ghora," meaning the "non-terrific" or "benign", aspect of that Deity and also as "na ghora yasmāt," signifying "the most terrific." Here the concepts of Life, Death and Regeneration are all concentrated in one Godhead. The God, who grants and sustains life as the all – beneficient, also transforms it through illusory destructions for the ultimate benefit and uplift of the organism so affected, through the process of evolution. In His beneficient aspect Rudra-Aghora is called "Dakṣiṇāmūrti," the embodiment of the sacrificial fee, who grants all Wisdom (Prajñā) and intelligence (Medhā) to His devotees. *The God in His most terrific aspect of "Aghora", is said to have destroyed Cupid (Kamadeva), the seed of creation, by consuming him to ashes at a glance.* He is, hence, resorted to, in this manifestation also, by great ascetics and adepts, who are anxious to overcome passion and all Worldly desire, the control and removal of which lead to inspired vision and wisdom. The sect of the "Aghora-

Śaivas", is separate from this school having links with "Vāmācāra". This form of the Lord is also worshipped to remove all malefic influence and hostile inclusions of planetary and other powers. This is mentioned to make the inclusion of ritual, connected with the counteraction of witch craft and appeasing of incensed planets, deities and powers in the Tantras, appertaining to both the "Vāmācāra," and "Dakṣiṇācāra".

### Tantra Yoga

There are nine kinds of Yoga. They are Jñāna yoga, Raja yoga, Bhakti yoga, Karma yoga, Haṭha yoga, Kuṇḍalini yoga, Tantra yoga, Japa yoga and Laya yoga.

Tantra yoga is a certain mystic process of generating Spiritual energy forces and vibrations within, with the help of Mantra, Yantra and Devata theory, as also of relating these to the forces without, through the symbology of specific sounds, formulas, diagrams and rituals intended to free human being from confinement to the lower nature and raise one to the regions of the higher nature.

### Sādhanā and Worship

Three stages of Sādhanā with five sub-divisions of discipline are accepted in Tāntric sādhanā. The three stages are : SIDDHI (purification), STHITI (illumination) and TARPANA (unification) corresponding to Karma, Bhakti and Jñāna. The five sub-divisions are SNĀNA (ablution), TARPAṆA (gratification), SĀNDHYA (meditation), PŪJĀ (worship) and HOMA (complete Self-abnegation).

Pashyachara sādhanā is Pañcamakāra practice, which is to be viewed with sacred mind and Spiritual approach. Madya (wine), Māṁsa (meat), Matsya (fish), Mudrā (postures of fingers) and Maithuna (sexual act) are not to be taken in their literal senses. The actual meaning of these terms are explained in "Agamasara," thus:-

Madya is the nectarine stream issuing from cavity of the brain which is the abode of the Soul.

Matsya is the suppression of the vital airs.

Māṁsa is the vow of silence.

Mudrā is the inter-weaving of fingers during worship.

Maithuna is meditation on the acts of Creation and destruction.

With efflux of time Tāntric people made goodbye to these moral practice and observed the enjoyment of the panchamakaras in their literally meaning.

In the "Kāmākṣyā Tantra," (5th patala) it is said: "With liquor, meat, fish, mudra and copulation with women, the great Sādhu (Saint) worships the Mother of the Universe."

In Tantra worship the images are based upon the germinal idea of double sexed divinity. This tāntric ideology is the genuine ancient tradition of Hinduism. The most common icon in Hindu temples is the Liṅga (phallic emblem) that displays the male sextual energy as the symbol of Cosmic Divinity. It is conceived as having occupied the "Womb Cell", in the temple, while the outer structure of the temple represents the feminine creative manifestation. The female aspect of the Deity is at the root of Creative activity. So it is Cosmic Śākti as the feminine power, energy that supplies inspiration to the Tāntrics in his Sādhanā. The masculine element, of course, plays its own natural part, but having been buried within the feminine element at final stage.

Control of Seminal fluid is thought to entail control of all passions and the achievement of desirelessness.

Several branches of Tantra like Śakta tantra, Śaiva tantra, Vaiṣhṇav tantra, Buddhist tantra and Jaina tantra developed in India.

## CHAPTER II

# Yoga of Sexual Transformation

According to Haṭha Yogic texts, man and woman represent Śiva and Śākti. These two Śāktis are known as ida and pingala. Ida is Śākti and pingala is Śiva. When they unite in ajna chakra that is the real union. The Seat of Śākti is in mooladhara and the seat of Śiva is in Sahasra cakras of the Kuṇdalini śākti in human body. When Śākti reaches ajna cakra, union takes place. The energy created in ajna cakra moves up to Sahasra cakra. When Śiva and Śakti unite together, Śiva begins to dance and that is the Nataraja aspect of Śiva.

Interaction between man and woman, tantra wise are three purposes —pleasure, procreation and Samādhi.

The subject of Kāma (desire) was taken up precisely with the same care, seriousness and objectivity as that of Dharma and Artha, or as any other technical topic, by the Vedic Risies. Brihadaranyaka upanisada of Sukla Yajur Veda symbolises woman as a medium of sacrifice, her lap as sacrificial altar, her hairs as sacrificial grass, her skin as Soma-Press and copulation as the act of sacrifice. It proclaims a series of rules and advises its followers to observe them unmistakably for a choicable progeny. Auddālaki Śvetaketu; apparently the Vedic Sage, first gave an exposition in five hundred chapters, which Pāñcāla Bābhravya condensed in a hundred and fifty chapters under seven definite sections (Adhikaranas), namely, General princples (Sādhārna), Sexual union (Sāmprayogika), Courtship and Marriage (Kanyāsamprayuktaka), the Wife (Bhrāryādhikārika), Wive of other people (Pāradārika), the Prostitute (Vaiśika) and secret love of extraneous stimulation (Anpaniṣadika). Of these topics, Dattaka, at the request of the Courtesans of Pataliputra, chose the sixth (Vaiśika) as his special subject and his example was followed by Cārāyaṇa, Suvarṇanābha, Ghoṭakamukha, Gonardīya, Goṇikāputra and Kucumāra, each of whom wrote a monograph on one of the remaining subjects in the order given above. In view of the fractional and specialised nature of separate treatises and the difficulty of mastering, Bābhravya's extensive work as a whole, the Śāstra was getting lost and Vātsyāna's professed object was the writing of a comprehensive compendium within a reasonable dimension.

Vātsyayāna's "Kāmasūtra," is the oldest literature surviving in India for pleasure of Sex. In contrast to the ideals of chastity and asceticism, Sex is not opposed to the attainment of the higher goal of Spiritual development.

All the works after Vātsyayāna, are just repetitions, with little variations, changes and additions. On Sexual morality, the physiology and the psychology of Sexual intercourse remain the same at present, as it was from the time immortality.

Dāmodaragupta, author of "Kuṭṭanimata", adorned the Court of Jayāpiḍa Vinayāditya, the King of Karkoṭaka dynasty, who ruled Kashmir circa. 779-810 A.D.

The other works on Erotic literature may be mentioned serially. The "Rati-rahasya," of Kukkoka was composed sometime before 12th century A.D. This work has generally come to be known as "Kukkaka alias Koka śāstra."

The "Nāgāra-sarvasva," of Padmaśrī, was written between the 10th and 14th century A.D. The "Pañcasāyaka," of the Maithili Jyotiriśvara Kaviśekhara was composed in the first half of 14th century A.D. Mahārāja Prandhadevarāya of Vijayanagara (15th century A.D.) composed "Ratiratnapradipika," in seven chapters which is an elaborate treatise on Sexual pleasures. The "Kāmasamūha," of Ananta, discussing almost all aspects of love, was written in 1457 A.D. "Kandarpacūdāmani", of King Virabhadra of the Vaghela dynasty was composed in 1577 A.D. "Anaṅgaraṅga", of Kalyāṇamalla was composed in 16th century A.D. and the "Rati-mañjari", in sixty verses only, of some unknown Jayadeva (different from the author of the Gita-govinda), are almost entirely with the subject of Sexual union (Sāṁprayogika). There are erotic literatures in Oriya language also.

Kavi Samrat Upendra Bhanja of Orissa had written "Pañcasāyaka," where he deals with "Candra-cālana," the erogenous zones of female during different Moon days. The Moon plays a very important role in each Woman's life. Women are said to be nine times more passionate than man. Different erotic center in the female body is awakened on each lunar day. If the Male concentrates his passion on that centre and arouses, then the female's passion will ignite very quickly and the organs will be far more intense. Finger feather touch of the clitoris and vaginal opening will be sufficient for average woman, after all the arousing art, to cause a female to have many oozings. In very rare cases, the erotic zone of female differs. For example, some females are fond of inner vaginal feelings.

The individual who is skillful in erotic art can give greater pleasure to the partner in mundane level. Arousing art for pleasure and tāntric act are same.

In the Tāntric context, the transcendental desire justifies the sexual undertone. Desire creates its objects, as Cosmic desire (Kāma) created the World. Desire multiplies and creates many objects. Withdrawn and being focussed on the Void of ultimate Reality, it becomes a Special inner radiance.

A Tāntric uses Sexual intercourse with a female partner as a mechanism for enhancing enjoyment in the direction of ecstasy, and does not conceive of Sexual intercourse as a quick scurry to orgasm. Control of seminal fluid is thought to entail control of all passions and the achievement of desirelessness.

In the Tāntric tradition, the woman is considered to be higher than the man. Lord Śiva is the first Guru (Master) and founder of Tantra and Yoga. His first disciple was Parvati, his counterpart, wife or Śākti. Sankaracarya wrote in his Tantra text "Ananda Lahiri,": "Without Śakti, how can Śiva create anything?" Śiva is only the silent witness, Śakti is the Creator. Therefore, in Tāntric tradition, the Women is the initiator. From Tantra it is known that Śiva is merely a Shava (a corpse), without Śakti. At the birth of the Cosmos Śakti is the Creator and Śiva is the witness. For practical physical union, "Maithuna," is prescribed in Tantra Yoga.

## Maithuna

Maithuna is not sexual union for pleasure, but it is union for Samādhi, the awakening of Suṣumna, raising the Kuṇdalini from mooladhara cakra and reaching the unconscious areas of the brain. Interplay of the energy is the Cosmic law to a Tāntric Yogi. Therefore, during the practice of physical union some Haṭha Yoga kriyas for the retention of the ejaculation and orgasm are to be practised. The vast energy (bodily fluids secreted at the time of climax) released should be conserved by retaining the bindu. This energy is directed from mooladhara to the higher energy centres by means of Vajroli mudrā, Sahajoli mudrā, Uḍḍiyāna bandha and Moolabandha.

According to Haṭha Yoga Pradipika:

"He who controls the bindu and keeps his own rajas separated through Vajroli is known as a Yogi. His rajas can never be destroyed and in his body the mada merges in the bindu. If in Vajroli the bindu and rajas can be kept separately in one's own body, then by the practice of Yoga, all kinds of Siddhis can be obtained." (This is applicable to female also.)

In usual sexual relationship for pleasure, the man is the active or aggressive partner and woman submits. It is the reverse in Maithuna, the Woman takes the top or leading posture and the man becomes her medium. It is the Woman who initiates.

Haṭha Yoga Pradipika informs:-

"That Woman who is able to keep her rajas above by means of retention of the orgasm is the real Yogini. - - - The practice of Vajroli gives Siddhi to the body – it becomes handsome, smooth, bright and attractive. This is the Divine practice of Yoga that gives liberation through enjoyment."

Vajroli means Spiritual practice of rechannelling Sexual energy, Sahajoli is female equivalent of Vajroli, Uḍḍiyāna bandha means abdominal contraction and Moolabandha means perineal contraction.

All these signifies, to a Tāntric that the vital energy or ojas should not be wasted in sensual enjoyment, because ojas is the unfoldment of the refined consciousness. So in Tantra there is Sexual transformation to different Samādhis.

Kuṇḍalini does not belong to the physical body, even though it is to be searched there, nor in the mental body or in the astral body, in the state of awareness where the concept of time, space and object are completely lost, it is the unconscious causal body and Kuṇḍalini in there. In the perineum, the seat of the unconsciousness of human being is found, which is known as Mooladhara in Yogic terminology. It is a gland, a muscle and a body in which all the unconscious powers and initiatives are hidden. Therefore, Mooladhara Bandha is the Master Key for Samādhi or Self-realisation. Unlock the Master Key and one becomes a realised Soul or Jivanmukta (liberated one while living) as known in Yogic terminology.

## Vajroli

The Spiritual practice of rechannelling Sexual energy is called Vajroli in Tāntric terminology. Anyone can learn Vajroli, but prior to it, one should practice. "Laṭa Mudrā", to be able to control oneself.

Because Śakti has emanated from Śiva and wishes to return to Him,

Śakti is impelled to come into close proximity of Śiva. Śiva is the center, the Liṅga, the fixed and unwavering nucleus. To become one with Śiva, Śakti gives up Her own independent characteristics and surrenders to Śiva. As a creeper has no support of its own, it takes the help of a tree, pillar or anything which stands erect. Once the creeper takes support to grow on, it doesn't change to another support. Similarly, when a man and woman come together for Laṭa Mudrā, the woman sits on man's left thigh and hold his penis with her right hand. The man must hold her left breast with his left hand, from the bottom of the breast, like a cup. Like a creeper the woman should drap herself around the Man and the man permits to be clung to, as her support. In this Laṭa Mudra, lot of sculptures of Umā-Maheśwara and Lakṣmī-Nārāyana are found. In the Spiritual aspect of this Mudrā, the man must control the woman to ensure that She does not become sexually excited. The couple should be able to sit together in this Mudra for a long time, without the least excitation. If this Mudrā is done properly, the woman goes to Bhava Samādhi. Her emotions will crescend until her mind becomes totally one-pointed directed towards man, and She will forget her worldly existence for a while. In this stage, if the couple direct themselves as Śiva and Śākti, they can reach Mahābhāva Samādhi also. In this manner the Man and Woman should learn to control their sexual heights.

To learn Vajroli one must clean oneself to suck water through the anus and urinary passages. This act is known as "Gaja Karma," because elephants (Gaja) suck up water with trunks and spray themselves.

For learning this, one should control "Apana vayu", the body force which causes the expulsion of urine, feces, flatus, semen, menses and fetus. An example can be given, when one wants to urinate, one can strain the flow of urinate, so in that manner one can learn Vajroli. After one is able to suck up water, one should proceed to use milk, then ghee (clarified butter), Honey and Mercury at last. Mercury which has been purified and prepared in the Tāntric way, should be used otherwise it is deadly poison. When one can hold the bladder full of mercury for three hours, without spilling a drop, one reaches to great heights, which is known to the Tāntric practitioner only.

When a man practices Vajroli on a woman, he sucks up with his penis the secretions which come out as She gets excited. The woman engaged in this purposes loses some years of her life span, because a great amount of her Śākti is removed. If the woman knows Vajroli, then she can "milk", a man of his semen with her suction over and over again, until nothing is left to eject. If both partners have full knowledge of Vajroli, there is mutual benefit and there is nothing like it in the mundane World. In such level one will forget Sex for a long time, except with one's partner. Vajroli is a mutual clashing, interaction and union of two individuals into one. Śiva and Śākti merge together into Sadaśiva, the proton and the electron reunite the form the neutren. As in physics, such a union is associated with much energy, the union of Vajroli is associated with tremendous Śākti, which can be used for Spiritual advancement.

Vajroli is only the beginning. There are Rajjoli, Sahajoli, Amaroli and Gaupya in Tāntric sādhanā. No one knows about Gaupya except Lord Śiva Himself. The love play, eroticism and the Sexual union of the Universal Soul continues for ever. A diagrammatic embodiment of the creative Sexual activity of the Universe is "Ś R Ī Y A N T R A", of Mother-Goddess.

## Yantra

Human beings can express in three ways, through signs, speech and writings. Yantra includes signs and writings. The Mantras and Tantras are co-partners of Yantras, because they are too expressed through these medias.

The expression "Yantra" is derived from the root "Yan," (Uṇādi 4. 133) or alternatively from the form "Yantrati" or ("Yantrayati") (Dhātu – pātha, 32.3), the meaning in both cases being "to restrain", "to compel", "to bend". The early context, in which the word was used relates to mechanical contrivances. The "Yantra", in this context is an engine, a machine, an appliance. This word is also applied to surgical instruments. So, it can be said that there are mechanical Yantras and Spiritual Yantras.

In Spiritual aspect "Yantra", is not a magic but a path or technique through which one can attain Siddhi, attain desires and is the shortest way, provided are followed with instructions and directions. Yantra Śākti is very wide, our Great (Mahā) Riṣis have practiced and attained perfection in it. They have showed us the way. In various Śāstras and mostly from Atharvaveda, Yantras has been held in high esteem, as it is the way of realisation of God and desires. It is said that different aspects of God reside in Yantras. The possible Yantras are innumerable with combinations of the geometrical forms, triangles, circles and four-sided figures, with association of Mantras.

The Tāntric ideology of the human being is constituted by several "Cakras" in the Kuṇḍalini, (viz: Moolādhara cakra, Swadhisthan cakra,

Manipur cakra, Anahat cakra, Viśuddha cakra, Ajna cakra and Sahasra cakra). Many Cakras are mentioned in different literatures, but these are the main Cakras for ascent of Kuṇḍalini. It is unprofitable to seek to identify the presence of these Cakras, within the anatomical and physiological constitution of human beings. The Cakras of Kuṇḍalini are in the Liṅga śarīra (astral body), otherwise known as subtle body, which contains the latent urges in an individual. "L I Ṅ G A," is a symbol of "something that is not yet revealed." The body made up of thoughts and their functions is composed of subtle elements, which have not yet undergone the process of grossification. To rise from the subtle elements, there is Sexual tāntric Kuṇḍalini Yoga sādhanā. For detail study and practice of Kuṇḍalini, Yoga is required and one should learn from a Siddha Tāntric Guru (Master).

CHAPTER III

# Evolution of Tantra in Orissa (Historical Prespective)

Orissa (parts of ancient Kaliṅga, Utkala and South Kōśala States), situated in the south - eastern part of India, whose main river in the Māhāṇadi river, has been the meeting ground of different faiths and sects, which has left behind a galaxy of religious monuments, temples, sculptures, icons, literatures and folk traditions which bear the cultural efflerescence.

Though Tantra had early origin, which is lost in mystery, from about early medieval period. Tantra as a special religious or philosophical concept gradually came into use in India. Religious cultural trends entered Orissa from all directions. The chief peculiarity of the Tantras is the prominence they give to the female energy of the Deity, his active nature being personified in the person of his Śakti or Wife. The majority of Tantras are devoted to one of the manifold forms of Devi, the Śākti of Śiva. Devi, as the Śakti of Śiva, is the especial energy concerned with sexual intercourse and magical powers and these are the leading topics of the Tantras. Each Śakti has a twofold nature, white and black, gentle and ferocious. Thus Umā and Gauri are gentle forms of the Śākti, while Durgā and Kāli are fierce forms. The Śāktas or worshippers of the Śakti are divided into two classes, Dakṣhināchāris and Vamācāris, the right handed and the left handed. The worship of the right hand Śaktas is comparatively decent, but that of the left hand is addressed to the fierce forms of the Śaktis and is most licentious. The female principle is worshipped, not only symbolically, but in the actual woman and premiscuous intercourse forms part of the orgies. One's own wife should be engaged as the partner in the sādhanā (for legitimate indulgence), but according to the left handed practice ritualistic intercourse can be held with a woman who is not one's own wife, another's wife and women of all castes are equally eligible.

According to the "Viśversāra Tantra", "what is here is there, what is not here is nowhere." Chāndogya Upanisad says, "as a man thinks that he becomes". Spiritual heights can be reached through Tāntric Yoga or Sādhanā as Śākti resides at Mooladhara cakra of the Kuṇḍalini With this background Śākti worship became popular in Orissa.

## BUDDHIST TANTRA

Jainism was a popular faith of Orissa since the earliest times, but it lost its ascendency after the death of Khāravela, due to lack of Royal patronage. Buddhism was dormant, but gradually spread its popularity. Mahāyānic form of Buddhism became dominant soon, with its Monastic institutions in eastern India, including Orissa, Tosāli, Bhorasaila, Tāmralipti, Chali Tā Le, Viraja and its environ, Ratnagiri, Jayāsrama Vihāra, Arghyakā Varātika, Bhō-rāhā, Muñjasi, Jagaddala Vihara, Boud, Ganiapali and many places of Orissa became centers of Buddhist movement.

Among the earliest Buddhist Tāntric temples of Orissa, mention may be made of the ruined temple of Tara at Bankada, the Capital of the old Koṅgada Maṇḍala, ruled by the Śailodbhava dynasty within 6th-7th century A.D. Though Buddhism was the religion of many, Buddhism was relegated to the background during that period.

Padmapur is a village to the north of Gunupur. Close to Padmapur there is Jagamunda hill famous for its antiquities. There are five Śiva temples dedicated to Manikeswar, Dhabaleswar, Mallikeswar, Nilakantheswar and Podukeswar. The little shrine of Mallikeswar at the top of the hill is peculiarly built by big blocks of stone without the use of mortar. The Shrine contains an inscription in the characters of the 7th century A.D. which preserves a small genealogy of three Buddhist Acharyas Chandrelekha, Bhuddhakhan and Dharmakirtti. It appears that the monastery of the famous Āchārya Dharmakirtti was located in this hill. It is known from Tibetan account that Dharmakirtti, the famous logician and philosopher, had his monastery in Kaliṅga and the inscription found in the Jagamunda hill clearly indicates the location of it.

In fact, till the coming of the Bhauma-kara dynasty in the 8th century A.D. notable Buddhist rulers do not seem to have flourished in Orissa territory and Mahāyāna Buddhism is known to have thrived here more on popular support than on any Court patronage. Most of the Sages and philosophers of Mahāyāna Buddhism belonged to Orissa.

Gradually there was unfoldment of Tāntric Buddhism. Tantrayāna of

Buddhism is generally divided into three distinct Schools, viz : Vajrayāna, Sahajayāna and Kālacakrayāna, which originated in Orissa and it is from this land that they travelled to other parts of India and even abroad. Therefore it can be said that Orissa is the land where Buddhist Tāntricism had its origin. Vajrayāna has no clear-cut definition in the Buddhist texts. Vajrayāna introduced the theory of five Dhyāni Buddhas and cult of Prajñā or Śākti. Vajrayāna considers Śūnya or vacuity as the ultimate reality and innumerable Gods and Goddesses as its manifestations. The five Dhyāni Buddhas emanated from the highest being Vajradhara or Vajrasattva. The Dhyāni Buddhas are Amitābha, Akṣobhya, Vairocana, Amoghasiddhi and Ratnasambhava. Vajrasattva is considered as the sixth Dhyāni Buddha. Each of the Dhyāni Buddhas has a Śakti. Besides the emanations of the five Dhyāni Buddhas, there are many other Deities in the Vajrayāna pantheon, with their Prajnā or Śakti. The number of Gods and Goddesses increases when Śūnya manifests itself in different forms; since the inspirations of these manifestations are innumerable, the Deities can alo be innumerable.

Sahajayāna is an offshoot of Vajrayāna. The Buddhist Sahajiyā dohā and caryā songs became popular in a very wide area during the period roughly from the 8th to 12th century A.D.

The grandiose conception of the idea of Sahaja, the Sahajayāna remained as a way of propitiating the primitive instincts and desires, i.e. sex hunger and the like, and in advocating the principle, it challenges all established religions with their rigour of discipline, orthodoxy and formalities. Thus Sahajayāna appeared as an open protest for all sorts of religions formalism and Yogic rigourism and it layed emphasis on developing the human nature for the realisation of Śūnyatā, the ultimate truth. So, the Sahajiās professed the principle of satisfying all the needs of the physical body which is the abode of all the tattvas, Pīṭhas and Deities, and without which no Siddhi can be attained. This idea or worshipping the physical body, is quite in keeping with the principle of propitiating human nature with its sex passions and other primitive propensities. It should not, however, be forgotten that the Sahajiās admit the primary importance of Sex instinct and primitive desires with a view to sublimating them by a natural Yogic process, rather than to suppressing them by unnatural and undue regulations. The whole Yogic process of the Sahaja school was found to be based on a highly sublime aspect of the Sex, where the Sādhaka is to embrace and sport with the female Śakti, variously called as the Cāṇḍāli, Doṁbi, Savari, Yogini, Nairātma, Sahaja Sundari etc. The Bliss that comes out of this sexo -

yogic practices was generally divided into four stages, viz : Ānanda, Paramānanda, Viramānanda and Sahajānanda and this final stage was known as the state of Mahāsukha, at the attainment of which "the senses are absorbed within, all thought processes are annihilated, all the seeds of existence are destroyed; it is full of the lustre of bliss, it is like the vacant sky and yet cool and sweet."

When a Sahajayānist entered into his Yogic practices, he accepts a female counter part as Mahāmudrā variously called Doṁbi, Cāṇḍāli, Śābari etcetera adores her, embraces her, kisses her and even penetrates his vajra into her lotus, but under no circumstances, he discharges his seed of creativity, for uttama siddhi, concomitant with Buddhahood, Mahāsukha or Nirvāṇa cannot be realied with the grose sensual pleasure caused by seminal discharges. Such a stability of Bodhi-citta enables its adherents to realise the supress Bliss, the summum bonum of the Tāntric Buddhists. Goddess Laṁkeśvari is depicted as a Tāntric Goddess in one of the Sādhanas of Sādhanāmāla. Her cult prevailed at Sonepur, on the rock bed Laṅkāvartaka in Mahāṇadi river.

Kālacakrayāna is also an offshoot of Vajrayāna. There is a Buddhist Tantra called "Śrī Kālacakra tantra", which introduces the cult of Kālacakra. This cult came into vogue in 10th century A.D. and spread to Kashmir, Tibet and China, where it became very popular. In the name of Kālacakra, Buddha came to be worshipped in the name of Heruka, Acala, Vajrabhairava etc. It is a system of Yoga which, with all its accessories of maṇḍala (magic circle) and concentration (abhiṣeka), is explained within this very body. . . . how all the Universe with all its objects and localities are situated in the body and how time with all its varieties (viz : day, night, fortnight, month, year, etc.) are within the body in its process of the vital wind. In the body of the text Sahaja has been fully explained and the details of the Sexo-yogic practices for the attainment of the Sahaja have also been described.

The word Kālacakra means the wheel of time. The theory of Kālacakra has also been explained by Abhinavagupta in terms of the wheel of time and the process of keeping oneself above the influence of the whirl of time. The process of controlling time is possible, according to this authority, by controlling the vital winds in the nerves through Yogic practices. In principle there is no difference between Vajrayāna and Kālacakrayāna. Lord Śrī Kālacakra is not different from Ādi Buddha or Vajrasattva or Vajradhara. Kālacakra is conceived as the nature of Śūnyatā and Karuṇā. Lord Śrī Kālacakra is regarded as the source of the Buddhas, possessing the three Kāyas, symbolical of the three times-past, present and future. He is the Bodhicitta, the ultimate immutable substance and is embraced by the Goddess Prajña in the absolute non-dual state.

According to Tibetan sources Ratnagiri was noted for pursuit of Kālacakara tantra in the later part of 10th century A.D. The Buddhist establishment at Ratnagiri was from 5th century A.D. to 12th century A.D. and played a conspicuous role in spreading the Buddhist - Tāntric culture far and near and attracted Scholars and Students from various parts of the Country.

Mahāyānic and Tāntric Buddhist centres developed in Orissa and the most important of these are the sites of Udayagiri, Lalitagiri, Ratnagiri, the Āsia hills, Solampur, Khaḍipada, Boud, Bāṇeśvara - Nāsi, Chauduār, Kuṇḍeśvara, Ayodhyā, Khichiñg, Bāripadā, Prăchi valley, Aṣṭarānga, Udlā, many sites around Chitrotpala valley, Ranipur - Jharial and many stray sites.

Evidently, the walls of the Buddhist temples were bare and simple, but in their large niches were fixed superb images of Mahāyānic and Tāntric Gods and Goddesses. Even with Tāntric influence, no erotic sculptures are found in Buddhist constructions in Orissa.

The evolution of Buddhist tantra led to the cononisation of the mode of icon making which achieved a high order of excellence. Kuru Kullā a tāntric Goddess is found at Udayagiri. If propitiated, Kuru Kullā is believed to make the Sādhaka capable of bewitching men and women of all status and positions. The Mantra of this Goddess is "Om Kuru Kullā Hum Hriḥ Svaha," and if it is muttered then thousand times, all persons will be bewitched. Thirty thousand would be sufficient for subduing a minister and one lakh for a king. She can even confer on her devotees the power of subduing all ministers and all kings.

Within the vicinity of Lalitagiri one four armed Tārā holding rosary in the upper right hand and vajra in the upper left hand, while her lower left hand carries the nilotpala and the lower right bestowing boon on the worshippers is found. According to N.K. Sahu, She appears to be a variety of Chaturbhuja Sita Tārā. Goddess Aparājita is found at Lalitagiri, standing in Ālidha attitude on two crouchant figures and holding a flower in her uplifted right hand, while an attendant goddess standing on a raised platform on her right, holds a parasol over her head. Charming images of Tārās are found at Ratnagiri with graceful tribhañga poses. Among the Buddhist tāntric deities found at Ratnagiri mention can be made of two armed Heruka and Vajrajvālānalārka.

Vajrapāṇi, Mānjuśri, Durgottārini Tārā, Avalokiśvara and Samkhipta

Mārichi sculptures discovered from Kendrāparā are exhibited at Indian Museum, Calcutta. One Vajrapāṇi sculpture from Lalitagiri is exhibited at National Museum, New Delhi. Khadaravaṇi Tārā from Udayagiri is kept at Patna museum. Vajrasattva from Solampur is preserved at National Museum, Calcutta.

The image of Prajñāpāranitā is found at Bāṇeśvaranasi. Beautiful female images of Prajnāpāranitā, Vajravārahi and Khadiravani Tārā are found from Chauduar. Tārā and Sambara images are found at Kuṇḍeśvara, Mārichi, Mānjuśri, Lokeśvara, Tārā and Vajya Tārā found at Ayodhya are fine works. Aparachana Mānjuśri and Aśokakānta Mārichi from Khiching are kept at Museum of Bāripadā. Trailokya Vijaya image is found at Amaraprasādgarh of Prāci valley. Mārichi is found at Astarānga, Chuṇda at Baṇia sai of Cuttack and Mārichi at Udlā.

Kings of Bhauma Kara dynasty ruled in Orissa from the middle of eighth century A.D. till the middle of tenth century A.D. The Mahāyānic form of Buddhism was a dominant faith of Orissa at the time of the rise of this dynasty. Some Bhauma Kara Kings bore Buddhist epithets Paramopāska, Paramatathāgata, Paramasaugata and Saugatāsrava. They extended royal patronage. Buddhist establishment at places like Khaḍipadā, Ratnagiri, Udayagiri and Lalitagiri flourished much during this period. Buddhism fast lost its importance in the later Bhauma Kara period, due to lack of royal patronage, but the main cause of its decadence was its connection with Tāntrism and its similarity with the Brahmanical sects like Śaktism and Śaivism.

All the Buddhist tantra Goddesses found in Orissa have prominent well developed sensual looking large breasts.

## JAINA TANTRA

The representation of seven Tirthaṅkaras and seven female figures guarded by Gaṇeśa in the Sataghara cave at Khaṇḍagiri and two rows of images, the upper showing 24 Tirthaṅkaras and the lower 24 Śāsana Devis, indicates that the female principle was fully adopted in Jainism in the beginning of the Christian era.

Lot of Jain antiquities are found in Koraput district. Ambikā, the Śāsana Devi of Neminātha, Yakṣa Gomedha and Yakṣiṇī Ambikā are found at Kachela. Four armed Tārā is found in one of the cells of a Jain monastetery at Suai. From Tibetian source, it is known that Jaina Tantra pīṭha (site) existed at Subai, which is situated near Semiliguda. The Jaina tāntric site of Subai is now situated isolated in the midst of scrub forest. Within an oval enclosure, with a low wall all around, is a series of about ten small shrines much damaged and only two of them are still standing. These Jaina tāntric shrines probably belong to the earliest phase of temple building in Orissa. There is invocation of Sarasvata power in Jainism also.

## Śākta Tantra

Mother earth has naturally taken form of Yoni and is worshipped as "Duarsani," near Partalgaṅga site of Nuapada district. It seems to be the earliest Śākti of Orissa.

Primitive people had invented mystic diagrams (Yantras) and sacred circles (Cakras) representing tools and weapons as Cult symbols, associated with fertility rites. These promoted the fertility of the earth and prosperity of people. As agriculture was thought to be in the province of Women, such rites were developed through them and earth came to be known as Mother earth. The erotic circles of Yogimath Donger, situated at a close distance of Khariar in Nuapada district is pre-historic rock shelter painting of neolithic period, is an evidence of primitive Śākti rite. Two YONIS are discovered from Maraguda valley and Suṇabeda plateau, which show the Śākti worship during proto - historic period. Megalithic people in Deccan used to make hole in a rock and worship it as Śākti. Such stones or huge rocks with holes are known as POT-STONE. One such POT-STONE is discovered at Podagarh, within Chaura mountains in Nuapada district of Orissa. It is the only trace of Megalithic Śākti worship in Orissa. This POT-STONE is now preserved in the private possession of the author at Khariar.

The Tantras call Śākti as Parā Prakṛti, i.e. the personified Divine Energy of the Supreme Deity, in other words, Brahma itself. Without the union of Śākti and Śiva there is no creation. The two are inseparable indeed. Śiva, the pure consciousness, is the silent Seer of all experiences while it is Śākti who brings forth the Universe, sustains it and destroys it to please Śiva.

The Supreme Deity of the Tantras is known as Śākti, inseparable from Śiva. Śākti and Śiva are not two or double stars, but are ultimately one and the same.

For a Śākta, the Supreme Deity is Śākti. The Supreme being of Śāktism is not a personal God. In its own nature it is more than that. The Śākta stand point posits the reality of God as the cause of the Universe. But it holds that while the effect as effect is the cause modified, the cause as cause remains what it was, what it is and what it will be. It holds that the Supreme being is manifested in one of its aspects in an infinity of relations; and though involving all relations within itself, is neither their sum total nor exhausted by them. Śākti, which is its functional aspect, works by negation, contraction and finitisation. As a Mother power She unfolds herself the World and again withdraws the World into herself. The purpose of her worship is to attain unity with her forms and this is the experience of liberation - a state of great Bliss (ānandaghaṇa). In the natural order of development, Śākti is developed in Worldly things but it is controlled by a religious Sādhanā, which both prevents an excess of Worldliness and moulds the mind and disposition (bhāva) into a form which develops the knowledge of dispassion and non-attachment. Sādhanā is a means whereby bondage becomes liberation.

In total there are 52 Śākti pīṭhas in India and its neighbouring areas, according to Tāntric literature. The distribution of Śākti pīṭhas throughout the Country shows that the unity of the Country was uppermost in the minds of the Seers of our Country from time immemorial, because they were dealing with Cosmic principals.

In "Tantra Chudāmani," a relevant mythological story is found, about these 52 Śākti pīṭhas. It says : Once Prajāpati Dakṣa performed "Brahaspati-sav Yajña," in Kankhal (near Hardwar). For it he did not invite his daughter Sati and son-in-law Śiva. Uninvited Śiva did not go to this Yajña: but inspite of Śiva's opposition Sati went to her father's home. There hearing unfavourable comments about her husband, Sati in the fit of anger discarded her life.

God Śiva thereafter began reaming about the Triloka carrying the life-less body of Sati on his shoulders. In order to revigorate Śiva,who became so much attached to the lifeless body, God Viṣṇu dissected the dead body through His cakrā. Wherever these dissected pieces of his body or ornaments worn by it fell, these places became famous as "Śākti pīṭhas." They are 52 in number according to Tantra Cuḍāmaṇi and Puri in Orissa, is one of them (Vide : Appendix - II). The Dakṣa's Yajña (sacrifice) finds mention in Vāyu purāṇa also. According to Vasudeva S. Agrawala, the limbs of the body of Sati dropped down severally by which one hundred and eight centres of Śākti worship (Śākti pīṭhas) were formed which are said to continue up to this day. The moral of this story is the broad - based apotheosis of the motherland conceived in the form of energised centres for Tāntric and Yogic sādhanā or for practising special meditation and Spiritual discipline.

The story goes on to say that Śiva after his roaming with the body of Sati had his consternation somewhat overcome and in order to attain peace he began to perform meditation or Samādhi. He sat down in the forest of devadāru trees in the Himālayas and went into Samādhi. It was an untensive exploration of the powers of his own mind and through unbroken meditation he desired to integrate them once again. His Samādhi continued for thousands of years and the fate of Gods against the asuras remained undecided. So they counseled and planned to break his Samādhi by the intervention of the God of love, Kāmadeva. He resorted to the place and created an atmosphere of disturbing the meditation of Śiva. Just then Pārvati as the female energy filled with the pride of physical beauty and outer charm wanted to wean away Śiva's mind like the magnetic needle doing to the iron. Śiva then thought within himself, "A Yogi who has got control over the power of the Cakras of the body and the mind, cannot fall a prey to the temptations of the senses and the God of love; how can physical beauty attract him to the World of sense pleasure?" Thus thinking, he opened his third eye of Wisdom in search of some extraneous centre of disturbance. He saw the God of love, Kāmadeva, aiming his shaft against Śiva in Samādhi. The Great God opened his eye of wisdom and consumed Kāmadeva to ashes, that is, burned his physical body so that all objective existence of Kāma was annihilated. The God of love became merely an idea that springs in mind and can be conquered by the illumination of the mental powers.

Two handed Mahiṣāsuramardinī Durgā which represents the earliest phase of chronological evolution of Śākti in Orissa are Virajā of Jaipur and one found at Someśvara near Kakatpur of Prachi valley. The Bhadrakali shrine is situated at a distance of about ten kilometers from Bhadrak. There is an inscription there assignable to 3rd century A.D. which refers to Parnnadevati, evidently the earlier name of the Deity now known as Bhadrakāli. These are the Śākta deities belonging to pre Gupta period in Orissa.

Four armed Mahiṣāsuramardinī images are mostly found in Praci valley. At Motia there is four-armed image which hold Śaṅkha and Cakra in upper tow hands, while the lower two hands pierce the trident to the breast of the demon. Such similar image is found at Mādhava temple of Niali and in the western wall of the Charchika temple at Banki.

There is Laṅkeśvarī Goddess at Junagarh of Kalahandi district. Laṅkeśvari is four handed, seated on a lotus and holding Śankha and Cakra in upper two hands, while the lower two hands are in vara and abhya mudrā. It is believed this Laṅkeśvarī deity to have been brought from Ravana's Laṅkā of Rāmāyaṇa fame. But in reality in medieval period there was rivalry between the followers of Buddhist tantra and Śākta tantra. Goddess Laṅkeśvarī is depicted as a Buddhist Tāntric Goddess in one of the Sādhanās of Sādhanāmala. Laṅkeśvari was the presiding Goddess of Laṅkā, identified with modern Sonepur area.

King Indrabhuti of Sambala, identified with present Sambalpur region, in Uḍḍiyāna organised the Mantrayāna Buddhism, while his sister Lakṣmikara was connected with the initial development of Sahajayāna in 8th century A.D. Princess Lakṣmīkara was married to the son of Jalendra, the ruler of Laṅkāpuri. Padmasaṁbhava the son of Indrabhuti was, in fact, a great religious reformer who preached Tāntrayāna in Tibet and organised the order of Lāmās in that land of snow.

The Śāktas established a Śākta Goddess Laṅkeśvari at Junagarh and it is a beautiful example of the tug of competition between Buddhist tāntrists and Śākta tāntrists in Western Orissa.

Four armed Mahiṣāsuramardinī Durgā is found at Jahambita in Keonjhar district. This image may be of post-Gupta period. There are many four armed images of Gaṅgā period (C. 1078 A.D.–C. 1435 A.D.) which have different iconographic features from the earlier once. Another image of this type is noticed in a ransacked house attached to Gaṅgeswati temple at Bayalisbati in Puri district.

Mahiṣāsuramardinī with six hands is not common in Orissa. One such image is known as "Dvāravāsinī," on the eastern edge of Vindu sarovara of Bhubaneswar. Three images of this variety are found at Bhubaneswar and the rest in Praci valley. Such a one is seen at Aṣṭarang, in peculiar sense, as it presses the mouth of Mahisāsura with one of her right hand, while the other five hands hold sword, arrow, bow, shield and trident.

Aṣṭa-bhujā (eight - handed) Mahiṣāsuramardinī became very popular during the reign of Bhaumakara dynasty (c. 736 - 948 A.D.) who patronised Tāntric Buddhism. Daśa-bhujā Mahiṣāsuramardinī was more popular in Orissa. Of the numerous Daśa-bhujā Mahiṣāsuramardinī mention may be made of the beautiful images found at Dalavada, Pitapura, Laṭaharana, Nivarana, Niali, Jogeswar and Vakatpur of Praci valley, Bhattarika near Baramba, Kanaka Durgā near Remuna, at Kiching, Padhuan near Basudevpur, at Bhubaneswar. Patnagarh and at many other places. Eight-armed variety are noticed in Vaital and Sisireswar temples of Bhubaneswar, Seragad Durgā temple and Durga temple at Baideswar also.

Twelve armed Mahiṣāsuramardinī are not much in Orissa. One such image is found at Bhubaneswar, near the eastern edge of Vindusaravara tank and is known as "Dvāravāsinī." The other one known as "Dakeswari," is near Chandabali in Bhadrak district and one is preserved at Orissa State Museum, Bhubaneswar.

Two eighteen armed Mahiṣāsuramardinī are found in Orissa so far. One is a parsva-devata of a Śaivite temple at Nirakarpur and the other is presiding Goddess in Praci valley.

One image of twenty armed Mahiṣāsuramardinī, which probably adorned a temple at Salebhata in Balangir district is now preserved at "DR. N.K. SAHU Museum," of Sambalpur University. All these images of Orissa belonged to a long span of period, from 7th to 16th century A.D.

Jajpur was the most important centre of Śaktism in Orissa. The Śākta temple of Viraja at Jajpur existed in the pre-Christian era, which is evidenced by the Mahābhārata, Harivaṁśa and Vāyu purāṇas. In the later stage of Orissan history, before the Gupta period, the Śākta shrine of Virajā was dominated by Buddhism. The Buddhist influence seems to have been eliminated in Gupta period and reconverted into a pure Brahamanical Śakti shrine.

The Śākta temple of Vīrajā was again influenced by Tāntric Buddhism in the Bhaumakara period. The Bhaumas had their Capital at Vīrajā and the earlier rulers of this dynasty were Buddhists, but the Buddhism of this period was a mixed form of religion in which Buddhism, Śāktism, Śaivism and Tāntricism had become amalgamated. So, it can be said that by the beginning of 9th century A.D. Religions elcticism had already started in Orissa. There are several Śākta images, particularly of Cāmuṇḍā at Jajpur.

Śaiva centre at Bhubaneswar has also a number of Śākta temples which show amalgamation of Śāktism, Śaivism and Tāntric Buddhism, built during Bhauma period. During this period Śākta temples sprang up on the four sides of Vindusarovara at Bhubaneswar and they are now known as Vaitāla or Kapalini situated in west of the tank, Mohini and Uttareśvara situated in the south and north of the tank enshrine Cāmuṇḍās, later Śākta temples on the east and west banks of the tank contain the images of Mahiṣāsuramardinī. The name of the Śākta temple on the east of the tank, which still exists, has been lost.

Vaitāla temple is the most important among these temples, because its sculptures and architecture indicates that the strange eseteric rites invluding human sacrifice were going on there. The name Vaitāla seems to have been derived from the word "Vetāla," or Spirit, with which the

Kapali Tāntrics used to do their Sadhana and attain Siddhis. In a literary work "Svarnnadri - Mahodaya," it is stated that venerable Goddess Cāmuṇḍā garlanded with skulls exists on a spot, on the west of Vindusarovara tank. She is of terrific form and is known as Kapalini. Though the Kapalikas were worshippers of Śiva, the other Deity of their worship was Cāmuṇḍā. The Cāmuṇḍā Deity now under worship in the Vaitāla temple is of terrific form. The basement of a stone "Yupa," which was utilised for the sacrifice is still found in front of the door of Vaitala temple. Unlike the cellas of other temples where light and shade intermingle, to create a serene atmosphere, the sanctum of Vaitala temple is intensely dark. The seriousness of the owful esoteric rites that were performed there, must have heighten by the darkness of the cella and by the presence of images of most terrific forms. In the inner walls of this temple, there is Bhairava in most hideous and terrific form. The form of Śākta tantra that is found at Vetāla temple seems to have allied itself with Tāntric Śaivism. Tāntric Śāktism and Buddhist tāntricism. The Kapalikas who followed this mixed form of religion were an extrect sect of Śāktism, Śaivism, Buddhism and Tāntricism.

The temple of Bhuasuni in the neighbourhood of Sisupalgarh and the other near the house of Satyapriya Mohanti at Bhubaneswar have the presiding images of Cāmuṇḍās, which have depiction of terrific forms with sunke bellies and with emaciated and sinewy bodies, garlanded with skulls and seated on corpses with jackels by their sides. The presiding Deity of the largest temple at Khiching is Khijjiṅgeśvari, in Mayurbhanj district, which is a Cāmuṇḍā having the characteristics of Bhaumakara period.

While these Śākta worships were continuing in eastern part of Orissa, in the western Orissa, the earliest Śākti worship is the natural YONI, worshipped as "Duarsani," near Patalganga site of Nuapada district. In historical period, from Terasinga charter (copper plates), of Parvatadvaraka kings of 5th century A.D. which records two grants of two different Kings, it is known that they were devoted worshippers of Goddess Stambheśvari. Terasinga is situated on the right bank of Tel river in Kalahandi district and is an early historical site with scattered archaeological antiquities. This charter of 5th century A.D. is the earliest reference of Stambhwsvari worship. The Sulkis who came after the Parvatadvarakas were all known as Stambheśvari-Padahbakta. The Bhañja rulers also worshipped this Goddess. Another Diety called "Lileśabhadrā Durgā" also appears in the character of a Bhañja ruler named Satrubhañjadeva. Stambheśvari is still worshiped at Sonepur, most part of Western Orissa, Aska in Ganjam district and as Khambheśvari near Sagada river near Bhawanipatna.

## SAPTA MĀTRIKĀS

According to a legend described in Īśānaśivagurudeva-paddhati (1. 52. 79 b), the Mātrikās were created to help Lord Śiva in his fight against Andhakāsura. When the Lord inflicted wounds on Andhaka, blood began to flow profusely from his body. Each drop which touched the ground assumed the shape of another Andhaka. Thus, there were innumerable asuras fighting against Śiva. To stop the falling of the blood, Śiva created a Goddess called Yogeśvari from the flames issuing out of his mouth. Brahmā, Viṣṇu, Maheśvara, Kumāra, Varāha, Indra and Yama also sent their Śāktis to follow Yogeśvari in stopping the flow of blood. Thus the Saptamātrikās originated. They embody the seven female potentials of the important Gods.

In the Suprabhedagama, the Mātrikās are said to have been created by Brahmā in order to kill Nirrita.

The Saptamātrikās are mentioned in the Rigveda (9. 102. 4), Gobhila-smriti, Mārkaṇḍeya purāṇa, Matsya purāṇa etc. Varāhamihira' Brihatsaṁhita mentions about the images of the Mātrikās. The sculptures of the Saptamātrikās are referred to in "Krityaratnākara." The Devī purāṇa mentions the names of the flowers used for the worship of the Mātrikās. Lexicographer Amar Singh has mentioned the names of Saptamātrikās in "Namaligyanusasanam", (vide : Amarkosa), which is assigned to 4th century A.D.

The several Tantra Sāstras such as the "Svachhanda Tantra," and "Yoginīhridaya," contain a detailed description of the Saptamātrikā and Aṣṭamātrikās which is both impressive and illustrative. Texts like Varāha purāṇa, Bāmana purāṇa, Devī Māhātmya of Mārkaṇḍeya purāṇa, Skanda purāṇa, Brahmavaivarta purāṇa, Devī Bhāgabat, Liṅga purāṇa, Jvalinikalpa and Prapañcasāratantra also deal with the origin of Saptamātrikā Goddesses, with their detail iconographic features.

While commenting on Varāhamihira's Brihatsaṁhitā, Utpala names the Mātrikās as Brahmāṇī, Vaiṣṇavi, Rudri (Māheśvarī), Kaumāri, Aindri, Yami, Varuṇi and Kuberi in the first instance: then says that there are other Mātṛ ganas like Nārasiṁhi, Vārāhī and Vainnyaki. In subsequent Hindu rituals the names of the sixteen Mātrikās with Gouri in the beginning are mentioned. The Purāṇas and Āgāmas mention Sapta Mātrikās to be seven in number, but Varāha purāṇa states that these

Mother Goddesses are eight in number and they represent eight mental qualities which are morally bad. According to Varāha purāṇa, Yogeśvari represents kāma or desire, Māheśvarī Krodha or anger, Vaiśṇavi lobha or coveteousness, Brahmāṇī mada or pride, Kaumāri moha or illusion, Indrāṇi matsya or false finding, Yami or Chāmuṇdā paiśūnya that is tale bearing and Vārāhi assaya or energy. In the Suprabhedāgama it is said that these seven Mātrikās namely Brāhmāṇi, Māheśvari, Vaiṣṇavi, Vārāhi, Indrāni and Chāmuṇḍā were created by Brahmā for the purpose of killing Nirrita. The Āgamā gives briefly the general description of these Goddesses in the following manner : Brāhmaṇi should be sculptured like Brahmā, Māheśvari like Māheśvara, Vaiṣṇavi like Viṣṇu, Vārāhī as short woman bearing a plough as her weapon, Indrāṇi like Indra and Cāmuṇḍā as a terrific woman. This last Goddess should have her hair in dishevelled condition, should possess a dark complexion and have four hands, She should wield the Triśūla in one of her hands and carry a Kapāla in another. All the Mātrikās are to be seated images and should have two of their hands held in the varadā and abhaya poses, while the other two hands should carry weapons approximate to the male counterpart of the female powers.

In Orissa the figures of the Saptamātrikās and Aṣṭamātrikās are frequently found carved in relief on the outer walls of ancient Śiva temples and as monoliths. According to H.C. Das there are 17 sets of Saptamātrikās in Orissa ranging from 7th century to 11th century A.D.

The earliest set belonging to 7th century A.D. is depicted alongwith Gaṇeśa and Vīrabhadra in the northern wall of the Jagamohana of Parasurameswar temple in Bhubaneswar without being associated with children. They are Cāmuṇḍā, Vārāhī, Indrāṇi, Vaiśṇavī, Kaumārī, Māheśvarī and Brāhmāṇī. These Mātrikā figures are four-handed. Gaṇeśa has got no mount here and presents an unique feature. Next to Gaṇeśa, Cāmuṇḍā in her most terrific form is found. In the upper right hands, it holds a lily and a bijapuraka, where as its left holds a long trident and a vase respectively. The drooping breasts, sunken belly and on the whole its emaciated body are the noteworthy features of its representation. The representation of this figure differs in many respect from the later group of representation of Cāmuṇḍā. Snake over the head of the Cāmuṇḍā is not found, which is invariably found in later group. Secondly in the pedestal an owl is found, but in later representations a corpse eaten by jackels are found. Vārāhī occupies the next compartment and has been represented with a lotus and a fish in the right hands and a Kuṭhāra and a vase in the left. The next Mātrikā Indrāṇi is being represented with its usual mount elephant and it holds a vajra in the left and vase in the right. The figure of Vaiṣṇavi has been represented with the usual attribute of Vishṇu and Kumāri holds a vijapuraka in his right hand and with a Gadā and Padma in the left. The next figure may be identified with the figure of Brahmāṇi and it holds an Akṣamālā.

Saptamātrikās are carved in the projecting rock about 30 feet long, about 5 feet in height near the village Ghoral in the Titilagarh sub-division of Balangir district. It may be tentatively assigned to 7th century A.D. Beglar (*Archaeological Survey of India*, Vol. XIII, p. 138) had visited this area during the year 1874 - 75 and 1875 - 76 and had wrongly identified these figures as Navagrahas. These figures were identified with the figures of Saptamātrikās with their two associates Gaṇeśa and Virabhadra in 1953 by K.N. Mahapatra. The figures are rudely carved and have been mostly obliterated due to weathering effect.

At Rānipur - Jhariāl site of Balangir district a rock piece of about 20 feet in height is situated at a distance of hundred feet to the west of Someśwar temple. The presiding Deity Cāmuṇḍā is chiseled, measuring 4 ft. 6 inches in height and 3 ft. 4 inches in width and is facing south, while the nine Mātrikās are chiseled and facing north- east, on the solid rock piece. There was a pillared Maṇḍapa in front of the presiding Deity, which has collapsed and its ruin is found at present. Cāmuṇḍā Deity has sunken breasts and nipples or the pap of the breasts, seems to be in high austerity, starved, bones and chest ribs visible, wearing a necklace and girdle of skulls, seated over a corpse and holding a knife by right hand and touching the lips by the left hand. Triśūla and Damarū are also found wraped by the left hand. The Cāmuṇḍā Deity of this monolithic temple seems to have been made according to the iconographic description of Kapalamalini tantra. Nine Mātrikās found on the north-east face of the same rock are the Śāktis of the principal Gods, which from left to right are : (1) Brahmāṇī or Sarasvatī, (2) Māheśvarī or Raudri, (3) Kaumari or Kārtikeyanī Vārāhi, (4) Vaiṣṇavi or Lakṣmī, (5) Vārāhi, (6) Indrāṇi or Māhendri, (7) Cāmuṇḍā, (8) Mahālaksmi or Yogeśvari and (9) Gaṇeśa or Gaṇeśani. In eastern India the Saptamātrikās were added with Mahālakṣmi or Yogeśvarī and Gaṇeśa or Gaṇeśani. Thereby nine Mātrikās became popular and the best example though much mutilated because of vagaries of nature is found here. It can be dated to 7th century A.D.

There was a very old temple of Saptamātrikās at Bhubaneswar, not very far away from the main gate of the Liṅgarāja temple. It was noticed by M.M. Ganguly (Orissa and Her Remains, 1912), who has mentioned," on the kumbha of the jungha it may be noted is seen a dori or bead, similarly met with in the temple of Saptamātrikās near the temple of Liṅgarāja." This notable dilapidated monument dedicated solely to the worship of Saptamātrikās has gone out of existence due to reckless dismantling of old structures.

Saptamātrikās are found in the Vaitāl temple of Bhubaneswar, assigned to circa. 8th century A.D. found in Yogāsana pose on full-blown lotus with their attributes. This group of Mātrikās headed by Vireśvara begins in the eastern wall and ends in the centre of the western wall. The presiding Deity and image enshrined in the central niche is an eight armed Cāmundā and has been depicted in her most terrific aspect, which is suggested by her sunken eyes, the hood of a snake on her head and a corpse under her feet with a jackal dragging it. Since the Deity is always covered with a piece of cloth her other terrific aspects cannot be studied. All the Mātrikās including Vireśvara and expecting the presiding Deity Cāmuṇḍā have certain characteristics common to them all. They are all seated in Yogāsana with full blown lotus and at their top, two flying Gandharvas. A holo surrounds the head of each Deity. The Saptamātrikās headed by Vīreśvara which begins in the eastern wall have been arranged in the following order : namely Vīreśvara, Brāhmiṇī, Māheśvari, Kaumārī, Narāyanī, Vārāhi, Indrāṇī and Cāmuṇḍā. From Cāmuṇḍā another row of seven Deities begin from the middle of the western wall, the first of which is a female Deity holding a trident and lily in the right and left hands respectively. The image may be identified with Śivaduti, who is invoked in association with the Mātrikās in the Mārkaṇḍeya Caṇḍi. The next niche is being occupied by Gaṇeśa, which has been represented here with other attributes, but no mount is found below the pedestal. No peculiarity is to be noted in the representation of the Mātrikā Deities of Vaitāl pemple except in the representation of Narāyaṇī or Vaiṣṇavi, that has no Garuḍa in the pedestal but a human figure with her left hand upraised. The other attributes of Narāyaṇī namely Śaṅkha, Cakra and Gadā are found in her hands.

The Saptamātrikā figures holding babies of Belkhandi, situated at the confluence of Utei and Tel rivers in the district of Kalahandi represent the next stage of evolution in 8th century A.D. While excavating Kedarnath Mahapatra, the then archaeologist of Kalahandi State brought out the lower portion of a temple of Saptamātrikās. The Mātrikās were arranged near the western wall in the following order :- Kaumārī, Māheśvari, Brahmāṇi, Vaiṣṇavi, Vārāhī and Cāmuṇḍā. The Deity

Vīreśvara was found to the south-west corner of the temple. Beglar had surveyed this area during the year 1874-75 and 1875-76, but had made no mention of this temple. Mātrikās of Belkhandi resembles in every respect, the Saptamātrikās of Dasāśvamedha ghat of the river Vaitaraṇi at Jajpur and those on the Mārkaṇḍeśvara tank at Puri. On the basis of its style K.N. Mahapatra believed that the Caṇḍi temple at Belkhandi was built by the Sōmavaṁśis.

Belonging to the same period of Caṇḍī temple of Belkhandi, the temple of Mukteśvara at Bhubaneswar, contains the figures of Saptamātrikās in its cusped and coffenel ceiling. According to K.C. Panigrahi the ceiling of the Jagamohana of Mukteśvara temple contains most beautiful sculptures. The decorations here have been conceived in the form of a canopy with an eight - petalled lotus at the centre, each petal being occupied by an Deity. These Deities constitute a group of Saptamātrikās with Vireśvara. All the Mātrikās except Cāmuṇḍā hold babies in their arms and that Vīreśvara holds a sword in the right hand. On the outer edges of the lotus there appear several panels of sculptures. Among these may be recognised Kārttikeya, Gaṇeśa, several narrative scenes, like Pārvatī's penance and dancing and musical parties. The representation of Saptamātrikās along with Vīreśvara differ from their early representation and Vīreśvara here holds a sword, but not a trident. The other associate Gaṇeśa has been omitted here and K.C.Panigrahi believes that this omission might have been necessiated by the lack of space in the lotus which contains eight petals for carving eight figures only.

Jajpur has two sets of Mātrikās. The first group consisting of three colossal images of Vārāhi (8ft. 10 inches), Cāmuṇḍā (8 ft. 10 inches) and Indrāṇi (8 ft. 8 inches) carved in chloritecist, now kept within the compound of the sub-divisional office of Jajpur. Of these three images Cāmuṇḍā is shown with three eyes, without flesh and reduced to a skeleton having hairs shooting upwards sunken belly, wearing the skin of an elephant, holding a pottisa and a decapitated head in her left hands and a spear and a sword in her right hands, seated on a corpse and adorned with garlands of skulls. According to a local tradition these three images originally stood on a platform with five others Mothers Brahmaṇī, Māheśvarī, Vaiṣṇavī, Kaumārī and Narasiṁhī of the same colossal size. Another set of life size Mātrikās is now found in a modern temple on Daśāśvamedha ghāṭa of Jajpur. They are associated with babies. On an average, the images are 6 ft. in height and 3 ft. in breadth.

To the north of this Shrine there stands the temple of Gaṇeśa with Gaṇeśa as the presiding Deity. In size, workmanship and the type of stone used, Gaṇeśa is similar to the mother Goddesses. It is obvious that Gaṇeśa might have been in the same group earlier. It is mentioned in Mātsya purāṇa that an image of Vināyaka or Gaṇeśa should always be associated with the Mātrikās. These are assignable to the Sōmavaṁśī period.

Similar set of Mātrikās or of the same variety is found on the edge of Mārdeṇḍeya tank of Purī. The figures made of chlorite stone resembles the Jājpur Mātrikās. Except Cāmuṇḍā all other figures are associated with babies and have four arms each. The facial expression of the Mātrikās while holding and caressing the child with their right lower hands have celestial smile in the facial expression, probably lost in meditation and bhava - samādhi. In Mādalāpāñji (Prachi edition) it is elucidated that a king named Bhīmakeśarī installed seven sisters on the eastern side of the Mārkaṇḍeśvara tank. Bhīmakeśarī has been identified with illustrious Bhīmarath of Somavaṁśī dynasty. The iconography of these images helps in assigning the images of this group to the glorious rule of Sōmavaṁśī Kings.

Ruin of a Saptamātrikā temple is found near the Alakā river in the Sanlapur village in Jagatsinghpur police station area. Its upper portion is broken, but all the images are found in sitting posture by holding a child on their laps and all the images are in a good state of preservation, except the figure of Vaiṣṇavi, the head of which is missing. These figures have several ornaments beautifully displayed and the introspective look on the faces have been beautifully shown. The images have been arranged in the following manner :- Vīreśvara, Kaumārī, Brahmāṇī, Māheśvarī, Nārasinghi, Vārāhi, Indrāṇī, Cāmuṇḍā and Gaṇeśa. These images resemble the figures of Vaitaraṇi valley and Mārkaṇḍeśvara group at Puri and therefore are assigned to Sōmavaṁśī period.

Saptamātrikās namely Vaiṣṇavi, Vārāhi, Indrāṇi and Cāmuṇḍā from Dharmasāla now find place at "Orissa State Museum." Except Cāmuṇḍā, all the figures have babies in their arms and seem to have lost in meditation or bhava - samādhi, like the figures of Mārkaṇḍeśvara tank at Puri. Therefore it seems that both the groups are contemporary to each other. The figures measure roughly (2 1/2' X 1 1/2' ft). The Crown and several ornaments of the figures have artistical display.

A set of Mātrikās (Māheśvarī, Vaiṣṇavī, Brahmāṇī and Cāmuṇḍā) along with a large number of beautiful images of Brahmāṇical and Tāntric Buddhist pantheons find place in Khiching museum. The making of facial expression of these images are elegant. These belong to an independent branch of Schools of Art in Orissa.

In the temple of Khajureswar near Sergarh in the Balasore district, in the lower panael of a plaque of unique Hara-Pārvatī carved in chlorite stone, the following Mātrikā images are found :- Cāmuṇḍā, Vārāhī, Kaumārī, Māheśvarī, Brahmāṇī, Vaiṣṇavi, Pārvatī, Vīrabhadra and Gaṇeśa. On the basis of architecture, the temple is assigned to last part of 13th century A.D.

One Gajalakṣmī image is also found in this temple.

The antiquity of the Mātrikās is shrouded in mystery. Eight Mātrikās has been mentioned in Devi Bhāgavata and Liṅga purāṇas. In the subsequent literature the names of as many as sixteen Mātrikās have been given, beginning with Gaurī, Mārkaṇḍeya purāṇa indicates that the Mātrikās helped Ambika to kill the Raktavija, a powerful demon, who was endowed with the quality of multiplying into demons of his stature and strength from the drops of his blood oozing from the wounds. The Agni purāṇa and Matsya purāṇa deal in detail about the iconographic features of these Mātrikās. The notable feature of the Mātrikā images of Orissa is that, the Mātrikās are never depicted in the shape of killing the demon for whom they were created but are found sitting at ease in their motherly affection on their mount with babies on laps.

## Cāmuṇḍā

Cāmuṇḍā in her terrific tāntric form is worshipped as presiding Deity at Vaitāl or Kāpāli temple and Mohinī temple at Bhubaneswar, as Kicakeśvari at khiching temple, as Jagulai at Chaurasi, as Carcikā at Banki, as Candaghanta at Niali, as Caṇḍī in the Caṇḍī temple of Kishorepur, as Caṇḍī at Asurswar and as side Deities in many Śākta and Śiva temples of other places. In the same temple of Kicakeśvarī o. Khiching there is also a figure of four armed Vaiṣṇavī with Garuḍa beneath her seat. It is a fine object of sculptural art. The Goddess gracefully holds the Cakra and Śaṅkha in her back hands, has her front right hand in the abhaya pose and claps the child with her front left hand. The several ornaments, including the artistic crown are tastefully displayed and the mellow, introspective look on her face has been beautifully shown. There is separate Cāmuṇḍā temple of solid rock at Ranipur - Jharial in Balangir district, which is made according to the description of Cāmuṇḍā in Kapālamālinī tantra

The Mother Goddess addressed as Devī and Śākti; the primal Cosmic energy is worshipped in Orissa, in her ferocious (Raudra) aspect as Kālī, Bhairavī, Bhadrakālī, Bhīmakālī, Cāmuṇḍā, Chandika etc. As inscription from Jajpur assigned to the 7th century A.D. mentions that Vatsadevi, probably the wife of one of the early Bhauma Kings, installed the image of Cāmuṇḍā, apparently in a temple at Jajpur. The above informations shows that Cāmuṇḍā flourished in Orissa as individual Tāntric cult. H.C.Das informs that during his survey, he has come across as many as 67 Cāmuṇḍās from four-armed variety to eighteen - armed one.

### Vārāhī

The Cult of Vārāhī flourished in Orissa as individual Tāntric cult. The huge image of Vārāhī, which is a beautiful image with fish in right hand and Kapāla in left hand is enshrined in the Vārāhī temple of Chourasi near the village Tilasipur. This colossal image measures (6'1" X 2'9"), Whose vāhana is a crouching buffalo. The Jagamohana of this temple resembles the Jagamohana of Parśurāmeśvara temple at Bhubaneswar, but the main temple is a replica of the Gourī temple of Bhubaneswar. The temple appears to be the sole surviving member of group of seven temples in the region, each dedicated to one of the Mātrikās. The Vārāhī temple at Chourasi is assigned on stylistic consideration, later than the Paraśurāmeśvara, but slightly earlier than the Mukteśvara.

A separate temple of Vārāhī once existed on the northern limit of Ekāmra Kṣetra, which was destroyed most probably during the beginning of the construction of New Capital. There is mention of this Vārāhī temple, which demarcated the area of Ekāmra Kṣetra. Bhubaneswar is known as Ekāmra Kṣetra in several Sanskrit works like Ekāmra purāṇa, Ekāmra Caṇdrikā, Śvarṇādri Mahodaya, Tirṭha Cintāmaṇi of Vachaspati Misra and Kapila Saṁhitā. Nāmostottarasata and Brahma Nila tantra mention Ekāmra Kṣetra as a Śākta pīṭha, which indicate the prevalence of Tāntric cult at Bhubaneswar.

Vārāhī of Chourasi variety is worshipped as Caṇḍi at Banchua village in keonjhar district. The Vārāhī of Narendrapur in Balasore district is more than 10 ft. in height and is in sitting position. Pancha Vārāhī at Satabhaya is situated on the sea shore of kanika area and Vārāhī is found in the Balisahi of Puri town. The Pancha Vārāhī at Satabhaya are two armed images with fish and wine cup in their hands and one is lost.

**Kātyāyanī**

Kātyāyanī, Vairocanī, Durgī and Kanyakumarī are first mentioned in Taittiriya Āraṇyaka. Goddess Kātyāyanī of later Vedic period gained wide popularity in Purāṇic period. Harivaṁśa, Vāyu, Brahmāṇḍa, Viṣṇu, Mārkaṇḍeya, Varāha, Vāmana and Matsya purāṇas give high epithets to this Śākti and conceive Kātyāyanī as a War Goddess.

In Skanda purāṇa She is said to be leading the unmarried life and residing in the Vindhya range. The action of killing Mahiṣāsura is accrued to her. She is said to be born of anger of the Gods and named Kātyāyanī. She is ascribed and attributed with many arms and holding the weapons given by Gods. Mounting on a lion given by Gauri, She went to kill demon Mahiṣāsura. As She is regarded as a War Goddess, She is worshipped mostly by the warriors at the time of actual fight. Bhaumakara Queen Tribhuvana Mahadevi III (c. 896 - 905 A.D.) wife of Bhaumakara King Śivakaradeva III assumed imperial titles of Parama - bhaṭṭārikā, Mahārājādhirāja Parameśvarī and compared herself with Kātyāyanī. She mounted the lion - throne like Goddess Kātyāyanī (Durgā) and her lotus - like feet were kissed by all feudatory chiefs with loyalty. This shows that Goddess Durgā in the name Kātyāyanī had become very popular in Orissa, during the period 9th to 11th centuries A.D. when religious electicism was prevalent in Orissa.

During that period Kātyāyanī gained vide currency and crept into Buddhist and Jain Pantheons. Apart from the Hindu tantras, the Buddhist tantra like Hevajra tantra, compiled around seventh century A.D. mentions the names of four Tāntric pīṭhas including Oḍḍiyāna which is convincingly located in Orissa and mentions that Jagannāth is worshipped as Bhairava and Kātyāyinī as Bhairavi in Oḍḍiyāna. The name "Jagannāth" used in Hevajra tantra, a Buddhist tāntric literature, is used for Lord Buddha. Even in Jñānasiddhi, Indrabhuti the King of Sambhala in Uḍḍiyāna during 8th century A.D. has made invocation of Lord Jagannāth, in many places of his work. It is to be observed that King Indrabhuti has addressed Lord Buddha as Lord Jagannāth.

In Oriya Kālikā purāṇa, composed in 11th century A.D. sixty-four Yoginis and Nabakoti (nine) Kātyāyanīs of fierce appearance are created to kill the demons. The legendary account of origin of Kātyāyanī as found in Kālikā purāṇa, indicates the triumph of Śāktism over Śaivism. As it is a Śākta upa - purāṇa, it gives great emphasis on the Śākti and highlights Śākti than other Gods. This Kālikā purāṇa identifies Orissa as Uḍḍiyāna alias Oḍradeśa and mentions that God Jagannāth and Goddess Kātyāyanī are wershipped there.

Further Kālikā purāṇa informs that Kātyāyana Muni first invoked Mahādevi and thus She popularly came to be known as Kātyāyanī.

In Brahmā purāṇa, Ekānaṁsā is identified with Kātyāyanī. In Purusottama Māhātmya of Skanda purāṇa, Subhadra, the central figure of Jagannāth trinity has been indentified with Kātyāyanī.

In "Bata Abakāśa," of Oriya Saint poet Balarama Dasa written in 16th century A.D. mentions that Lord Jagannāth is attended upon by sixty four Yoginīs, Kātyāyanī, Sapta Mātrikās, Vimalā, Vīrajā and referes to seventy-two local Goblins. Kātyāyanī images are rare in Orissa. Nine images of Kātyāyanīs are found in the outer surface of the enclosure of sixty-four Yoginis temple at Hirāpur. They are two-armed standing on the trunkless head of the Demon with skull cup and dagger in their hands associated with jackals or dogs flanked by their attendants holding Chhatra over their heads.

Kātyāyanī is associated with sixty-four Yoginīs Cult and find mention in the following lists of 64 Yoginīs :

1. Kālikā purāṇa.
2. Bṛhada-Nandikeśvar Purānokto Durgāpūjā paddhati (Viśvokoṣa - (?), Vol. 16, 1312, p. 73).
3. Caunsaṭha Yogini Nāmāvali (2nd and 3rd lists).
4. Durgāpūja ( A palm-leave manuscript of Orissa State Museum, Dh. No. 345, folio 22-23).

## YOGINĪ CULT

According to "Haṭha Yoga Pradipika", of Yogī Swatmarama, a Yoginī is one who practises Vajroli. In Chapter 3, verse 99, it is stated, "If a Woman practise Vajroli and saves her rajas and the man's bindu by thorough contraction, She is a Yoginī." It seems the Yoga of Sexual transformation had become very popular among the ladies of Mahānadi river valley. Therefore the Yoginīs had developed as folk-goddesses. The Skanda purāṇa describes that there are as many Yoginīs as there are Gotras. These Yoginīs are sometime represented as eight fairies or sorceresses created by Durgā and sometimes there are as mere forms of that Goddess, sixty or sixty-five in number and capable of being multiplied to the number of ten millions.

In Skanda purāṇa two different lists of the names of the Yoginīs one consisting 48 names while other is having 64 names. Lists of 64 Yoginīs are found in different texts like : Kālikā purāṇa, Bṛhada - Nandikeśwar

Puranakta Durgāpūjā paddhati, Caunsatha Yoginī Nāmāvali, Caṇḍi purāṇa alias Caṇḍi Yudha by Saralādasa and Durgāpūjā ( a palm leaf manuscript preserved in Orissa State Museum) and Briha Nila Tantra.

Matsyendranāth in view of popularity of the Cult gained over the period, systematised and expounded it in his famous work "Kaulayānanirṃaya," which has become the authoritative text of the Cult.

While dealing about the "Saints of Sahajayāna, their Chronology and Ideology", Ram Prasad Mishra very successfully informs that so far as Luipā who is called Matsyendra in Tibetan list is concerned, there were two different men of the same name in the tradition of Sahaja Siddhas and Nātha Siddhas. The elder Luipā is a Siddha of Sahajayāna and is different from the younger Luipā called Matsendranāth in the list of Nātha Siddhas.

R.P. Mishra informs that according to Kaulajñāna Nirnaya, Matsyendra was called Matsyaghna or a killer of the fish, when he killed a big fish in Candradvīpa and rescued the text of sacred wisdom from its belly. Candradvīpa where Matsyendra rescued the text of the sacred knowledge from the belly of a fish was most probably the Candvāli-dhāmrā region of Orissa, which is even at present a popular citadel of the Cult of Śaivism and the Nāthas. The Nātha as a school of Śaivism appears to have accultured much from different religious systems in the primary days of its genesis. It admitted the influence of Upaniṣads, Śāktism, Vaiṣṇavism and Tāntric Buddhism although its adherents criticised a number of religious systems, its supreme reality is called "Saccidānanda", the Absolute Truth, the real Truth transcending all dualism and non-dualism and thus carries on the influence of Upaniṣadas. Śākti figures as inseparable from Śiva in this Cult. The Supreme Reality in this Cult is accompanied with Viṣṇu from the right hand side and with Śiva from the left hand side. So Śiva as the Supreme reality of this Cult is quite different from the Śiva of other Śaiva School.

Yogini temples in various parts of India belong from the eighth to twelfth century A.D. Therefore, it can be supposed that Matseyendranāth existed within 8th-9th century A.D. The place from where he rescued the text of the sacred knowledge of Yoginis was Candvāli-dhāmrā in Orissa. Now this area is known as Chandbali Dhamra area, which comprised the area of Balasore district portion, now Bhadrak district portion of old Kanika estate in Orissa.

N.N. Bhattacharyya informs that the great Tāntric teachers, regarded in the Nātha tradition as Ādisiddhas, came from the lower section of Society. Mīnanātha, also known as Matsyendranātha-identified by the

Buddhists with Avalokiteśvara and by the Muslims with Machandali or Mocharā Pir was a fisherman. Gorakṣanātha, with whom such Tāntric works as Gorakṣasaṁhita, Gorakṣasid-dhāntasaṃgra, etc., are connected, was either a fisherman, or a Keotiya or Kaivarta.

Matsyendranāth and Gorakṣanāth, the Natha Yogis were connected with the religious culture of Orissa and therefore it is interesting to quote R.P. Mishra :- "In Akulavira Tantra ascribed to Matsyendranāth, Sahaja is described as a state of Supreme equilibrium which transcends all perceptual knowledge with positive and negative attributes. In this state, the Yogi becomes one with the whole Universe and realises a non - dual existence. From Tārā Sādhanā of Vaśiṣṭha depicted in Rudrayāmalā and Brahmāyāmalā and the direct reference to Śiva and Śākti in Advaya Vajra Saṁgraha, it may be suggested that both the Buddhists and the Hindus within the fold of Tāntricism had developed a mutually tolerant attitude during this period. It appears that the Nāthas also would have taken this advantage of toleration during the primary days of their Cult. Matsyendranāth, though originally a Śaiva, seems to have favoured this toleration. From Orissa he appears to have proceeded to different parts of India and even to Nepal and Tibet. He was most probably called Luipā, the younger, owing to his tolerant attitude towards Buddhist Tāntricism. His tolerant attitude became wider in Nepal, where his doctrine representing an amalgamation of Tāntric Śaivism and Tāntric Buddhism became so popular that he was deified as Avalokiteśvar Buddha and the Nepalese continued to believe that "to worship Buddhas is to worship Śiva." From Nepal Matsyendranāth most probably travelled to Tibet where he wrote jointly with Dipaṁkara Śrī Jñāna "Abhisamaya Vibhaṅga Nāma." The jont authority of this Tāntric text has rightly prompted some Scholars to suggest younger Luipā or Matsyendranāth as a senior contemporary of Dipaṁkara. Dipaṁkara is generally suggested to have been born in the last quarter of tenth century A.D. He proceeded to Nepal as well as Tibet in the first half of the eleventh century A.D."

The discussion shows that Matsyendranāth was most probably two hundred years senior to Dipaṁkara. So, it seems that the work started by Matsyendranāth "Abhisamaya Vibhaṅga Nama," was given final shape by Dipaṁkara in later years within 10th - 11th centuries A.D.

In a work named "Tantraloka", Abhinavagupta prays Macchaṇdabibhu for his mercy. Tantralōka is accepted as a work of eleventh century A.D. According to "Tantra Mahārnava", Gorakṣanāth had his sacred seat in the forest of Jagannāth in the East. These prove that Matsyendranāth and Gorakṣanāth being intimately connected with the religious culture of Orissa during the middle age thus exerted a profound influence on its religions.

Yoginī pīṭhas (centres) became popular and according to H.C.Das, the remains of Yoginī temples in various parts of India belonging to the period from the 8th to 12th centuries A.D. clearly reveal that the exponents and followers of this esoteric Cult made vigorous attempt to popularise it in all parts of India. Nine Yogini temples discovered so far are distributed in Orissa, Madhya Pradesh, Uttar Pradesh and in Coimbatore district of Tamil Nadu. Of these five were discovered before 1875 by the foreign archaeologists–Cunningham, Beglar and Col. Macferson : Bherāghat and Khahurāho in Madhya Pradesh, Ranipur – Jhariak in Orissa and Coimbatore in the south. The remains of other five Yogini temples are found at Shahdol in Madhya Pradesh (images now preserved in the Dhubela museum in Chattrapur district), at Mitauli and Dudahi in Lalitpur district of Uttar Pradesh, at Lokhari in the Banda district of Uttar Pradesh and at Hirapur near Bhubaneswar in Orissa, discovered by K.N. Mahapatra. All these temples except that at Khajuraho are hypaethral in appearance and are open to the sky. In this connection we may mention that the temple at Suruda in the district of Kalahandi as mentioned by Cunningham has not yet been located.

The Cult of Yoginī, as an extreme exuburance of Tāntricism developed in Orissa. The two traced sixty-four Yogini temples so far, are at Hirapur and Ranipur - Jharial. In the Yogini temples Kula is described as Śākti and Akula as Śiva, the union of two is Kaula, the process establishing the relationship in Kaula marga. Śiva or Bhairava, the central figure in Yogini temple is represented in Supreme poise and beatitude and Yoginīs encircle his in a Maṇḍala exhibiting their individual feature in terrific posture.

Very likely the Kāpālikas, the followers of Śiva and Śākti were attached to the ritualistic services of Yoginīs. The penances, spells and magic rituals of the Kāpālikas were based on the principles of mysticism and esoterism. To acquire occult power the Kāpālikas resorted to pañcamakāra Sādhanā which comprises madya, māṁsa, matsya, mudra and maithuna. It seems the Kāpālikas were expert in Vajroli practice.

To the neighbouring southern area of Cāṅdavāli - Dharma (modern Chandbali and Dhamra area) of old Kanika estate area, is situated Auḷ. From the earliest period to the end of the medieval age, Indian literature shows a set of ideas and corresponding practices, different from the officially acknowledged norm, which have found expression in the beliefs and rituals of the Auls, Bauls, Sahajiyās, Kāpālikas, Nāthas, Lokāyatas and various other Sects. All these come within the purview of Tantra.

The AUL system of tāntric practice was most probably very popular in AUL region, therefore settlement grew up in coastal area as AUL. In north Orissa, a number of villages were grouped to form Vishaya (Bisi) or Khanda. A group of Biṣis or Khanḍa constituted a Daṇḍapāṭa. The Daṇḍapāṭa of AUL alias ALI became popular.

According to tradition, Kapilendra, the Sūryavaṁśī Gajapati (A.D. 1435 - 1467) of Orissa had eighteen legitimate Sons, and one illegitimate son named Puruṣhottama. The Mādalā Pāñji mentions three of his sons, namely Hamvira, Puruṣottama and Madhusudana Rāy. Madhusudana Rāy was made the Chief of Aul (Ali). So, it is definite that by 15th century A.D. Aul alias Ali had developed as an Daṇḍapāta or administrative unit.

After Madhusudana Rāy, the succession of Aul Daṇḍapāṭa is not known. The last Hindu Gajapati of Orissa was Mukundadeva (A.D. 1560-1568) of Chalukya dynasty. After the death of Mukundadeva, his Official Ramchandra Dev placed himself as the Raja of Khurda and became the founder of Bhoi dynasty. The surviving two sons of Mukundadeva were Tailanga Ramchandra Dev and Chhakari Bhramarbar, who attacked the newly formed Raja of Khurda, but were defeated by Gajapati Ramchandra Dev. These two sons of Mukundadeva appealed to Emperor Akbar, who deputed Raja Man Singh to make arrangements regarding rents and to commence a survey of then Orissa.

Raja Man Singh chose Ramachandra of Bhoi dynasty as Raja of Khurda and during that period Aul (Ali) fort was surrendered to Raja Man Singh in 1592 by a Pathan Chief. Raja Man Singh gave it to the eldest son Tailanga Ramchandra Dev of Mukundadeva, who waited on him at Kalkalghāṭi. The second son Chhakari Bhramarbar received the fort of Sarangarh (Patia). While doing this transaction Raja Man Singh had camped at Dera Bisi. After he left the site of his camp, came to be known as Dera Bisi.

From the family tradition of the Raja of Aul, it is known that just after Raja Man Singh went back, the then surviving Mahānta (Guru) of Matsyendranāth's "Yogini Cult," and "Nāṭhism," had approached the first Raja of Aul, Tailanga Ramchandra Dev, for gifting some land, for establishing a Math, of their Cult. Accordingly land was granted and the Math of "Matsyendranāth", was set up at Dera Bisi in 16th century A.D. Further survey, finding and research are required to give more details of this MATH.

## LAJJĀ GOURI

The epithet LAJJĀ for Śākti refers to abstract quality and may be traced in the Vedas. The Śākta principles find expression in the Devimāhātmya section of the Mārkaṇḍeya purāṇa, and here She bore the name LAJJĀ as one of the traditional epithets. Even Lakṣmi bore the name Lajjā. No literature has been discovered so far, which gives the detail iconographic details of Lajjā Gouri. This is because, India was exposed to foreign raids and her ancient libraries have been burnt and destroyed.

The Tantras speak of three temperaments, dispositions, characters (bhāva), or classes of human beings, the pāśu-bhāva (animal), vira-bhāva (heroic) and divya-bhāva (deva - like Divine). These divisions are based on various modifications of the guṇas (qualities as they manifest in human beings (Jiva). In the pāśu the rajo-guṇa operates chiefly on tāmas, producing such dark characteristics as error (bhrānti), drowsiness (tandrā) and sloth (ālasya). It is however, an error to suppose that the paśú is as much a bad individual, on the contrary, a jiva of this class may prove superior to a jiva of the next. There are also numerous kinds of paśú, some more, some less tāmasik than others. Some, there are at the lowest end of the scale, which marks the first advance upon the higher forms of animal life. The paśú is in fact the individual who is bound by eight bonds (pāśa), of which the Kulārṇava tantra enumerates eight -namely pity (Dayā), ignorance and delusion (mohā), fear (bhaya), shame (lajjā), disgust (ghṛṇā), family (kula), custom (śila) and caste (varṇa).

Sir John Woodroffe gives an example of shame (Lajjā) from the Hindu scruptures and states that when, to take the Svāmi's example, Śrī Kṛṣṇa stole the clothes of the bathing Gopis or milk-maids and cowherds and made them approach Him naked. He removed the artificial coverings which are imposed on man in the sāṃsāra. The Gopis were eight, as are the bonds, and the errors by which the Jīva is misled are the clothes which Kṛṣṇa stole. Freed of these Jīva is liberated from all bonds arising from one's desires, family and society. Formerly it was sufficient to live in worldly fashion according to the morality governing life in the World. Now the Sādhaka must go further and transcend the World, or rather seek to do so. One rises by these things which are commonly the cause of fall. When one has completely achieved the purposes and liberated from all bonds, the individual reaches the stage of Śiva (Śivatva).

After rising above the eight bonds (pāśa), mentioned above, an individual can overcome one's paśū - bhava or animal instinct. Each bond is meaningful and to overcome shame, LAJJĀ Deity worship developed. In Devi Mahātmya (v. 12- 33) it is mentioned that Śākti is also embodiment of various virtues and abstract such as Lajjā (shame or modesty) etc. This concept of the Devi Māhātmya greatly enhanced the prestige of the Great Mother and established her superiority over other Gods and Goddessess.

The Mother has no shame or modesty, when She gives birth to new life. So, in that stage She is above paśū - bhāva, for that moment. In the sophisticated Tantras with Śākta orientation the whole process is explained with reference to the human body. The space holding the thousand petalled lotus in the cerebral region is called Brahmārandhra or Śūnya. It is the breeding spot of Icchā-Śākti and Para-Nāda. It is a part of the Visargamaṇḍala, which is great causal state of Brahman or Samvit symbolised by Sabalabrahma or Kulakuṇḍalini.

Two Lajjāgaurī Deities are discovered in Orissa so far. One was discovered at Kortipadar village area, in the vicinity of Khariar township and the other at Komna in Nuapada district, situated at the extreme western border of Orissa. The icon of Lajjāgauri represents nude seated female in spounting position (in pre-delivery position, with secretion of pre-delivery fluid) and lotus headed. The fully blossomed lotus with petals signifies Sahasrāra cakra of Kuṇḍalini yoga. The icon of lotus replacing the head is specially mentioned in the "Vishṇudharmottara (3, 82, 8)," as "devyāścha mastaka padmaṁ tathā kāryam manoharam saubhāgyam tad vijānihi." Because of this reason, the lotus over the neck, instead of the human head in these figures. Pregnant lady should have large swelling of the belly. Strangely enough, the Lajjā Gouri images are not shown with swelled belly. Most probably the iconographical details were forgotten by the artists and they were chiselling Lajjā Gouri images traditionally, without knowing its details. In the Lajjā Gouri image discovered at Kortipadar; in the vicinity of Khariar, cloth is worn at lower body. The artist has wrongly done it. The icon of Lajjā Gouri image discovered at Komna is in its proper description, without swelled belly.

The worship of Lajjā Gouri was prevalent in India during medieval period mostly in Rajasthan, Mahārāṣṭra, Madhya Pradesh, Andhra and South India. In South Kōśala region of upper Mahāṇadi river valley Lajjā Gourī sculptures are found at Malhar (Bilaspur district) which belong to circa. 9th-10th centuries A.D. and on the Jain temple of Arang (Raipur district).

The practice of Lajjā Gouri worship has extended till Nuapada district area of western Orissa, which area once comprised the area of South Kōśala.

## TĀRĀ

The word "TĀRĀ", means Star. The name of this Goddess has similarity with the celebrated Mother Goddesses of Western Asia. In India "Tārā," signifies protection and thereby Saviour... Buddhist tradition, She saves or protects her devotees from eight great fears (aṣṭamahābhaya). Her early history in India is in mystery but from Subandha's work "Vāsavadattā," it is supposed that by 6th century A.D. her Cult became popular in India. Goddess Tārā made her way into Buddhism and came to be known as Śākti or energy of Boddhisattva Avalokiteśvara.

Tārā cult passed from India to Tibet and in various Goddess forms went to China within 7th and 8th centuries A.D. corresponding with the female principle worshipped in Buddhism, in the Hindu pantheon Tārā, Ugratārā, Ekajaṭā and Mahā Nilasarasvatī Goddesses are found. The dhyānas of these Goddesses as found in the Hindu tantras correspond to those found in the Buddhist tantra Sādhanās.

In Buddhist pantheon Tārā became the consort of Amoghasidhi, who was destined to play great role. Tara's colour is green here and She is embodine of the element of air.

Goddesses emanating from Akṣobhya consists of those belonging to the Tārā group. Foremost among these Deities is Mahācinatārā, who is also known in Buddhist tāntric literature as Ugratārā. Tārā has been incorporated in Hindu pantheon under the name of Tārā and is regarded as one of the Ten Mahāvidyā Goddesses. It is interesting that the dhyāna of Tārā, as is found in the Tantrasāra of Kṛṣṇānanda Āgamavagisa, is directly borrowed from the Sādhanamālā. Even the association of Akṣobhya with Tārā is maintained in the Śākta Tantras. Ekajaṭā is also a form of Tārā whose cult is reported to have been brought to India by Siddha Nāgārjuna from Bhoṭadesa or Tibet.

Of all the Goddesses of the Vajrayāna pantheon of Tāntric Buddhism, Tārā became the most celebrated as the consort of Avalokiteśvara. Goddesses of the Tārā group in Buddhism are Khadiravani Tārā, Mahāśri

Tārā, Saḍbhuja Sitātārā, Dhanda Tārā and Sitā Tārā. Tārā is the common name applied to a large number of Goddesses such as Jāinguli, Parṇaśabari, Mahācinatārā, Ekajaṭā and others. Khadiravani Tārā is also known as Śyāma Tārā because of her green colour. She is endowed with two hands and shows the varada mudrā with the right and utpala in the left. This is the most common and most popular iconographical trait of Tārā. Khadiravani can be recognised by the figures of the two attendant deities. Aśokakāntā Mārici and Ekajaṭā. Marāśri Tārā has two more attendants, Jāṅguli and Mahāmāyāri and She is also green. Vaśya Tārā, also known by the name of Ārya Tārā, looks exactly like Khadiravani Tārā with the exception that She sits in bhadrāsana with both legs dangling. Tārā also has many-handed forms. Sitā Tārā is a white variety of Tārā with one face and four arms. Ṣaḍbhūja Sitā Tārā, as her name implies, is a six-armed form of white Tārā. Dhanada Tārā is one of the four-armed varieties of Tārā. The special features of the Goddess are that She rides an animal, and like Vajra Tārā is surrounded by eight goddesses.

Female emanations of Ratnasambhāva also consist of two deities of the Tārā group, Vajrā Tārā and Prasanna Tārā. The former is conceived of in the middle of the circle of eight mothers. She is eight armed, four-faced and decked in all ornaments. She has numerous forms. Prasanna Tārā is of terrible appearance. She is yellow and has eight faces and sixteen arms.

There are Tārās of five colours in Tāntric Buddhism. In practice most of the Buddhist male deities of the later period came to be known as Avalokiteśvara or Lokeśvara and all of the female deities came under the general name Tārā. Different forms of this goddess were classified from the viewpoint of her colour. To the red Tārā group belonged Kurukulla to the blue group Ekajaṭā and Mahācinatārā; to the yellow group, Vajratārā, Jāṅguli, Parṇaśabari and Bhṛkuti; to the white group Aṣṭamahābhayatārā, Mṛtyuvañcanatārā, Caturbhūja Tārā, Ṣaḍbhuja Sitā Tārā, Viśvamātā, Kurukullā and Jāṅguli; and to the green group Khadiravani Tārā, Vaśyatārā, Arya Tārā, Mahāttaritārā, Varada-tārā, Durgottāriṇitārā, Dhanada-tārā, Jāṅguli and Parṇaśabari. It is definite that all the major Goddesses of Vajrayāna form of Tāntric Buddhism came to be known as Tārā.

Some Hindu Deities as Mahākālā, Gaṇapati, Gaṇapatihṛdayā, Sarasvati, Indra, Yama, Varuṇa, Kubera, Iśāna, Agni, Nairṛti, Vāyu, Brahmā, Viṣṇu, Maheśvara, Kārttikeya, Vārāhi, Cāmuṇḍa etc. have been incorporated in the Vajrayāna pantheon of Tāntric Buddhism.

In one of the cells of a ruined Jain monastry at Suai, situated in the road between Semiliguda and Nandapur in Koraput district; one image of four-armed Tārā, adorned with bangles upto the elbows is found. Due to ravages of weather, the whole monastery is in a dilapidated condition.

Tārā cult became so much popular that in the Śākta tantra, She has been given the position of the Supreme being; as second Goddess of Daśamahāvidyās.

## DAŚA MAHĀVIDYĀS

Mahāvidyā is the great Śākti. She is māyā because it is Her māyā which produces Saṁsāra. As Lord of māyā She is Mahāmāyā. The truth consists of both Vidyā and Avidyā, and this Tantra Mahāvidyā is a symbolic representation of this whole truth, whose worship would not only bring happiness in this so called ephemeral world but also release from death and attainment of Bliss. Because pure existence means nothing, the existent must know that one is existing. This is sentience and it arises out of consciousness - force (cit - śākti). This consciousness force in the Supreme Being is known as Mahāvidyā without which there is no difference between Being and Non-Being. The consciousness-force or power in the Supreme a logical being flows to creation for ānanda (Bliss) in three streams icchā, kriyā and jñāna symbolically represented by the three premier Mahāvidyās – Kāli, Tārā and Tripura Sundari Ṣoḍasi. In order to comprehend the tāntric concept of Mahāvidyā, there is clear idea of what māyā and avidyā means in Tantra as concept of Vidyā brings in only half truth. Therefore Mahāvidyā, the Cult of Daśamahāvidyā (ten malevolent manifestations of the Goddess) exposed the extreme form of Tantrism. These are held to be ten in number and the number being probably selected to match the ten chief incarnations of Viṣṇu Mahāvidyās are the sources of all that is to be known and these are the most important Deities of the Tantras.

Orissa is a State where a large number of Śākti - tāntric pīṭhas like Ugratārā at Nirākarpur, Ugratārā at Berhampur, Carcikā at Bānki, Mangalā at Kakatpur, Vimalā in Puri inside Jāgannāth temple, Sāralā at Jhaṅkaḍa (Kanakapur) and Vīrajā at Jajpur.

The Deities of Daśamahāvidyās have all different attributes and their designation are thus :-

1. Kāli (sometimes called Śyāmā), is black in colour and fierce in character.

2. Tārā, is a benign manifestation.
3. Sodaśi, the Goddess as a beautiful girl of 16 (also called Tripurā).
4. Dhuvaneśvarī.
5. Bhairavī.
6. Chinnamastā.
7. Dhūmāvati.
8. Vagalā.
9. Mātaṅgi.
10. Kāmalatmikā or Kamalā.

Of these the first two are especially the "Mahāvidyās," the next five on the "Vidyās," and the last three "Siddhavidyās." The spiritual aspects of the Goddesses of Mahāvidyās are dealt by D.N. Bose and Hiralal Haldar thus :-

"Kāli is pure ecstacy, a feeling of perfect satisfaction. There is no question of such a thing that this much I have got and this much I require. She is above all senses of positivity and negativity. When She first awakens with the sense of positivity, She becomes Tārā. She sees herself as Brahmā, the fountain source of many. She stands in the midst of a funeral pyre in which the World was reduced to ashes in the previous Kalpa. The seeds of the previous manifestations germinate here. She it is who serves the eternal into many. Then the Goddess appears as Ṣoḍaśī, complete in sixteen Kalās or phases of Śākti to give shape to her wishes. The wish descends through five senses of perceptions, viz. : sound, touch form, taste and smell and hence the conception of five Gods found along with the Goddess. Then the Śākti further descends to assume names and forms and is then known as Bhubaneśvari, who is the Goddess of the World phenomenon. She stands for the forces that will constitute the material World. The Śākti then appears in each unit of creation so that the process of multiplication may continue unhampered. She is then known as Bhairavī, I require this, I want that, etc. etc. She it is who moulds the individual appearances and her pose of bringing about the changes is called Kuṇḍalini. It is She who takes up each individual self to Śiva from which it comes. Under her influence individuals are running for fulfilment of Worldly satisfactions and even for God realisation. To do this the Śākti has to sever herself. This is meant by Chinnamastā. She severs even her head so that the mount can drink the very blood that comes out of her trunk through the neck. On her either side are two Nāyikās, Ḍākini and Varṇini who represent names and forms. All the individuals are so many Chinnamastās. They have their being in the

Mother and yet they do not know that they are virtually sucking the life-blood of the Mother. She represents the Śākti by which the Great Mother sacrifices herself for the happiness of her children. She severs her love for the children and feeds them with her own blood. She is unique in both her aspects. In one hand she holds her own head and feeds it with her own blood, which represents that she is turned inwards and is in eternal communion with self-knowledge, here figuratively taken as the head, the crown of creation. Outwardly she is constantly taking up such forms e.g. I am angry, I am thirsty, I want knowledge on the one hand and again she brings about fruition of these desires. The Śākti then further gets down and makes the individuals forgetful of all these and think themselves as quite helpless, afflicted with thirst and hunger and suffering the pangs of birth and death. She is then known as Dhūmavati, a widow, seated on a chariot on which mounts a crow, cowing eternally demanding this and that. Here the Śākti has reached the nāḍis of her downward course and then She turns inwards to carry the individuals steeped in ignorance and misery to a state of Bliss. Smarting under pains from Dhūmāvatī when the individuals pine for relief, Goddess Bagala revives in them the sense that they are Brahmā in essence. She is therefore, represented as holding by one hand the tongue of the Asura, i.e. our World mindedness and belabours the Asura with a mallet in her other hand. She instils a desire in the individuals to shun their worldly propensities and control the loose thoughts that have dragged them downwards. The Goddess appears with a mallet in hand to bring about the enjoyments of the individuals according to their necessity and also in their proper sequence. The next Mahāvidyā is Mātaṅgi whose steps are like those of an infuriate elephant. Her eyes are rolling under the influence of drink and her movements bespeak of herself as engrossed in her own feelings. She has been called the Dharmapatni, the eternal consort of Śiva and is running after him to be one with him. In the Dhyāna mantra She has been called as the presiding Deity of the "Words." She has been called Mantraśākti; a force that makes the words come true, pervading the Universe. Finally the Śākti appears as Kāmalā, who represents pure Self-consciousness, herself bathing in the calm ocean of happiness. The four elephants pouring ablutions of nector over her are knowledge, wealth, virtue and Godmindedness. She is herself the enjoyer and the enjoyed. The conscious force thus merges again into consciousness. The work of the Mahāvidyās is going on in this way in the macrocosm and the microcosm and is flinging the creation to a state of stern materialism and then again observing the same within herself."

The iconography of the Daśamahāvidyās or the ten forms of Goddess are described in religious Śākta literatures. All these Goddesses are considered as the manifestations of Śākti (Mahākāli). All these Goddesses have their own Yantras, Manṭras and mode of worships. The "Śāktisaṅgamatantra," says that among the Mahāvidyā Goddesses Kāli, Tārā, Ṣoḍaśī alias Sundarī, Bhairavī, Chinnamastā, Mātaṅgi and Vagalā are fond of Vamācāra, while Kamalā, Bhuvaneśvari and Dhūmāvatī may be appeased by Dakṣiṇācāra.

In Orissa the images of all the Goddesses of Daśamahāvidyās are not found. At Puri there is one early image of Kāli known as Shyama Kāli, belonging to 15th century A.D. This image conforms to the iconography of Dakhina Kāli. She is four-armed, holding sword in one upper arm while raising the other upward and the lower arms are in abhaya and varada poses. She is black in complexion adorned with garland of severed human heads and standing on Śiva in viparitarati or maithuna, practicing Vajroli, as prescribed in, "Haṭhayoga Pradipika."

There is another image of Tārā (15th century A.D.) worshipped as Ugra Tārā at Bhusandapur of Puri district. She is of dark blue complexion placing her left leg on the breast of Śiva, who is lying like a corpse on the funeral pyre. She is of short stature, terrible in appearance and dressed in tiger skin, she wears a garland of severed human heads, she is four-armed, three-eyed.

There is Ugra Tārā temple at Berhampur. Goddess Bhubaneśvari is worshiped inside the Jagannāth temple of Puri. Bhubaneśvarī is four-armed, seated on a white lotus in padmāsana pose. She holds aṅkuśa in the upper-right hand, the lower right being shown in varada pose. She holds a nāgapāśa in the upper left, the lower one being in abhaya mudrā. She is three eyed and has the cresent moon in her crest.

There is one Tāntric Kāli temple at Pitala, about two hundred years old, built by a Raja of Dharakote, in Ganjam district. One Kāli temple, about more than hundred years old, built by a Raja of Kalahandi is situated at Bhawanipatna. One monolithic image resembling Śhyāmā Kāli of Puri, is discovered by J.P.Singh Deo (author), by the side of a hill stream, at Dunguripali village area of Nuapada district of Western Orissa. It is much weather beaten.

There are few other Kāli and Tārā temples scattered in Orissa. The images of other Mahāvidyās are not available in Orissa, although the tradition of Daśamahāvidyā worship is still continuing. Every villages, towns and cities in Orissa have their own Goddesses, mostly worshipped as prescribed within Daśamahāvidyā puja rituals. So, Tantra is living religion of Orissa. In "Mahānirvāṇa Tantram," it is mentioned, "The river Gaṅges, the Mahāṇadi, the residence of the Spiritual guide, and the celebrated Shrines, these are the Tirṭhas or the holy places of pilgrimage in the Kali Yuga."

The svarūpa of the Mahāśakti has been revealed in Tāntric texts and in the Dhyāna mantras of the Adya Śākti Kālikā. The destructive force is one of Her aspects. As She destroys Mahākāla at the time of Pralaya, She is called Kāli. She is worshipped as Ādyā, as She is beginning of all. After mahāpralaya she alone remains as Tama or Avyakta Prakṛti in a state inconceivable by words or mind. Though formless She assumes various forms; though without beginning she is the origin of all. She is the Great Creator, Protector and Destroyer and Commander of all. The Goddess Kālikā, or Ānandamayi as She has been called, residing in the heart of Mahākāla (the Eternal Time), at her independent will appears as Mahākāli, Mahālakṣmī and Mahāsarasvatī to fulfil Her sport of Creation, Preservation and Destruction.

## ŚAIVA TANTRA

Śiva is the great God, Mahādeva, who is the eternal life principal. He is unmanifest in Universal form, but manifest in each individual or every form of life force. Also known as Mṛtyuñjaya, he is the Death-conquering Deity. Vedic cosmogony has identified Rudra-Śiva with Agni (fire), because it is the life-principle and therefore Cosmos was regarded as the fire-altar. Even the human body corresponds to it as the altar in which the fire of life is burning and kept constantly enkindled throughout the duration of earthly existance.

There is two fold of Agni, i.e. hot and cold, which are destructive and benevolent. Similarly God Śiva in his Bhairava or terrible form is dreadful and disintegrating, but in the form of Śiva is auspicious and sustainer of the life-process. In the Vedas and Vāyu purāṇa, mention have been made of innumerable Rudras. The conception of the Eleven Rudras was already developed in the Rigveda. The explanation of Rudras is clearly given in the Upanishads that the Eleven Rudras are symbols of eleven prāṇic energies by which both the individual and the universal are made capable of their dynamic functioning. The list of eleven Rudras are found in several purāṇas like Matsya purāṇa, Liṅga purāṇa, Harivaṁśa purāṇa, Bhavishya purāṇa and Śiva purāṇa. The Eleven

Rudras are (1) Aja-ekapād, (2) Ahirbudhaya, (3) Virūpaksa, (4) Tvashtā, (5) Raivata, (6) Hara, (7) Tryambaka, (8) Savitā, (9) Jayanta, (10) Aparājita and (11) Pināki.

The Rudras are all different manifestations of Agni. The Eleven Rudras as the principles of prāna in its diversified forms, are closely associated with the sacred Ekādaśi day or the eleventh day of the bright and dark halves of the month. It is enjoined that proper fasting should be observed on the Ekādaśi day to propitiate and worship the Eleven Rudras which means the purifying of the metabolic fire and obtaining for it new strength by drying away the toxin and which voluntary fasting brings about. The chemistry and physiology of a regulated fast in the regimen of life are well known in modern science and they were equally well realised by the ancients who prescribed two fast days, on the two Ekadaśi tithis (days) in each month. This creates a rhythm of purāṇic vibrations which is full of health and peace for body and mind.

The great exploit of Śiva was drinking of poison, he is Gaṅgādhara or the carrier of thousand fold floods of the river Gaṅgā, he is well known for smearing ashes on his body, and is known as Mahā Nagna or the Great Nude in (Atharva Deva 20. 136. 11.), an epithey of the transcendent Puruṣa or Creator, and his infinite nature or the Prakṛti styled as Mahā Nagni, the eternal Nude Eoman. Absolute Puruṣa is nude and Prakṛti or Nature is his covering. The five fross elements of matter known as Bhūtas (space, air, fire, water and earth) form the cloth which becomes the covering of the principles of Divine consciousness (Chinmaya Puruṣha). The nude God is Mahākāla - Absolute Time and the nude Goddess is Mahākali - the Black Mother.

Śiva is the Lord of all creatures and hence known as Pāśūpati. The word Pāśu is significant denoting a prāṇic centre. Each pāśu or living creature is an examplar of the life - principle. In their differentiated aspects the pāśus are numberless and Śiva as the archetypal Divine principle of life is the Lord of them. The bonds that keep them together are known as pāśu. Unless these bonds are loosened both by the grace of the Lord and the endeavour of the devotee, no one can get rid of them and the Soul that is soiled by matter remains bound in the snares of death.

Śiva is the arch-yogin, the Lord of all the Yogic practices and therefore known as Yogeśvara. The conception of Śiva in his Kāmāntaka form or conquering the God of love is the greatest exploit of the Great God. The foremost teacher of Yoga is Śiva and Yoga discipline is above all learning and knowledge of the Scriptures. Yoga is intensely practical requiring perfect mastery of the physical, vital and psychić powers that are in one's personality. An individual who has mastered Yoga becomes immune against all temptations and pleasures of the senses and becomes established in one's own Spiritual centre unmoved by the extraneous attractions and virtually become identical with the nature of Śiva as Sthaṇu, the changeless and stable Deity fixed in one's own centre.

In "Nāsadiya Sūkta", (Hymn of Creation) of the Rigveda (10. 129.) it is stated that Kāma was the first to be created and it was the seed of the Creator's mind from which sprouted the entire Cosmic creation. Love is the predominant impulse in the heart of all creatures and therefore its regulation, control and purity are of the highest significance for the integration of one's personality.

God Kāmadeva is said to hold a bow by which he shoots his five arrows of the various mental conditions which torment all beings. Kāmadeva as the power of Sex has been considered to be the greatest disturber of Yoga, it was therefore essential for Śiva to sublimate the instinct of love before it could be able to effect his Samādhi. This is the meaning of the burning of Kāma, known as madana - dahana.

The motif of the Kāmānta form of Madana-dahana exploit of Śiva was adopted by the Buddhists as the great event of the conquest of Māra (Māra - Dharṣaṇa). It is said that when Buddha sat on his diamond throne in an unmovable pose and was to realise the highest point of his meditation all the dark influence of matter rose up in a tidal flood headed by the leader Māra, the genius of evil and temptation. He brought with him his beautiful daughters to seduce the Master and a host of demons to attack him and rain on him their different weapons of potentialities for evil, but Buddha remained unmoved and his mental concentration did not succumb to any one of these devilish forces. Thus Māra or the genius of temptation could not prevail against Buddha and Buddha obtained Sambodhi or Enlightenment, that is, the realisation of the Divine principle of Light; he became in a real sense the victor of Jina. The description of this event in religious literature and its portrayal in art are very florid and inspiring and form a beautiful motif of Buddhist religion similar to that of Māra dharṣaṇa in Brāhmaṇīcal literature.

Śiva as Yogin must therefore be realised within the heart of each individual who aspires to conquer death, darkness of matter and limitation in all its basic forms, and who wishes to ascend on the higher world of light. Divine Powers and Immortality. All Yogis pay homage to Yogeśvara. It is after this mastery of Kāma that Śiva attains perfection of Yoga and Samādhi and becomes entitled to join his female energy Kuṇḍalini or Śākti or Pārvatī and attain the form of Ardhanārīśvara.

## ARDHANĀRĪŚVARA

In iconography there are many examples of Ardhanārīśvara Śiva, in which the right half is Śiva and left half is Pārvati or Husband and Wife, sharing the two halves of the same maṇḍala (Vāmārdhajāni).

This form is the aspects of Śiva and Pārvati in whom the respective Kuṇḍalini or Serpent powers in their male and female forms open their coils for an upward ascent and reach to combine with each other, the highest centres of the brain, which is symbolised as Kailāsa.

The two aspects were conceived in the Vedas in many ways. The single egg or germ of creation was split into Prāṇa and Bhūṭa. He was called Hiraṇyagarbha in which hiraṇya or gold is the symbol of prāṇa and garbha that of matter. The female germ is fertilised by the male energy and the two together are known as Hiraṇyagarbha. Bṛihan-Nāradiya purāṇa, Matsya purāṇa, Liṅga purāṇa and Śiva purāṇa have conceived of the Ardhanārīśvara form.

It is the basis truth of both physiology and psychology that each individual is half-male and half-female. The characteristics of each sex are co-extensive in the whole body and each individual self partakes of the two features of the male and the female. The two fold sex impulse is present in the whole body. In man the male part is predominant and in the woman the female; and both elemental passions need to meet with their counterparts. The truth of the Psyche must become the truth of the physical body. Cupid and Psyche form an inseparable pair and are but archetypal of the two opposite sexes forming a single pair for the purpose of the highest perfection of the human Soul and begetting the progeny through a complex mechanism of chromosomes or mysterious cell-division.

It is stated in the Rigveda : "What you describe to me as Male are in reality also Feṃale. He who has the penetrative eye of the mind discerns this truth and not the blind who sees with the physical eye only."

The integration of the male and female elements of the personality is symbolized in India i.e. Bharat by the androgynous Deity Ardhanārīśvara. The sculptures and carvings of this Deity are half male and half female. Śiva on the right and Śākti on the left. This Deity embodies the ancient truth that Divinity is neither male nor female, but a transcendental fusion of the two.

## THE BULL (NANDI)

The seed in human beings, animals and plants is a vast world of all the subtle forms that become manifest in creation of nature. The great Bull (Nandi) of Śiva is Kāma, the sprinkler of Seed. The Seed is the refined substance; it permeates the whole body and its various sheaths, like blood, tissues, bones, marrow and all the secretions of the endocrine glands and the spinal canal. This seed is the great power of Śiva Mahādeva and is symbolised as the Nandi Bull that is the sprinkling agent of the God of Love or the erotic impulses that appear in bodily rhythm.

The vehicle of Śiva is Nandi the Great Bull and Śiva loves to ride on his Bull, who is a member of the Lord's family. Nandi Bull represents the fecundating energy of Kāma, the God of Love. Śiva as the Lord of Yoga (Yogeśvara) conquered Kāma and naturally, it is he, who became the Rider of the Nandi Bull and is called Nandiśvara also. Usually Sexual energy flow downwards, but the other Yogic aspect through Vajroli is that of the upward flow of the Sex power, when that ascends to the brain and saturates the highest centres of the mind and thus contributes to the Samādhi of Śiva. The Nandi Bull is thus both a sprinkler and preserver of the energy that is with Śiva.

## ŚAIVA TANTRA

According to R.K.Upadhyaya, the expressions, "Śaiva tantra," and "Śaivagama," are synonyms and as such they are coextensive in meaning and usage. The Śaiva tantra has postulated three basic concepts and it is arranged into four sections (pādas). The subject matters of these four consecutive sections are (1) direct experience of external objects (bhoga), (2) emancipation (mokṣa), (3) initiation (dikṣā) and (4) performance or religious rites and ceremonies (caryā). The three basic concepts may be stated as follows :(1) Paśūpati (Śiva), (2) individual Self (paśu) and (3) fetter (pāśa). The association with delusion is responsible for the non-realization of intrinstic nature of the Self. In this state an individual Self receives the designation of Paśu. This pasuhood is indissolubly bounded with dualistic outlook. The fetters which enmesh on individual Self with the worldly existence are susceptible of a five fold classification.

"Paśu is of three distinct types : (1) Kala, (2) Talapākala and (3) Sakala. The first variety of paśu, namely, Kala is endowed with dross (male). And the second type of pāśu which is termed as talapākala, is endowed with dress and action. Likewise the third kind of paśu which is designated as Sakala is endowed with dress, action and ignorance (māyā). Again the type of pāśu which bears the name of Kala and endowed with dress is further liable to a twofold subdivision (samāsakaluṣa and asamāskaluṣa). The second sort of paśu namely, talapākala, which has been declared to be endowed with dross and action, has been arranged into two distinct orders :(1) mature dress (pakvamala) and (2) immature dress (apakvamala). The two classes of paśu styled Kala and talapākala are accorded the epithets, Vijñānakala and pralayākala when they move in pure and righteous religious path. The remaining variety of paśu which is called Sakala remains enclosed within thirty-six categories beginning with Kala and the like and is subject to the cycle of birth and death. Its biophysical existence in different order of animal life is determined by inexorable law of Karman.

"The fetters have been classified under five heads : (1) fetter engendered by dress (malaya), (2) fetter engendered by action (karmaja), (3) fetter engendered by māyā (māyeja), (4) fetter engendered by the power, obscuring the light of the Soul (tirodhānaśaktija) and (5) fetter engendered by Vindu (Vinduja). Now dross which engenders fetter is one and is endowed with the innumerable powers. It veils the power of knowledge and the power of action. It brings into existence the physical body which is the veritable wrapper of the Soul. The body which owes its existence to this type of fetter resembles a husk of some fruit or seed, (Bhojaraja's Tattvaprakāśika Kārikā 18). And Karman which gives rise to the specific type of fetter is of two varieties, namely, merit and demerit. It is conductive to the experience of results of chequered character. It is eternal and infinite. It has no beginning or an end like the series of relation holding between seed and sprout.

"Now the true nature of the fetter engendered by Vindu is going to be dealt with. It is remarkable that the Supreme Self is the ultimate cause of this entire Universe. He is one and omnipresent. He is called the primordial Being and the Lord of all. Undoubtedly His Divine power is comprehensible by mind; but it is characterized by the absence of any visible manifestation. And it paves the way of the renunciation of worldly things. Besides, this power is of the nature of knowledge and action. It is owing to the influence of this Śiva-Śākti that an individual Self succeeds to reach the blessed region of the Supreme and becomes worthy of experiencing infinite perennial Bliss.

"Śaivāgama declares in indubious terms that a conscious Self may achieve Spiritual liberation through the grace of Śiva (God) even without enduring the consequences of his actions. Divine acquittal is all-powerful to release one from sorrow and suffering imposed by the fetters of action (Karman). — The Vedic hymns have loudly proclaimed about the existence of God. They have also glorified the majesty of the Supreme. But the method of worship of the Supreme has not been elaborated in the Vedas. It is the Vedic Śaivāgamas that have dealt with the different ways and forms of worship in a clear and comprehensive manner."

Śiva is believed to be the first Guru and the founder of Tantra and Yoga. Parvati his counterpart, wife or Śākti was his first disciple, therefore the knowledge of Tantra and Yoga was first imparted to a Woman. In Hindu and Tibetan traditions of Tantra there were eighty-four Siddhas and out of these, sixty-four were Yoginis. In "Ananda Lahari", Śaṅkarācārya states, "Without Śākti, how can Śiva create anything?" Śiva is only the silent witness, Śākti is the creator. Therefore, in Tāntric tradition, Woman is the initiator.

Cosmic power is called Śākti (from the root meaning "to be able") in Tantra and is given different forms and names according to the specific function and sphere of operation. Śākti is the creative impulse that manifests the Universe in response to inspired consciousness. Creation is the play of energy before consciousness, the dance of Śākti before Śiva. In a Universe that is increasingly recognized by material science as a matrix of interlocking energy fields. Śākti is all. In the Mahānirvaṇa Tantra Śiva addresses Śākti thus :-

"You are the Supreme manifestation of Brahman, the Supreme consciousness and from you has come the entire Universe. You are its Mother. You are the origin of all manifestations. You are the form of everything. Your root is in Brahman who is actionless. It is you, moved by his desire, who creates, protects and withdraws this World with all that moves and is motionless. Therefore, by worshipping you, your devotees will surely reach the Supreme."

Śākti has a dual nature. It is Śākti as "MĀYĀ," who enveils us in this World of sensual experience and delusion. Yet it is the direct personal perception of the Śākti Kuṇḍalini that leads to enlightenment.

Tantra recognizes that the Supreme is one, beyond polarity, but that it manifests as Śiva (male), consciousness and Śākti (female) energy. However, Tantra emphasizes the rituals of the Goddess Śākti, for these constitute the practical means (Yoga Sādhanā) for the arousal and unification of the energies that are necessary to propel us to the peaks of expanded consciousness.

## BHAIRAVAS

It is known from Viṣṇudharmottra, III.48.4 -6 that the southern face of Śiva holds a fierce shape and is called Bhairava. Bhairava is also associated with śākta pīṭha. Ānandabhairava or Mahābhairava, which is the name given to Śiva, is the Soul of, or is composed of, the nine collections of things of which the World is made up, such as time and its various forms (Kālavyūha), existing things like the blue substance (kulavyūha), names (Nām-vyūha), perception (Jñānavyūha), the five faculties, viz. consciousness, heat, will, intelligence and mind (Chittavyūha). Mahābhairava is the Soul of the Goddess; therefore She also is the Soul of, or composed of, the nine collections. Both, therefore, constitute one entity. When there is Sāmarasya, or community of joy or intense love between them, creation follows. The Female element, or Mahābhairavi, however, is predominent in the process of creation and the Male element, or Mahābhairava, in the work of destruction.

The Cult of Śiva has two aspects, benevolent (Saumya) and malevolent (Ūgra). Among various types of the terrific or Ūgra forms of Śiva; mention may be made of his Bhairavas, Aghora, Virabhadra and Birupākṣa forms. According to āgamic texts there are sixty-four Bhairavas, divided into eight groups and they are the counterparts of the sixty-four Yoginis.

The origin of the mystic Bhairavas is known from Vāmana purāṇa, which states that there was a fierce battle between Andhakāsura and Mahādeva. Andhakā hit the head of Mahādeva with his mace. With this blow, blood oozed out from the wound and flowed down the four sides. From the stream of blood that gushed out of the head of Mahādeva, the Bhairavas were created. From the blood flowing to the east was born Vidurāja Bhairava, decked with beautiful ornaments and looking like a blazing fire. Fom the flow of blood of Mahādeva to the south was born Rāmaraja Bhairava, deep black in colour associated with preṭas. From that flow to west; Nāgarāja decorated with leaves and Atasi Kusuma in colour and from that of the north was born Svachchandarāja Bhairava black in colour; holding Triśūla (trident) and lastly from the total flow of the blood, came out Lambitarāja Bhairava.

The eight Bhairavas according to Tantrasāra are Asitaṅga, Ruru, Chanda, Krodha, Unmaṭṭa, Kapāli, Bhisaṇa and Samhāra. Bhairavas are also mentioned in Mahāvidyās. Mahābhairava, Sambārabhairava, Asitāṅgabhairava, Rurubhairava, Kalābhairava, Krodhabhairava,

Kapālabhairava and Rudrabhairava are worshipped in the occasion of autumnal Devi worship.

In course of time, the eight Bhairavas such as Asitāṅga, Ruru, Chanda, Krodha, Unmaṭṭa, Kapāla, Bhiṣana and Samhāra multiplied into sixty - four Bhairavas.

## HARI - HARA

Hari - Hara is the composite form of Viṣṇu and Śiva. In this composite form Rudra -Śiva is named as Harihara or Śaṁkara-Nārāyaṇa. In this aspect the right half is Śiva and the left half is Viṣṇu. There is a short description of the Śiva-Nārāyana form in Matsya purāṇa (2. 60. 21 - 27).

There is metaphysical exposition of this composite form (Śarira - Yoga) in the Harivaṁśa purāṇa (1. 25. 27) which states that Brahmā obtained a vision of the joint form of Śiva and Viṣṇu and saw Śiva in the form of Viṣṇu and Viṣṇu in the form of Śiva. It was a miracle that Śiva wore the Pitāmbara and held in his hands conch, wheel and mace and Viṣṇu took the robe of a tiger's skin and attributes of a trident and spear. Śiva accepted Garuḍa as his vehicle and Viṣṇu took the banner of a bull.

Brahmā declared that Brāhman was one (ekam Brahma) and there was no opposition between Viṣṇu and Rudra who shared the single aspect of the transcendent Self.

Brahmā interrogated Mārkaṇḍeya about this mystery and the latter replied: "I see no difference between the Viṣṇu aspect of Śiva and the Śiva aspect of Viṣṇu. Both are the differentiated aspects of the transcendent Akṣara Brahmā. In fact, what is Viṣṇu is Rudra and what is Rudra is Brahmā. One Divine reality becomes differentiated as the three Gods - Brahmā, Viṣṇu and Rudra. All three are Self-existent creators and lords of theWorlds and all of them are Ardhanārīśvara.

"As water mingles with water so Viṣṇu in his composite form becomes of the same aspect as Rudra. As fire mingle with fire and assumes the form of a single flame as Rudra mingles with Viṣṇu and becomes Viṣṇumaya. We should think of Rudra as of fiery aspect and realise Viṣṇu as Soma and thus the whole World is the composite form of Agni and Soma. They both create and destroy the creation together. Both are Supreme Gods. Maheśvara showing benevolence to the created World. The Gods Nārāyaṇa and Maheśvara become the past, present and future. This is the highest secret to be realised. Rudra holds Viṣṇu as the

Supreme deity and Viṣṇu regards Śiva to be the same. The one transcendent being has differentiated himself in the form of the two Gods. There is no Śiva without Viṣṇu and no Viṣṇu without Śaṅkara and therefore Rudra and Viṣṇu assume a composite form as Harihara.

"I, therefore, bow to Rudra and to Viṣṇu moving together, On the one side I bow to the three eyes and to the two eyes on the other. On the one the red eye and the lotus eye on the other. On the one father of Kumāra and on the other of Pradyumna. On the one holding the Gaṅgā and on the other the mountain. On the one wearing the garland of skulls and on the other Vanamāla. On the one holding the trident, on the other a discus. On the one holding the Brahma-daṇḍa and the other a golden club. On the one wearing the skin and on the other yellow robe. I bow to the lord of Pārvatī and also to the lord of Lakṣmī. I bow to him who holds the Khatvāṅga and the club in his composite aspects ; who smears the ashes and the black agaru; who lives in the cemetery and who sleeps in the ocean; who rides on a bull and who rides on the Garuḍa.

"I bow to Rudra who has many forms and to Viṣṇu of many incarnations. I bow to the one who supports the World and to the other who brings about the dissolution. I bow to one who is of a benevolent form (Saumya rūpa) and to the other of a terrible form (Bhairava rūpa). I bow to one who destroyed the sacrifice of Dakṣa and I bow to the other who brought about the bondage of Bali. My obeisance to one who destroyed Tripurā, Kāmadeva and Andhakā and to the other who destroyed the Asuras named Mura, Naraka and Kaiṭabha. The one has a thousand arms and the other also has infinite hands. Obeisance to Lord Viṣṇu and to Lord Śiva. The one is worshipped by the mantras of Yajurveda (viz. Śatarudriya for Śiva) and the other by the Śāma chants (i.e. Viṣṇu)."

This Hariharātmaka stotra was held dear for recitation by Sages like Vyāsa, Nārada, Bhāradvāja, Garga, Viśvāmitra, Agastya, Pulastya and Dhaumya. The composite principle of Viṣṇu and Rudra who was also named as Indra, was first enunciated in Rigveda (73. 68). Imagery of Indra and Viṣṇu functioning in one centre was liberally written in Purānic literatures and the sculptures gave it a composite form in the Harihara Mūrti. This signifies that in knowledge of the Absolute there is no difference of cast, creed, nationality and Religions. As knowledge is for knowledge sake, in the same manner the knowledge of Absolute is for the Absolute realisation, which is possible to achieve in human birth, for liberation.

## ŚIVA'S TRIŚŪLA

Śiva's trident, Triśūla is the symbol of the triadic pattern of Creation and the three spikes of this irresistible weapon correspond to the three Guṇas (Satva, raja and tama) or tensions which bring the Cosmos into existence and also make for its disruption when they are discordant. In this manner, the Creation continues and there is no end to Creation.

## AṢṬMŪRTI ŚIVA

Great God Śiva has an epithet "Aṣṭamūrti," which denotes eight forms both in his Cosmic manifestation and on the individual level. The eight manifest forms of Śiva are (1) Water, (2) Fire, (3) Earth, (4) Air, (5) Space, (6) Sun, (7) Moon and (8) Sacrificer (Yajamana), the initiated Priest (Dikṣita-brāhmana), or the giver of Libation.

These eight forms are divisible into three categories, (1) Five gross elements of Matter (bhūta), (2) Sun and Moon symbolising prāṇa and apāna, that is, the hot and cold aspects of a single vital power (prāṇa-mātrū), (3) Yajamāna or Brāhmana or priest of the bodily sacrifice which is the same as the principle of Mind (manas) or consciousness (prajñā-mātrā).

In Śaiva tantra Śiva in his absolute form is one, but in his differentiated form he becomes Trimūrti (Triple form - Bhrama, Viṣṇu and Māhesh) and is conceived of as Aṣṭamūrti, the owner of Eight forms. Eight-fold pulsation is put in the Brāhmanas in a rather obscure style saying that sleeping babe, RUDRA, was awakened and began to cry for a name to be given to it and it cried eight times so that eight names or eight different appellations were given to it as follows : (1) Rudra, (2) Śarva, (3) Pāśūpati, (4) Ūgra, (5) Aśani, (6) Bhava, (7) Mahādeva and (8) Iśāna.

The Linga purāṇa (II. 13- 17 and 26 -27) elaborates the Aṣṭmūrti doctrine as an item of the faith of the Pāśūpata teachers and enumerates the Eight forms as Śarva, Bhava, Pāśūpati, Iśāna, Bhima, Rudra, Mahādeva and Ūgra, there is slight transposition of this order in Mārkaṇḍeya purāṇa.

## PĀŚŪPATA, KĀPĀLA AND KĀLĀMUKHA SECTS

In the well known sealing of Mohenjodaro, Pāśūpati is depicted in his conspicuous form, sitting as cross-legged Deity, surrounded by four wild animals, viz. elephant, tiger, unicorn and bison. In Vedic times, the conception of Pāśūpati was wisespread in folk-lore and folk-cult. One of the names of Rudra was Pāśūpati in Vedic literature.

The body is the paśu par excellence. In essence the Vedic doctrine was that Prāṇas or the life-forces are verily manifesting as animals. Prajāpati created the animals with his own Prāṇas, thus Prajāpāti himself in the form of Agni and Rudra -Śiva became known as Pāśūpati. In purāṇas deep metaphysical exposition and meanings of Pāśas or bonds and their deliverance brought about only by Śiva-Rudra are explained. All the Dharmas and Adharmas, the relative ordinances of good and evil, are the bonds from which individual should seek freedom in order to obtain Salvation, through the grace of God Śiva. This is the great Pāśūpata Yoga, whose fountain head and source of knowledge is the great God Śiva, whose sure and transcendent aspect cannot be soiled by any modification of matter.

The founder teacher of this Pāśūpata school of thougnt was Lakuliśa, who was born at Kāyāvarohana in western India and regarded as the incarnation of Maheśvara. He had four eminent disciples named Kuśika, Garga, Mitra and Kaurusya or Rusta. They started roaring campaign against false beliefs and preached the religion of Bhakti to Śiva and his worship in the form of Liṅga. Facts about Lakuliśa, the great exponent of the Pāśupata sect, are found in an inscription of 380-81 A.D. (Gupta ers 61), belonging to the reign of Chandragupta II, from which it appears that he flourished about the 2nd century A.D. in the Kathiawar region. The earliest text dealing with the principal tenets of the Pāśupata system is known as the "Pāśupatasūtra". The name of its author is not known, but it was commented by Rāśikara Kauṇḍinya, who flourished in the Gupta age. One of the important streams of the ancient Pāśūpata system later culminated in what may be called Āgamānta Śaivism. This Schooi possesed a considerable literature called "Āgamas," a number of which are preserved in manuscripts of the 8th and 9th centuries A.D. numbering eighteen; according to one tradition and twenty-eight, according to another.

According to N.N. Bhattacharyya, the eighteen Āgamas, which are also called Śiva Tantras are : Vijaya, Niśvāsa, Svāyambhūva, Vātula, Vīrabhadra, Raurava, Mākuṭa, Vireśa, Candrahāsa, Jñāna, Mukhabimba, Prodgita, Lalita, Siddha, Santana, Sarvodgita, Kiraṇa and Parameśvara. A list has also been found which mentions ten more Śiva Tantras: Kamika, Yogada, Divya, Karaṇa, Ajita, Dipta, Sukṣma, Sahasra, Aṣṭa and Amśubheda. According to the tradition twenty-eight Āgamas were produced from the five mounts of Śiva. From the mouth known as

Sadyojāta came the five beginning with the Kāmika, from that known as Vāmadeva came the five beginning with Suprabheda, from that known as Āghora came the six beginning with Vijaya, from that known as Tatpurusa came the six beginning with Saurava and from that known as Īśāna came the six beginning with Kiraṇa. It should be remembered that these traditional twenty-eight Śiva Āgamas are regarded as authoritative by all Śaiva sects, even by the later social reformistic Vīraśaivas. The Āgamānta Śaiva appear to have contributed to the development of Tāntric ideas in Tamil Śaivism. Contribution of Āgama to art of Śaiva Tāntric architecture is remarkable.

Two extreme offshoots of Pāśupata system were the Kāpālikas and Kālāmukhas. These sects represented a special ritualistic trend, a tradition of hoary antiquity, containing many obscure elements. These Sects had no literature of their own; whatever is known about them comes from the writing of ancient writers belonging to the upper level of society who did not like their rituals and ceremonies and hence described them in a distorted and derogatory way. Even a master mind like Śaṅkarācārya did not hesitate to distortion and fabrication which is proved by the mode of his presentation of the views of his opponents. These sects were basically worshippers of the Female principle. They had no faith in patriarchal and authoritarian Social values, nor in the Caste system.

But to Śaṅkarācārya,though the material World was unreal, the Caste system was real, like Brahman and in the Social field his authority was Manu.

The Kāpāla and Kālāmukhas are two distinct Sects, though they were often confused with one another. According to Rāmānuja, the Kāpālikas maintained that a man, who was advanced in their doctrine, could attain the highest bliss by concentrating one's mind on the Soul seated on the female organ. They worshipped Bhairava as the Great God and attributed great virtues and occult powers to drinking wine and eating disgusting substances as food. They performed human sacrifices and believed that by the practice of Yoga they could achieve miraculous powers of speedy movement.

The Kālāmukhas held that happiness in this World and Salvation in the next could be attained by such practices as (1) eating food in a human skull; (2) besmearing the body with the ashes of the dead and also eating those ashes ; (3) worshipping the God as seated in a pot of wine and (4) holding a club. Men of other castes could become Brahmaṇas by performance of certain rites and one who undertook the vow of a Kāpāla became a holy saint. The religious devotion of these outlandish sects was reserved for the horrid God Bhairava with his wife Caṇḍika, wearing a garland of human skulls and requiring human sacrifices and offering of wine for his propitiation. Demoniacal practices of these Sects form a "ghastly picture of the wild aberrations of the human intellect and spirit."

## MATTAMĀYŪRA SECT

Āchārya Purandara Swami propounded a form of Śaivism in the city of Mattamāyūra in Central India and after the site's name, the faith came to be known as Mattamāyūra sect. A tribe known as Mattamāyūra is found mentioned in the Mahābhārata (II. 32. 4-5). In Central India this sect became popular and in the whole Mahāṇadi valley, during the period of Pāṇḍuvaṁśī alias Sōmavaṁśī King Mahāśivagupta Bālārjuna (Circa. 595 -655 A.D.), this sect of Tāntric Śaivism became very popular, which later came to be called Mattamāyūra and it is assumed that Mahāśivagupta Bālārjuna had accepted the doctrine of this Paśupatadharma. Many Śaiva ācāryas of this Sect preached their doctrine. Many Tāntric Śaiva temples were built during this period, which came to be known as "Kōśali style of temple architecture," in upper Mahāṇadi valley.

This Sect held a liberal view regarding religious practices and insisted on Yoga and Social work like feeding the poor, building hospitals, establishing Schools etc. Somasambhu, a teacher and Ācārya of the Golakimāth of this sect, composed a treatise called "Somaśambha-paddhati," in which a comprehensive account of Śaiva Āgamas is given. Īśānaśivagurudevamisra's" Īśānaśivagurudevapaddhati," is one of the Tantra text, belonging to this Sect, composed about 1100 A.D. or little later.

Āchārya of this clan or sect took up the mission of popularising Tāntric Śaivism in western and eastern India. In Tripuri and its adjoining regions in Central India there are evidences of inscriptions belonging to the 10th-11th centuries A.D. about this Sect. This Sect controlled a number of temples and mathas. The genealogy of the Mattamāyūra Ācāryas can be arranged in the following manner:

## NĀTHA SIDDHAS

Nāthism originated from lower level of Society, which was influenced by Ājvikism, Jainism, Buddhism and Tāntrism. Mīnanātha also known

- Kadambaguhādhivasin
  - Śaṅkhamathikādhipati.
    - Tērambipāla.
      - Āmardakatirṭhanātha (alias Rudra Śiva)
        - Purandara (alias Mattamayūranātha)
          - Kavachaśiva
            - Sadāśiva
              - Hṛidayaśiva
                - Vyōmaśiva alias Gaganaśiva
                  - Pataṅgaśambhu
          - Dharmaśambhu Sadāśiva
            - Purnadara alias Mādhumatēya
              - Chūḍaśiva
                - Hṛidaraśiva
                  - Aghōraśiva
                - Prabhāvaśiva
                  - Praśāntaśiva
                    - Īśānaśambhu
                      - Vyomaśiva II alias Gaganaśiva II.
                    - Prabōdhaśiva

GENEALOGY OF THE MATTAMĀYŪRA ĀCĀRYAS

as Matsyendranātha was a fisherman, Gorakṣanātha was either a fisherman or a keetiya or kaivarta and Hāḍipā alias Jālandharipā, was a Hāḍi (or a net-holder according to another tradition) who served as a stable sweep in the palace of Queen Maināmati of Pāṭikā.

In northen, western and southern India centres of Nāthism had spread. In theoretical matters they depended on the Śaiva and Śākta Āgamas. Their aim in practice was to attain Siddhis (which is achieved through different Samadis, according to Kuṇḍalini yoga) and for attaining, they took to esoteric practices. They believed that by the Yogic control of breath, disciplining of the body and use of drugs made of mica and mercury, it was possible to attain immortality. Their religious discipline was that of Haṭhayoga. The Śākta pīṭhas were the sacred places of pilgrimage and their religious theories and practices contained many Śākta Tāntric elements.

According to the Natha Cosmology, as described by N.N. Bhattacharyya, before creation everything was dark and void. In that vacuity came into being a bubble from which an egg was formed. The yellow portion of the egg was the earth and the white portion the sky. From the sweat of the primal God, Ādinātha was born, his lover Kotaki or Manasā, and from their union sprung Brahmā, Viṣṇu and Śiva. In order to test them Ādinātha assumed the form of a mutilated corpse. Having seen the corpse Brahmā and Viṣṇu avoided it, but Śiva recognised it as the body of his father and took it to the cremation ground. When the body was in flames, Mīnanātha sprang from its naval, Gorakṣa from its head, Hāḍi-pa from its bones, Kānu-pā from its ear and Caurangi from its legs. They are the five original Nātha Siddhas. According to the South Indian tradition, nine Nātha Siddhas (Navanāthasiddha) founded nine sects each of which numbered one crore members.

The above mentioned Nātha Cosmology mentions that before creation everything was dark and void. In that vacuity came into being a bubble from which an egg was formed. This egg tradition, reminds about the egg of a pean-hen, from where the Purāṇa tribe and Bhanja were born in Mayurbhanj area of Orissa. Even in "Ethnology of Bengal," Dalton has recorded thus : "There is a tradition that the Kharias with another tribe called Purans were the aborigins of Mohurbhanj, one of the Katak tributary Mahals. They aver that they and the family of the Chief (Bhañja) were all produced from a pea -fowl's egg, the Bhañja from the yolk, the Purans from the white, the Kharias from the Shell." (Vide : Acharya, Padmasri Paramānanda - *Studies in Orissan History, Archaeology and Archieves*, Cuttack Student's Store, Cuttack, 1969, pp. 540 -544). As the egg born traditions are prevalent in Orissa, there are much possibilities that Nāthaism had started in Orissa and mostly in the area ruled by the Bhañja dynasty.

Mīnanātha is nobody but junior Luipā Matsyendranātha. N.K.Sahu states that the origin of the Nātha cult is attributed to Luipā - Matsyendranātha who is known as the first Siddha in the Tibetan text. The Yoginikula Tantra was introduced by him and he rescued the text of the knowledge from the belly of a fish, at his birth place Candradvipa, which has been identified as Cāṁdavali-Dhārma region of Orissa, i.e. the Candbali - Dhamra region of old Kanika estate, now located as sea-coast in Bhadrak district. It seems therefore that Nāthism, as a school of Śaivism originated in Orissa and as the neighbourhood of Delhi was the primal sect of this school, the Nāthas treated Kurukshtra as the seat of their primal Lord or Ādinātha Śiva.

In the Tantra-Mahārṇava, quoted in the Gorakṣa Siddhānta Saṁgraha, Gorakṣanātha is described as residing in the forest of Jagannātha (Orissa). This proves that Gorakṣanātha was connected with Orissa region.

Kṛṣṇācārya, Kṛṣṇapāda or Kānhupā, came out of a Brāhmana family of Orissa and Tārānath believes on the authority of his Guru that even Lord Buddha had once prophesised the birth of this Ācārya to be in the country of Uruviśā (Orissa).

Out of the five original Nātha Siddhas, two were born in Orissa and one was closely connected with Orissa. In Nāthism, words like Viśvanāth, Lokanāth and Jagannāth are used for describing the Absolute and Nāthism has much influence in Orissa.

The Nātha Siddhas believe that Ādinātha is the first Nātha, the founder of all esoteric sciences. He is very often equated with Śiva and Vajrasattava. The Hara-Gouri conception of Nāthism is an adaptation of both the Mahāyānic Karuṇa and Śūnyatā and the Vajrayānic Upāya and Prajñā. The Śūnyavādā of the Mādhyamika system is also accepted in Nāthism. According to Nāgārjuna Śūnya or vacuity is of four kinds – Śūnya, Ātiśūnya, Mahāśūnya and Sarvaśūnya. The followers of Nāthism believe in three kinds of Śūnya – Ādiśūnya, Madhyaśūnya and Antaḥśūnya. This Śūnya is to be realised through Yoga. The process has been described in a text called "HĀḌAMĀLA," which says that by the Yogic control of breath and thirty knots in the spinal cord can be loosened, as a result of which the two vital winds, prāna and apana, can enter the spinal cord and move upwards as Hamsa through the Six nerve plexuses - mūlādhara, svādhiṣthāna, manipura, anāhata, viśuddha (vaisandhari) and ajñā (ādya) - and on reaching the Sahasrāra region assume the nature of Śūnya. There are 72,000 nerves within the body of which 64 can be distinctly located and 15 utilised for Yogic purposes. In the Yogacintāmani section of the Gorkavijaya, we have the concept of navacakra which is the addition of three extra stages to the Tāntric Ṣaṭcakra. These extra stages are the three forms of Śūnya – Adi, Madhya and Antyah. It also deals with ultā-sādhanā which is a yogic method of making the vital fluid flow upward. This shows that the Nātha Siddhas practiced VAJROLI.

Some believe Nāthism probably started as reactionary movement against the erotic practices of Tāntric Buddhism, but in their Haṭha-Yoga practice, there is esoteric Vajroli Yoga. Nātha Yogis tried to keep away from women as far as possible, but in their Yogic practices they had to use women as mere instruments, because they took to Hāṭhayoga esoteric practice like Vajroli. In spite of this, Gorakṣanātha is celebrated for his celibacy, which he practiced in his later years.

It is interesting to know information from N.N. Bhattacharyya, when he states that Śiva possessed mahājñāna, the knowledge which could make a man immortal. Śiva determined to impart this knowledge to Gauri and took her to the middle of a Sea to do so. Mīnanātha guessed Śiva's intention. Assuming the form of a fish he was able to learn this knowledge. When Śiva came to know this he cursed Mīnanātha that he would forget the knowledge. Meanwhile, Gauri desired to make the five Siddhas worldly minded. She used her erotic tricks so that they might be attracted to women. Except for Gorakṣanātha, the passions of other four Siddhas were aroused by her gestures, as a result of which Mīnanātha was snared to become the ruler of women in a country called Kadalideśa, Hādi-pā to become the stable sweep of Queen Mainamati, Kānu-pā was banished into Dāhuka country and Caurangi cohabited with his step-mother. Gorakṣa, however, was married to a princess and had a son by her known as Karpaṭinātha.

According to the legend described in the Gorakṣavijaya, also known as Minacaitanya, Gorakṣanātha rescued his teacher Mīnanātha from the influence of a woman of Kadali. There are many contradictory accounts relating to Mīnanātha or Matsyendranātha. In a Tāntric text called "Kaulayana- nirṇaya," he is described as the founder of the Yogini-kaula. In the Buddhist tradition he is identified with Luipāda. Mina or Matsyendra is also mentioned in the Tibetan Buddhist lists of Siddhas. In Nepal he is identified with Bodhisattva Avalokiteśvara. Even today a Cart festival is celebrated in his honour. Among the Muslims of Bengal he is known as Machandali or Mochrā Pir. In Munidatta's Caryāgitikośa a few verses have been ascribed to him. In the texts of Vajrayāna Matsyendra and Gorakṣa are regarded as Siddhas. In the north Indian tradition Gorakṣa was a fisherman by caste, while in the Bengal tradition he was a Cowherd. A few Tāntric texts such as the Gorakṣa Saṁhitā have been associated with his name. In north India Gorakṣa-panthā is regarded as an esoteric system connected with Tantra and Yoga.

It seems the Spiritual enlightenment of the Nātha Siddhas became very popular in Society and because of this reason the Buddhist Tāntrics could not afford to loose them and included some of them and the 64 Yoginis founded by Matsyendranātha, in the list of Tibetan Buddhist list of Siddhas. It is Swami Muktananda Saraswati who informs that in the Tibetan and Hindu traditions of tantra there are eighty-four Siddhas and out of these sixty-four were Yoginas. From the traditions at Keonjhar, it is known that one of the Bhañja – King of Keonjhar was one of these 84 Siddas. Tārānath has described that Vajraghaṇṭa belonged to a royal family of Oḍiviśā (Orissa). It is said that Vajraghaṇṭa met the Yogini Vilāsavajra in Uḍḍiyāna, who showed him the incomprehensible way of Mahāmudrā Siddhi, and then the Ācārya meditated for long twelve years in a thick forest in Oḍiviśā, taking as his Mudrā a brandy-selling woman who possessed all the signs of a Padmini. After acquiring Siddhi he devoted to the work of propogating the Guhya tantra and converted large numbers of people into Tantrayāna.

Saraha or Sarahapāda who is also known as Rāhulabhadra is stated in the "Bsṭāṅ-ḥgyur," as belonging to Uḍḍiyāna, which according to Tārānath, was born in the country of Oḍiviśā. As he lived probably in the Rahul river valley of Western Orissa, flowing within Kondhmal and Kalahandi districts, the river has been named after him.

Virūpa hailed from Orissa and was residing on the banks of river Virūpa flowing in contiguity in Asia range of hills, probably named after him. In the accounts of Tārānath, he is depicted as a drunkard and debauch. He is narrated to have been expelled from the Buddhist Saṅgha for his moral laxity.

The mother land of Kaṁbala is known as Oḍiviśā (sometimes written as Uḍḍiyāna).

Ācārya Pitopāda, who was a teacher of esoteric Yoga in Ratnagiri monastery of Orissa is credited with the introduction of Kālacakra tantra in Buddhism and he was without doubt a famous author of a large number of Tāntric books on Kālacakra, many of which are unfortunately lost at present. Among his six great disciples, the names of Avadhūti, Bodhuśrī-

and Nāropā are well known in the Tāntric world and all of them learnt and practised Yoga philosophy in the great monastery of Ratnagiri.

Ācārya Abhayākara Gupta was another famous Siddha, who was born at Jhāṛkhanda in Orissa from a Kāyastha father and a Brāhmaṇi mother. He was educated in Nalanda where subsequently he became an abbot and he was also for sometime the Chief abbot at Vikramaśilā. This Ācārya is known to be the preceptor of King Rāmpāla (c. 1077-1119 A.D.), whose Queen dedicated to his pleasure the temple cloister of Edapura, which is probably the same as Ādipura of Mayūrbhanj.

Ācārya Mokṣakāra Gupta, Vibhūti Candra, Dānaśila and Subhākara were the four great luminaries of Jagaddala-vihāra, a great monastic institution of medieval Orissa. In the Bengali "Chaṇḍi," of Mukunda Rāma Kavi Kaṅkaṇa (1577-78 A.D.), it is suggested that Jagaddala was situated towards the south of Triveṇi and Saptagrāma, somewhere within the limits of medieval Orissa. The location of Jagaddala - vihāra is not yet identified satisfactorily.

Another monk of Jagaddala, named Jñāna Mitra, who hailed from Tripurā, was very widely known in Orissa, and he was proficient not only in Gūhyatantras, but also in various Mahāyānic scriptures. "He learnt profoundly the collections on Yamāntaka, Saṁbara and Heruka, the Gūhya Candra Tilaka, Mahāpāṇitilaka and Kālacakra." He was a great devotee of God Jagannāth and very often he was getting into the temple of Puri, where he performed various miracles and Tārānath believes that when this Ācārya was once ill-treated inside the temple, the images of Jagannāth lost their hands and feet, as well as their former magical efficacies.

All the names of Nātha Siddhas, Śākti Siddhas and Buddhist tāntric Siddhas are interfused together in the list of 84 Siddāchāryas and it is very difficult to differentiate them. Therefore a separate detail study on these Siddāchāryas is essential.

Nāthism had great influence in Orissa. In the "Ākula-Vira Tantra" ascribed to Matsyendranāth, the Sahaja state is described as a state of supreme equilibrium which transcends all perceptual knowledge with positive and negative attributes, while in that state the Yogi becomes one with whole Universe and realises a non-dual existence. In the "Gorakṣa Saṁhitā," a work attributed to Gorakṣa, Sahaja is likened with the boundless sky and is characterised as the absolute truth and although this work is regarded by some Scholars as of late quasi - Hindu origin, it may be said to have embodied the teachings of Gorakṣa. Even in the Haṭha Yoga Pradipika, we find the theory of four kinds of Śūnya

– Śūnya, Atiśūnya, Mahāśūnya and Sahaja Śūnya – associated with four stages of sounds produced in Yoga and so it is not difficult to see that the conceptions of Sahaja and of Śūnya in Nāthist literature are exactly the same as we meet in the Buddhist - Tantra texts, Dohās and Caryā songs.

N.K. Sahu informs that moreover, Charpaṭinātha, another great teacher of Nāthism is regarded in the Tibetan tradition as one of the 84 Siddhas and the "Devamanusya Stotra," supposed to be written by him is a beautiful hymn to Avalokiteśvara, which is in circulation even at present among the Buddhist community of Nepal. The great yogic philosophers like Acyuta, Ananta, Yaśobanta, Bārańga and others, who flourished in Orissa in the 16th century A.D. based their Yoga system on the Haṭha Yoga of the Nātha Cult and drew inspiration from its great Siddhas.

H.Bhattacharya in his edited work *The Cultural Heritage of India*, Vol. IV, p. 270, has given the names of eighty-four Siddhas, according to the Tibetan tradition thus : (1) Luhipā, (2) Lila-pā, (3) Virupā, (4) Ḍombipā, (5) Sabara (Sabaripā), (6) Saraha (Rahula-bhadra, (7) Kankali, (8) Mina, (9) Gorkṣa, (10) Caurangi, (11) Vina, (12) Santi, (13) Tanti, (14) Carmari, (15) Khaḍga, (16) Nāgārjuna, (17) Kānha-pā, (18) Kanari (Āryadeva), (19) Thagana, (20) Nada-pada, (21) Sali-pā (Segala-pāda), (22) Tilo-pā (Tailika-pāda), (23) Chatra, (24) Bhadra, (25) Dvikhaṇḍi, (26) Ajogi, (27) Kada-pada, (28) Dhovī, (29) Kankana, (30) Kambala, (31) Tenki, (32) Bhade, (33) Tandhi, (34) Kukkuri, (35) Cujbi (Kusuli), (36) Dharma, (37) Mahi, (38) Acintya, (39) Babhahi, (40) Nalina, (41) Bhusuku, (42) Indrabhuti, (43) Megha-pada, (44) Kuthari, (45) Karmara, (46) Jalandhari, (47) Rahula, (48) Garbhari, (49) Dhakari, (50) Medini, (51) Pańkaja, (52) Ghaṇṭa, (53) Yogī, (54) Celuka, (55) Vaguri (Gundari?), (56) Luncaka, (57) Nirguṇa, (58) Jayananda, (59) Carsati, (60) Campaka, (61) Visana, (62) Bhali (Teli, Taili), (63) Kumari,(64) Carpati, (65) Manibhadra, (66) Mekhala, (67) Mankhala, (68) Kalakala, (69) Kanthadi, (70) Daudi, (71) Udhal, (72) Kapala, (73) Kiḷa, (74) Puṣkara, (75) Śarvabhakṣa, (76) Nagabodhi, (77) Darika, (78) Puttali, (79) Panaha, (80) Kokila, (81) Ananga, (82) Lakṣmīkarā, (83) Samudra and (84) Bhali-pā. These Siddhas or Siddhācāryas flourished between 10th and 12th centuries A.D.

The above list of Siddhācāryas is furnished by H.C. Das, directly from H. Bhattacharya's work, but it seems to be defective, because the name of Vajraghaṇṭa is not found among the names. In the "Account of the Pēg Sām Jon Zāńg," the name of Vajrahaṇṭa is mentioned. Because of this reason N.K.Sahu was of opinion that it seems extremely difficult to present a chronological account of these Siddhas as the traditions about them are full of curious confusions and as some of the names are believed to be borne by more than one among them. For instance, the traditions of more than one Savara, Duipā (Luhipā), Saraha, Kṛṣṇa, Śāntideva, Śāntarakṣita and Dipañkara, which have been mixed up by the Tibetan and Nepalese writers providing sufficient scope of confusion for the modern Scholars (Vide : R.C. Mazumdar, History of Bengal, Vol. I, p.339). The Chronological accounts of some of the Siddhas in the order of precepters are disciples are, however, found in the Bstañ-ḥgyur Catalogue, the Pāg Sām Jon Zāṅg and the History of Tārānath, and these require a careful scrutiny in the light of the available historical evidences.

This shows that a proper detail study of the 84 Siddhācāryas has not yet been done. A laborious and careful study of these realised Souls or Siddhācāryas, their chronology and ideology; of these Saints of Sahajayāna is essential to enrich the study of the jivan-muktas of this School of Spiritual thought or marg. The beauty is that most of the Śaiva and Śākta Tāntric Yogis are included in this long list.

## ŚAIVA TANTRA IN ORISSA

Śiva has been worshipped from proto-historic period in Orissa. Among uneven numbers, the graphic variant of (III) is found used as strokes in Proto-Indian, Proto-Elamite and Sumerian scripts. But the beauty is that three lines are found at Pre-historic rock shelter painting of Yogimath Donger, near Khariar, in Nuapada district of Western Orissa. This pre-historic Rock shelter painting has been dated to neolithic period, because it is painted in red-tint colour and show the domestication of Bulls, Cow and Calf. Gods formed Triad in consideration of their functions. Triad occupied highest honour in the Hindu pantheon. But the idea of Triad sprung from Śiva-Yoga. Though the basic idea of Triad goes to the credit of Triple-forms of Proto-Śiva, the term itself owes much to Babylonian Trigon. Baripada area of Mayurbhanj district had contact with Babylonia, as known from the discovery of an "Ivory Babylonian Seal," at Baripada in 1953 (Vide : *Hindusthan Standard*, daily English paper, Calcatta, dated 13th October 1953). In the conception of Hindu Triad Śiva became the fourth entity from whom Brāhmā, Viṣṇu and Rudra came forth representing the principal elements of Haṭha-yoga, the air (water), the fire and the combination of the two. The latter came as the microcosm of the fourth entity. As studied earlier Śiva and Rudra are different aspects of same God Lord Śiva.

The origin of Śiva Liṅga is mythical. In Śiva purāṇa, it is mentioned that once Śiva was wandering naked. Śiva entered into Dāruvana. There was a Janasthana (abode of Seers) in that Dāruvana. At the sight of naked Śiva a commotion was created and all cursed him, out of hatred that his penis would fall down. All of a sudden his penis was detached from his body and it began to move from place to place burning everything that came on its way. Neither it could be stopped nor could it be extinguished. As a result, the World began to be burnt. At last the people took shelter with Pārvatī. Pārvatī became pleased with the prayers of the Brahmacāries and She held it in her Yoni. Then according to the advice of Brāhmā, all began to worship Śiva in the form of Liṅga. Liṅga worship is very popular in Orissa. Generally, Linga stands as a formless from of Śiva.

Bansidhar Biswal has studied the feasibility of Ka-Liṅga name and states that in the Śaiva theology, there is no mention of Ka-Linga. But among various Liṅgas Jyotirliṅga and Svayambhuliṅga are held high. In the esoteric literature the term, Jyoti is accepted as the Sun. In the Śaiva purāṇa the Jyoti and the Sun mean "Ka". In pre-Vedic days there was worship of Liṅga, symbolising the Sun. The Vedic Seer, Dirghatamas, is the main source of Kalinga kingdom. According to his philosophical view Kalinga means Ka-Linga (Surya-Śiva) and Kalinga means the worshipper of phallic Deities. Śiva Liṅga is worshipped in every village and where-ever there is human settlement in Orissa.

The Naṭarāja image discovered at Asanapat, in Keonjhar district is the second inscriptional evidence of Śiva worship in Orissa, because in recent years a fragmentary inscribed slab dated to 4th century A.D. has been excavated from a Śiva temple mound at Maraguda valley of Nuapada district. The Śiva Deity of this mound is a huge Śiva liṅga about 25 feet in girth. The Asanapat Śiva image depicts Śiva in naṭarāja posture with eight hands, of which two are engaged in playing the Viṇā across the chest and two in holding the snake over the head. Of the rest four hands, one displays the varada mudra, while the three others hold the triśūla, akṣamālā and ḍambaru. The image is in naked ūrdhavaliṅga form and is in tāṇḍava dance pose. The ūrdhavaliṅga symbolise Vajroli. Śiva's attendants Nandi and Bhṛkuṭi are represented on both the sides of this image. At the bottom of this Śiva image of Orissa, is the inscription of 13 lines, which speaks of erection of a temple (Devayatana) for Lord Śiva by Mahārāja Śrī Śatrubhañja of Nāga dynasty and is assigned within 5th-6th centuries A.D.

Archaeological remains at Dengaposi and Sitabinji, the two neighbouring villages in the Keonjhar district, where Caves and a number of natural rock shelters in the hills are found, show that Śaiva ascetics lived there and practised penance. The important object of worship of the ascetics was a Mukhāliṅga with four faces of Śiva, which is still to be found at Sitabinji. The inscriptions of 5th-6th centuries A.D. with temporal paintings found at Sitabinji record the names of Śiva as Saśidhara and Saśalāñchanadhara. K.C. Panigrahi is of view that there are evidences to show that by 5th century A.D. Śaivism became dominant form of religion of Orissa. The huge Śiva liṅgam, now to be found in the Bhaskareśvara temple at Bhubaneswar, was originally an Asokan pillar and the fragmentary Lion capital dug out, at the close proximity of the temple, was its capital. There are distinct evidences in the body of the Liṅgam and the Lion capital that both were deliberately destroyed and there is a line of inscription on the Lion capital, in the script of the 5th century A.D. (now preserved in Orissa State Museum), showing that such destruction took place in the 5th century A.D. The pillar, after heavy chiselling was converted into a Śiva liṅgam and the capital after deliberate breakage was buried in front of the temple, within a very short distance from the Liṅgam. The manner in which a Buddhist monument was converted into a Phallic emblem indicates a violent struggle between the Buddhists and the Śaivas, of which a tradition seems to have found place in the Ekamra purāṇa, one of the sacred texts which describe the history of Bhubaneswar from the orthodox standpoint. So, it can be understood that 5th century A.D. was a period of conflict between Buddhism and Śaivism in which the latter triumphed. It may be noted that in the 5th century A.D. there was a revival of Hinduism in India under the great Gupta emperors of the north and the same revival also took place in Orissa.

Caves found in the close vicinity of the temple of Bhāskareśvara, mostly to the west of it, at Bhubaneswar, can be assigned to 5th-6th centuries A.D. The most remarkable group of these Caves, known as Pañca Pāṇḍava Guṁphā, which is still in a tolerably good condition, consists of three spacious chambers with specious verandahs. These Caves clearly indicate that they were intended for the abodes of the Śaiva ascetics. As the glorification of Sex energy is a concept of Pāśupata

Śaivism it can be supposed that the shrines at Sitabinji and round about Bhāskareśvara temple at Bhubaneswar were established by the Pāśupata sect of Śaivism.

At Gupteśwar cave in Koraput district there is a Liṅgam of 6 ft. in height and 10 ft. in circumference, held very sacred by the people. H.C. Das informs about an unique Śiva liṅga at Kumbhira-gadhi situated on the eastern bank of the river Subarnarekha in the Bhogarai block of Balasore district. The Śiva liṅga made of chlorite stone and finely polished in twelve feet high with upper most part, four feet in cylindrical shape showing curved limbs, locally stated to be the sacred thread of the Deity. The middle portion of the Liṅgam is an octagonal shape and the basement is square. The circumference of the Śākti is 36 feet. There is a square size stone Vedi (6 ft. in size) which is stated to have been set with the liṅga in earlier period. The Vedi shows the workmanship of lotus flowers, holes and other scroll works. Sometime back the Vedi was separated from the liṅga and the latter was raised straight from a slanting position. The stricking importance is the unusual size of the Liṅga. It is a colossal liṅga next is size and magnitude to that set in the Bhāskareśvar temple at Bhubaneswar. It appears that originally it was Buddhist Stupa and was converted to a Liṅga when Śaivism spread in the area. The date of installation of this Stupa may tentatively be assigned to post - Gupta period when Swetavalika Buddhist Buddhist Mahāvihara discovered in the village Jayarampur, located about 5 km. to the east of this Shrine, which was established by Achuta, a feudatory Chief under Mahārājādhirāja Gopacandra whose kingdom extended from Faridapur in the east to Balasore in the west.

Narendrapur not far from Chandabali (Dhamra area), the birth place of Matseyendranāth was an eminent worshop for production of Śiva-Liṅgam. The site has yielded numerous Śivaliṅgas from 6 ins. to 6 ft. in height, varved in sand and chlorite stones, many of which are still found in the village. Probably Śiva-liṅgas were transported from this place to the south-east Asian countries through sea-route and to different places.

The early Nala Kings of South Kōśala (Western Orissa), Bhavadatta-varman and Arthapatiraja in 5th century A.D. were worshippers of Śiva and they declared in their charters that their kingdom was bestowed to them by Maheśvara and Mahāsena. C.B.Patel is of opinion that we have established that the Nalas were originally forest tribes (Niṣādas) of Vindhyan region after whom the region perhaps came to be known as "Niṣādha," and were palpably the early worshippers of Rudraśiva. — However, to us, it appears that Śaivism perhaps, made its advent here with the advent of the Nalas since the last part of 3rd century A.D. or early part of 4th century A.D. prior to the invasion of Samudragupta.

In Kalinga (South Orissa), though the Māṭhara Kings in 4th and 5th centuries A.D. were patrons of Vaiṣṇavism, they had no dislike for Śaivism. Satrudamana of Simhapura who was probably a subordinate ruler under Māṭhara King Śaktivarman, was a worshipper of Damaneśvara Śiva (E.I. Vol. XXXI, pp. 89-93). The Vāśiṣṭha King Anantavarman, also called himself a devout worshipper of Maheśvara (E.I. Vol. XXIII, pp. 56-61 and Vol. XXIV, pp. 47-52).

Eastern Gaṅgas established their rule in Kaliṅga in 498 A.D. who were great patrons of Śaivism. Indravarman I, the earliest King of this dynasty had payed homage to Parameśvara who is described as creator, sustainer and destroyer. Gokarṇasvāmī Śiva, installed on the crest of the mount Mahendra was the tutelary Deity of the Gaṅgas. The Gaṅgā Kings believed in the synthesis of Vaiṣṇavism and Śaivism. It seems the synthesis of Vaiṣṇavism and Śaivism in Orissa had begun from the 6th -7th centuries A.D.

The Gaṅga King Indravarman like his predecessor Hastivarman, was a devout worshipper of Śiva. Under Devendravarman, the successor of Indravarman, there was landmark in the growth and development of Śaivism in Kaliṅga. During his region Bhagavana Pataṅga Śivacarya of the Mattamayūra school is known to have visited Kaliṅganagara and initiated him in the Gaṅga era 184. This Śaiva Siddhānta teacher Pataṅga Śambhu or Bhagavāna Pataṅga was the disciple of Vyomaśiva alias Gaganaśiva-I. Under the early Gaṅgas Vaiṣṇavism, Śaivism and Buddhism seemed to have flourished in the extent land from the Vamshadhara river to the Godavari river. With this background the success of Śaivism and other religious sects at the expense of Buddhism in Kaliṅga has to be attributed to the activities of the Śaivacharyas of the Mattamayura cult and the patronage of the Gaṅga Kings. With the stewardship of the early Gaṅgas of Kaliṅga, Śaivism spread throughout Kaliṅga, from the peaks of mountains to the coastal plains. Temples dedicated to Śiva, Viṣṇu, Śākti and Sūrya were constructed in all parts of the farflung Gaṅga Kingdom.

The fortunes of Śaivism in early 6th century A.D. cannot be traced, but it can be supposed that triumphant progress of Śaivism continued in this century. In Uttara Tosali section of Utkala (North Orissa), during the last quarter of sixth century A.D. Mahārāja Śrī Śambhuyaśa of Mudgala dynasty was a devout worshipper of Lord Śiva. In his Soro copper plates (dated early 7th century A.D.) for the first time, the name of Uḍraviṣaya as an administrative unity in Uttara Tosali is mentioned. Uḍra or Oḍra people of Utkala were people of developed stage. Uḍra seems to have been derived from the stem, "Ut," which means to fly up and it may be accepted that Udrayāna bandha as a Yogic practice of Śaiva tantra, grew up among the Uḍras of Utkala. The phallic deities of Uḍra developed into classical form under Uḍrayāna, as a Haṭha-yogic austerity. Uḍḍiyana bandha was discovered in Uḍra, which signifies abdominal lock practice of Vajroli, i.e., Spiritual practice of rechannelling sexual energy as dealth in chapter-II. So, it seems that Uḍra people of Uḍra-viṣaya had practised the Sexo-yogic practice and invented "Uḍḍiyana bandha," therefore Orissa made a great gift of "Uḍḍiyana bandha," to the great Yogic tantra science, which is recorded in "Haṭha Yoga Pradipika." If any woman once tastes this Yogic coitus, can never forget the pleasure derived out of it, her life long and attain Samādhi, if she practices Vajroli yoga.

There was Rise and fall of the Śailodbhava dynasty in Orissa who ruled Koṅgoda maṇḍala, i.e. the territory around Chilka lake, during the period circa. 550 A.D. to 736 A.D. Śaivism was the religion of the Royal house of Koṅgoda. They built some Śiva temples at the foot of a hill called Kṛṣṇagiri located at a distance of about 15 miles from Khallikota in the northen part of Ganjam district. There are fourteen temples at Kṛṣṇagiri belonging to different centuries, with Uma-Maheśvara images. It is interesting to quote S.C.Behera, when he states that in his Ganjām plates of 620 A.D., Mādhavarāja II calls himself "Parama Brahmāṇya," and devoted to the feet of the blessed Lord of the three Worlds (viz. : Śiva), who is the cause of existence, creation and destruction, whose arms are placed on the hump of the great Bull (viz. : Nandi) and on the pillow of a Couch, (and) whose matted hair is illuminated in one place by the crescent of the moon. In his Khurda plates, he is a devout worshipper of Lord Maheśvara's feet.

"But the question arises : how and under what circumstances Śaivism, in place of Vaiṣṇavism was accepted by the kings of Koṅgoda? Although the Māṭhara rulers of Kaliṅga were devotees of Lord Nārāyaṇa, yet we notice that at least one ruler, namely Anantavarman, of that family was a "Parama Māheśvara." This is known to us from his Śṛiṅgavarapukuṭā grant, palaeographically assigned to the fifth or sixth century A.D. It was during this period that the early Gaṅgas established their hegemony in upper Kaliṅga and began to worship "Lord Gokarṇeśvara."

"In the first quarter of the seventh century A.D. Śaśāṅka, King of Karṇasuvarṇa and overlord of Mādhavarāja II, appeared in the Eastern

India as a great patron of Śaivism. His coins bear the emblems of Lord Śiva, Bull and the Full moon. They obviously indicate his acceptance of Śaivism. Tradition as recorded in Ekāmra purāṇa, also informs us that Śaśāṅka constructed a massive temple of Śiva at Tribhuvaneśvara.

"Thus we note within a period of about one century Anantavarman of the Māṭhara dynasty, Eastern Gaṅgās of Kaliṅga, Śailodbhāvas of Koṅgoda and Śaśāṅka, the overlord of Mādhavaraja II appeared in Eastern India as strong upholders of Śaivism. This introduction of Śaivism in Orissa in the period under review is indeed very significant. This becomes more conspicuous, when we find that in this period Cālukyas in the south and Pāṇḍuvaṁśīs of Kōśala were devout worshippers of Lord Viṣṇu. So the question arises : where from did the Śaiva Gurus or Ācharyas migrated to Orissa? What form of Śaivism was accepted by the Śailodbhavas of Koṅgoda?

"It seems the Śailodbhavas were not the upholders of the Lakuliśa-Pāśupata cult. This becomes clear from a statement made by Ācārya Haribhadra, in his "Saddarśana Samuchchaya," regarding the characteristic features or worship in this cult. He says : the Lakulis' Paśupatas; worship that form of the Almighty, contemplated by the ancient sages where there is neither the celestial river, cobras, the garland of skulls, the digits of the moon, Pārvatī, matted hair, ashes nor anything else. "But from the preamble of the Śailodbhava charters, we learn that the royal house of Koṅgoda worshipped the matted hair of Śiva, which is embraced by the moon with his tender beams, resembling the clean fibres of a lotus stalk, whose radiance is besmeared with the tawny rays of the bright gem of the great serpent, whose tie becomes lose when Pārvatī seizes Śiva by hair, and from which the particles of ashes are washed away by the leaps of the Gaṅgetic water. Thus it is clear that all the elements, which are discarded in Lakuliśa cult, are remarkably meditated upon by the Śailodbhavas. It may be pointed in this connection that one Nettabhañja, known to us from his Baṇatumba plates, who flourished about this period in the Ghumsar region, was a "Parama Maheśvara" and we learn from his charter that he worshipped Śiva with digits of moon (Śaśāṅka) and the garland of skulls (Kapālamala). Thus it is now obvious that during the period under review in Koṅgoda, Lakuliśa cult was not in vogue. The Lakuliśa images of the Orissan temples appear to be of a bet later date.

"From the Chandrehe inscription of Prabodhaśiva, we learn that the Śaiva Ācaryas of the Mattamayūra clan worship Lord Śiva with his Snake (Phaṇi), celestial river (Amara Nadi), matted hair (Jaṭā), Moon

(Chandra) and the garland of Skulls (Kapālānaṁ - mālā). Thus it seems that the Śailodbhavas, Śaśāṅka and Neṭṭabhañja (of Baṇatumba plates), who worshipped Śiva with all the above quoted features, were all followers of Mattamayura form of Śaivism. This view maintained by us is supported by other corroborating evidences. From the Bilhari and Ranod inscriptions, we are having a long genealogical list (according to Guru Parampara) of the Śaiva Ācāryas of this clan. From it we learn that Rudraśiva was the Lord of Āmardāka tirtha. Āmardāka tirtha is probably the same as the modern Āmardā of the Mayurbhanj district of Orissa. Thus we find that one of the Śaiva Ācāryas of this clan, namely Rudraśiva was having his stronghold in the northern extremity of Orissa, which came under Śaśāṅka's zone. Again from the verse 49 of the Bilhari inscription, we learn that Purandara alias Mattamayuranātha, disciple of Rudra śambha, "communicated supreme splendour of the King of Avanti by initiating him in the Śaiva faith." In this connection, it is further interesting to note that Devendravarman I of Kaliṅga or Gaṅgā era 184 in A.D. 682, according to his Dharmaliṅgeśvara plates, granted a village to his royal preceptor Pataṅga Śivācārya, learned in Vedas, Vedaṅgas, Itihāsa and Purāṇas, as the token of Gurupūjā on the occasion of the Mantradikṣā of the King. And from the Bilhari and Ranod inscriptions we find that Pataṅgasambhu, disciple of Vymośiva alias Gaganaśiva - I, was a famous Ācārya of the Mattamāyūra clan. So we are inclined to identify Pataṅgaśiva of Dharmaliṅgeśvara plates with Pataṅgaśambhu of Mattamayura sect of Śaivism.

"Thus from inscriptional sources we find that Ācāryas of the Mattamayura clan had taken up the mission of popularising Śaivism in western and eastern India. Purandara in Avanti, Rudraśiva in north Orissa and Pataṅgaśambhu (circa. 682 A.D.) in Kaliṅga proper took up leading roles in this cause. These Ācāryas must have exerted their overwhelming influence on the Śailodbhāvas, who like the Ācāryas of Mattamayura clan worshipped Śiva with his matted hair, crescent, Gaṅgā and snake. It may be further pointed out that both Gaṅgās and Śailodbhavas refer to Mahendra as a sacred seat and so both must have been influenced by the same Ācāryas.

"Now the question arises : where from did these Ācāryas migrated ? According to Mahābhārata they lived in Rohitaka, which may be identified with modern Rohtak, 43 miles north -west of Delhi. We further learn from the Lodhia plates of Mahāśivagupta Bālārjuna that Pramathācārya (probably of the Mattamayūra clan), who was responsible for the introduction of Śaivism in South Kōśala migrated from a

"Topavana," in Dvaitavana, very near to Delhi. Thus it seems that Śaiva Ācāryas of Mattamayūra clan migrated from this region and established in Central India, where from they extended their influence in the East coast including Koṅgoda.

"What was the philosophy underlying the Śaivism, accepted by the Śailodbhavas of Koṅgoda? Pulindasena, the progenitor of this family worshipped the Lord, who is "Śāśvata" and "Svayambhu." Many scholars including Dr. Kielhorn interpreted Svayambhu as Brahmā. But this interpretation does not seem convincing as the Śailodbhavas were Śaivites. In Sanskrit lexicons Svayambhu is a general term referring to the Trinity—Brahmā, Viṣṇu and Śiva. Besides this, Śāśvata is a name of Śiva. In the verse number 16 of the Banpur plates of Madhyama-rāja-I, it is noticed that "Śambhu," is Śāśvata and Śānta. In this form of worship as we learn from line 12 of the Bugudā plate, "Citta" and "Guṇa," are two essential factors. These two terms have been interpreted in a general sense by all the editors of Śailodbhava charters. But it seems that they have technical connotation, as pointed out by Gaṇa Kārika.

"Again this type of philosophy is explained in verse 17 of the Bānpur plates of Madhyamarāja - I. Here the God (Śiva) is thought to be "the great Lord of the Divines, whose inevitable lustre (jyoti) is the root cause of the World's rise, existence and decay." This fully agrees with the famous Brahmā Sūtra "Janmadyasya yataḥ", of Bādarayāna. The same Lord, whom Śailodbhavas worshipped was meditated upon, in the Upanisadic spirit as "Vyakta as well as Avyakta and omnipotent."

Although the Upanisadic contemplation was known in that period there were also people, who believed that hard penances and self torture lead to the attainment of Divinity. It is known from the Bānpur plates that "for the attainment of the Divine status, some people left their abodes and practised Yoga in the caves. Some of them inhaled smoke, others lived by taking air, fruit and water, while others lived without taking anything."

"However, Koṅgoda in the seventh century A.D. played a very important role in the revival of Brāhmanism at the cost of Buddhism."

The study of S.C. Behera shows that in 7th century A.D. Yogic Śaivism was very popular. The tradition about Śaśāṅka building the temple of Tribhavaneśvara is found in Kapila Saṁhita, the Svarṇādri Mahodaya and Ekāmra Candrikā also. This shows that the worship of Self-revealed (Svayambhu) Liṅgam was popular in Bhubaneswar (Ekāmra) long before Śaśāṅka, who constructed there the temple of Tribhavaneśvara with a view to giving Śaivism a prominent position.

Just after this happening, a large number of Śiva temples raised their heads at Ekāmra and the area came to be known as a great Śaiva kṣetra in India, which assumed the name of Bhubaneswar after the Deity Tribhāvaneśvara. K.C.Panigrahi believes that the temple built by Śaśāṅka has been replaced by the present great temple of Liṅgaraj.

Satrughneśvara, Bharateśvara, Svarnajāleśvara, Lakshmaneśvara and Parasurāmeśvara early temples of Bhubaneswar, were built by the Śailodbhavas. During this period Lakuliśa Pāśupata cult found its way to Orissa. Lakuliśa is given a conspicuous place at Rāhāpaga in the front part of Bharateśvara temple at Bhubaneswar and in the low relief of the base of Jagamohana in Parasurameśvara temple. This Śaiva cult did not receive any patronage from Śailodbhava Kings and its influence is not remarkable.

Lakuliśa Pāśupata cult gained ascendency during the time of the Bhauma-Karas (circa. 732-945 A.D.). Although the early Bhauma-Kara Kings were devout Buddhists, they did not refuse patronage to Śaiva cult. Lakuliśa images found in the temples of Bharateśvara, Parasurāmeśvara, Vaitāl, Śiśireśvara, Mārkaṇḍeśvara and other temples of this period at Bhubaneswar are assigned to Bhauma-Kara period.

Mādhavi Devī, queen of Buddhist King Śubhākaradeva-I, of this dynasty, is known to have built the temple of Madhaveśvara Śiva and appointed a Śiva Ācārya for conducting the worship. In the Hindol plate of King Śubhākaradeva - III, donation of a village Naddilo in Uttar Tosali, for the worship of the God Vaidyanatha Bhaṭṭāraka installed in the Pulindeśvara temple built by Pulindarāja, is found. This shows that Śubhākara-III was a great champion of the Śaiva faith. Śubhakaradeva-IV was a Śivaite King and he was the first Bhauma King to declare himself as "Parama-Māheśvara," the devout worshipper of Lord Śiva. Two Boud charters (E.I., Vol. XXIX, p.220 f.), of Bhauma ruling Queen Prithvi-Mahādevi (894 A.D.) record the grant of villages for the worship of Ūmā-Maheśvara enshrined in the temple of Nanneśvara Śiva built by Sasilekha in commemoration of her deceased father, Nanna. Number of examples from the epigraphic records can be shown from Bhauma-Kara period to show that Śaivism was popular during their period. The "Virajā Māhātmya makes references to some Śaiva temples, known as Kusumeśvara, Laliteśvara and Daṇḍiśvara at Virajā (Jajpur) which do not exist now. The art tradition of Bhauma-Kara period was influenced by Buddhism, Śaivism and Tāntric, which formed a strange amalgam.

During this period the Siddheśvara and Nilamadhava temples at Gandharāḍi, situated about 12 miles to the north-west of Baud were constructed. This shows that Hari-Hara cult had its influence during Bhauma-Kara period.

Many of the feudatories of the Bhauma Kings were ardent advocates of Śaivism. The Śulkis had Goddess Stambheśvari as their tutelary Deity. At the same time the Śulki inscriptions begin with an invocation to Śiva. Raṇastambha, Jayastambha and Kulastambha of this dynasty were great devotees of Śiva and bear the epithet "Paramamāheśvara." It is interesting to point out that the manifestation of the Universe is effected through the power (Śākti) of Śiva and that power is not different from the possession thereof. In the words-Śākti is Śiva's creative energy and is regarded as his feminine aspect.

Several Kings of the Nanda and Tuṅga dynasties were also great followers of Śaivism. Devānanda, Vinitatuṅga and Gayāḍatuṅga were devout worshippers of Maheśvara, as is revealed by their own copper plates.

During Bhauma-Kara period, as Lakuliśa-Pāśupata cult of Śaivism became popular, its off-shoots Kāpālika and Kālāmukha had their influence in Orissa. These two sects worshipped the Female principle, even though their great God was the shaggy Bhairava.

It is mentioned in the Devī-māhātmya section of Mārkaṇḍeya purāṇa (87. 5-23), Cāmuṇḍā (Kāli) sprang from the brow of Kauśiki (Ambikā) to destroy Caṇḍa and Muṇḍa, servants of Śumbha and Niśumbha. In the process She swallowed elephants, horses, chariots and other occupants and then presented the heads of the two demons to Kauśiki. She has many names and forms, more varied then other nine mātrikās which are enumerated in the Agni purāṇa (50.21-22, 30-40, 144.30-37): (1) Rudra Carccika, (2) Rudra-Cāmuṇḍā, (3) Mahālakṣmī, (4) Siddha-Cāmuṇḍā, (5) Siddha Yogeśvari, (6) Rūpa-vidyā, (7) Kṣamā, (8) Danturā and (9) Kubjikā.

The Kāpālikas and Kālāmukhas worshipped the Bhairava aspect of Śiva and his consort Cāmuṇḍā. So, it can be supposed that the activities of the Kāpālikas and Kālāmukhas were prevalent where ever Bhairava and Cāmuṇḍā images are found, throughout Orissa. All the Khakkara temples and sixty-four Yoginis temples, which were the Śākti worship sites in Orissa seem to be the centres of their worship with sexo-yogic practice of Vajroli (the tāntric sexual secret of Self-transformation). The popularity of these types of Śaiva tāntrism was due to widespread indigenous beliefs and practices throughout India, which was prevalent within 8th-12th centuries A.D. and gradually became extinct or two lost Śaivite sects, as it was not favoured by the higher societies and general people.

During 7th-8th centuries A.D. Mahāśivagupta Bālārjuna ruled South Kōśala, with his Capital at Śripur, (modern Sirpur) on right bank of Mahāṇadi. Being a great devotee of Śiva, he enjoyed the epithet "Paramamāheśvara," in his charters and also "had the Śaivite emblem of the Bull on his Seal." He, being a worshipper of Śambhu, constructed a temple of Śiva at the village (modern) Sēnakapat and made it over to an ascetic, Sadaśivācārya who was probably the Spiritual successor of Sadyaḥśivācārya, hailing from the penance grove, entitled "Amaradaka." In Lōdhiā plates, the donee Śūlapāṇi was a disciple of Pramathāchārya who is said to be an inhabitant of Pañcayajña - tapōvana in Dvaitavana. Here, it is sufficient to say that these Śaiva-ācāryas probably belonged to a sect of tāntric-Śaivism which later came to be called Mattamayūra and as such, it may be assumed that Mahāśivagupta may have accepted the doctrine of Mattamayūras and settled Śaiva Ācāryas in his kingdom. There seems to be synthesis of various religious faiths like Viṣṇuism, Śaivism, Buddhism and Tāntric Śaivism during the period of Mahāśivagupta Bālārjuna. During this period, with Śaiva tāntric influence, a style of tantric temple architecture with plan of two squares placed diagonally and intersecting each other at angles of 45 degrees developed. This plan is based on Yantra and came to be known as "Kośāli style of rekha temple." One such temple is found at Bodhi-komna in Nuapada district and another in Ranipur-Jharial archaeological complex of Balangir district.

R.P. Misra is of opinion that from sixth century A.D. Titilagarh region comprising Titilagarh proper, Ranipur-Jharial, Ghodar and many other places of Śaivite culture was a citadel of Mattamayūra Śaivism. In ancient time Ranipur-Jharial was named as Ranipadra. It was associated more or less with the religious mission of Mattamāyūra Śaivāchāryas- Mattamāyūranath Purandara, Sidāśiva Vyomaśiva-I and Vyomaśiva-II (alias Gaganaśiva-II). As Kapālamalini Tantra suggest Taitila or Titilagarh had accepted Goddess Ghaṇṭāsini as its presiding Goddess as early as seventh century A.D. The Cult of this Goddess was not merely a ritualisation with different materials of worship but was associated culturally with different branches of learnings, music, yoga and Mattamāyūra Śaivism. Mattamayūra Śaiva theology appears to have contained a dynamic concept of humanism at its root. As Mahāyāna and Tāntric Buddhism believe in inherent potentiality of Buddhahood in all beings, this Śaivism also believes in the possibility of everybody becoming a Muktatma Śiva, irrespective of caste, creed, colour and profession. The central doctrine around which the comprehensive theology of Mattamayūr Śaivism has developed in the doctrine of

Siddhānta. In theology of Śaivasiddhanta, emphasis is always laid upon the principles of three material bases of Tripadartha Tattva and Quadruple means or Catuspada Tattva. The doctrine of three material bases defines three basic principles of Mattamāyūra Śaivism as Pati, Paśu and Pasa. In the traditional annotation of the Siddhanto doctrine of Śaivism, Paramaśiva is treated as Pati or Supreme Lord of Universe. He is absolutely independent, eternal, owner of unfailing will power and both transcendent and immanent at the same time. Although he is conceived as an indefinable Śūnya like the Omnipresent sky, he is not devoid of a body and his body is extraordinary in the sense that it is beyond all worldly limitations and is composed of the five mantric powers named as Īśāna, Tatpuruṣa, Aghora, Vāmadeva and Sadyojata. These Mantric powers enable the adherent to achieve the means of living meritoriously in this World and to realise the spiritual advance towards the status of Muktātmā Śiva. In the philosophy of Mattamayūra Śaivism all Jīvas whether in the body of a Sudra or Vaisya or Kshatriya or a Brāhmin or a prince or a poor are considered as pasus or unenlightened Soul. The doctrine of this school names the attributes which increase attachment towards material enjoyment and aggravates Spiritual ignorance as Kalas. Jīvas accompanied by these Kalas are called variously as Sakal Jīva, Apakvakalusa Jīva, Pakvakalusa Jīva, Apakvapasa Pralaykala Jīva and Asamaptakalusa Vijñānakala Jīva according to the grades of their Spiritual advance. The Jīva which surposses all these attributes of defilement in all aspects of its functioning is named as Samaptakalusa Jīva and owner of such a Jīva or Soul becomes Aṣṭavidyeśvara or master of eight Spiritual powers and finally a Muktatma Śiva. In this final stage he perceives every being as one and the same and thinks everybeing as the manifestation of Parama Śiva believing the principle "Yatra Jīva Tatra Śiva." In this respect, it is evident that no better humanistic ideology can be traced out elsewhere in comparison with this Śaivite doctrine of equal vision towards all creatures.

Belkhandi situated at the confluence of Utei and Tel rivers was a prominent site of Śaiva tantra in Kalahandi district. A huge Bhairava image is lying down there. Andhakāsuravadha - mūrti, Cāmuṇḍā, Mahiṣāsura - mardinī, maithuna, vidyādhara couple, chattri fragment, pūrṇa - ghaṭa, broken ornamental pillars and three varieties of Saptamātrikās sculptures found there are of interest. The old Śiva brick temple has fallen down since relote past, but over its Liṅga Deity, which is a Mukha-Liṅga a modern temple is built. From ruins, it is known that the old brick temple structure had a stone pillared Maṇḍapa, in its front, beautified by beautiful sculptures. The antiquities of this site are dated to 8th century A.D. The Śiva images here have ūrdhva-liṅga (penis erectus) signifying the upward flow of seminal fluid, through Vajroli. Control of seminal fluid is thought to entail control of all passions and the achievement of desirelessness. The control of mind is tantamount with the various terms denoting the Supreme achievement of the tāntric Yogī, intuitive wisdom and freedom from re-birth. In Tantra Lord Śiva is regarded as the Great Yogī or Mahāyogi. Few Umā-Maheśvara images with ūrdhva-liṅga are also found there.

Hari-Hara Bhairava, an image of local style with ūrdhva-liṅga (penis erectus) and Padma-yonis are found at Sankushgarh site of Kalahandi district. One Naṭarāja image was stolen from Sankushgarh and is not to be found there now. Three model tri-ratha temples made of stone pieces are also found there. These and scattered antiquities there shows that many tāntric temples once stood there. Sankushgarh site situated at the confluence of Rahul and Budhanala near Urladani seems to be a Śaiva tāntric site of medieval period.

The Kōśaleśvara temple at Baidyanath and the Kapileśvara temple at Charda, both Śiva temples of Western Orissa can be bracketed between circa. 875 A.D. and circa. 950 A.D.

In coastal Orissa Śaivism suffered a set-back due to the rise of Buddhism in 8th century A.D. but soon there was revival of Śaivaite activities. During Bhauma-Kara period Śiśireśvara temple was built at Bhubaneswar, dated circa. 800 A.A. by K.C. Panigrahi. Vaitāl temple (circa. 775 A.D.) though a contemporary of Śiśireśvara at Bhubaneswar is a Śākta temple, built in Khakhara style. The growing popularity of Śaivism is evident from the presence of Śiva images in the Tāntric temple of Vaitala. Apart from the composite image Śiva and Pārvatī (Ardhanārīśvara), the imge of Śiva and Pārvatī (Umā-maheśvara) seated side by side on a lotus seat is found. Śiva is four armed, holding a lyre, a trident and a japamala, where as Pārvatī is two-armed placing her right hand on the shoulder of her consort. Śiva in terrific form (Bhairava) is found inside Vaitāl temple, wearing a garland of shulls and possesses sunken eyes, open mouth, protruding tongue and hollowed belly. Being seated in fighting posture, rests the body on the left knee and holds a kharpara and a dagger in both of his hands.

Taleśvara temple is situated in ruin in the paddy-fields in the neighbourhood Parasurameśvara temple at Bhubaneswar, several sculptural specimens of this temple have been removed to Orissa State

Museum, of which one is an image of Lakuliśa and another is of Ardhanarīśvara, both built in sections. The latter is a close prototype of the image of the same Deity to be found in the western vada of the Vaitāl temple. Taleśvara temple belongs to the Vaitāl-Śiśireśvara group.

According to K.C. Panigrahi two small temples, now in ruined condition, stand to the north of the Śiśireśvara, in the compound of the family home of the Paramagurus at Bhubaneswar and they exhibit the same architectural dispositions of Taleśvara, Vaitāl and Śiśireśvara group of temples, belonging to Bhauma-Kara period. The Śiva Liṅga at Soro contains a Buddhist Dharani (*The Orissa Historical Research Journal*, Vol. XI, p.16), which proves that Buddhism lost its identity and merged itself completely in Śaivism.

The Śaiva temple of Śiśireśvara could not, however, escape the influence of Buddhism. The pedestal of Lakuli is occupied by a tri-ratna superimposed by a lotus and flanked by deer. A wheel in place of the lotus would make it a complete Sarnath device, which is clearly a Buddhist symbol. K.C. Panigrahi remarks, "A sculptor trained in the Buddhist tradition and accustomed to carve a Sarnath device on the pedestals of the Buddhist images has, by force of practice, allowed himself to carve the same device here and then has tried to camouflage it by putting a lotus in place of a wheel." Buddhist figures of Amoghasiddhi, Avalokiteśvara and Jambhāla are noticed very close to the aforesaid figure of Lakuli.

Śaiva tāntric sect of Mattamayūra became dominant in Western Orissa with the rise of Ācārya Vyomaśiva -II alias Gaganaśiva-II, in the last quarter of 9th century A.D. Gaganaśiva is also known by other names of Gagaṇeśa, Vyomeśa, Vyoma-Śiva, Gagana Śaśimauli etc. He built the temple of Someśvara Śiva at Ranipur-Jharial (Rani padraka) with the patronage of Somavaṁśī King, who seems to be Mahābhavagupta Janamejaya-I. It was probably because of this that the Śiva temple which he built was named as Someśvara temple and the place came to be regarded as Somatriṭha. The inscription of Gaganaśiva in this temple, is a great evidence of Mattamāyūra sect of tāntric Śaivism. Gaganaśiva -II visited many places for propagation of Śaivism in India and at last became the Chief Ācārya of Mattamāyūra sect. Ranipur-Jharial at first seems to be a Buddhist centre, as Buddhist images are found there. With the constructions of Viṣṇu temple; locally known as Indralath brick temple, Someśvara Śiva temple of Mattamāyūra sect and Chausathi-Yogini temple there, Buddhism seems to have been wiped out there.

In 9th and 10th centuries A.D. the Bhañja Kings of Khiñjali maṇḍala and Khichinga maṇḍala were great patrons of Śaivism. The early Bhañjas of Boud were devotees of Viṣṇu. Raṇabhañja in the first part of his reign was a Vaiṣṇava King, although his Chief Queen Vijayā Mahādevī was a devotee of Śiva. It is during this period, according to some Scholars that the twin temples of Nīlamādhava and Siddhesvara at Gandhatapati (modern Gandharadi) were built in fulfilment of the religious desires of the King and Queen. Raṇabhañja in the last part of his reign became a devout worshipper of Lord Śiva. After Raṇabhañja, the Bhañjas shifted to Ghumsar region and made Vanjulvaka their headquarter. The invocation of Lord Śiva is found in the charters of the Ghumsar Bhañjas, which shows that they were patrons of Mattamayūra sect.

At Boudh town there are three small temples within the compound of Rameswar temple, which are Śaiva tāntric temples, standing in a triangular formation assigned to Somavaṁśī period. The triangle is pointed to east direction. The temple standing at the southern and northern ends of the base line of the imaginary triangle are known respectively as Bhubaneśvara and Svapneśvara. Both of them are facing east. The name of the temple at the apex of the triangle is Paścima Somanātha, which faces west. Except the difference of orientation, these three temples are otherwise identical in respect of their plan, elevation and embellishment. All these three temples are dedicated to Śiva and their Śāktis are made in the design of two squares placed diagonally and intersecting each other at angles of 45 degree. This plan is a tāntric yantra, borrowed from "Kōśali style of Rekha temple architecture," of upper Mahāṇadi valley. Even the Śāktis of the Liṅga Deities of these three temples are made in the design of interesting two squares at angles of 45 degree. According to Śivānandalahari's tāntric thought, Lord Śiva likes to stay in fortresses i.e. the yantra plan and Śākti is the ritualistic fort of Lord Śiva, fit to be worshipped in Tāntra method. These three temples are assigned to early perod of Sōmavaṁśī rule in Orissa, to later part of 9th century A.D.

According to Arjun Joshi, during this period the Bhañja Kings of Khijjiṅgakoṭṭa were great worshippers of Lord Śiva. The copper plate grants of these Kings begins with invocatory verses like, "May Bhava, the Lord of Bhavānī, sole sovereign of all the Worlds, dispeller of Worldly fears, conversant with the numerous modes of meditation, the omniscient, be to our prosperity." These copper plates contain at the top a copper seal with a round rim. On the medallion are a crescent, a bull, a trident and generally the legend of the king such as Śrī Pṛthvibhañjadevasya or Śrī Satrubhañjadevasya etc. all moulded in relief. Some of the Bhañja Kings of Khijjiṅga officially described themselves as Parameśvara i.e. devout worshippers of Lord Śiva. Śrī Pṛthvibhañjadeva was sinless on account of his devotion at the feet of Hara enshrined at Khijjiṅgakoṭṭa. This figure of Hara exists in the present museum at Khijjiṅga, which was enshrined in the original temple.

"Besides the temple of Hara, which is now rebuilt and known as Khijjiṅgeśvari temple, the Bhañja Kings of Khijjiṅga built a number of shrines for Lord Śiva, but unfortunately almost all have disappeared owing to the ravages of time or destroyed by iconoclastic Muslim invaders. This is testified by the large number of Śaivaite images excavated at Khijjiṅga and preserved in the Museum. There are, however, some specimens of Bhañja monuments still found at Khijjiṅga, such as the Khaṇḍiya deul and the temple of Chandra-śekhara inside the Ṭhākuraṇī compound. There are also some ruined temples like the shrine of Nīlakaṇṭheśvara popularly known as Kutai Tundi, at a distance of nearly five hundred yards from the Khijjiṅgeśvarī temple.

"Worship of Śiva liṅgas existed in Khijjiṅga before the Bhañjas and is widely prevalent in the region even today. The worship of Śiva has been assimilated by the Sun-worshippers who worship Bhabha, a form of Śiva, as one of the twelve Ādityas.

"In the Khijjiṅga Museum there are three beautiful figures of Ūmā-Maheśvara dating to the 10th century A.D. These figures are in the Aliṅgana pose and seated in Sukhāsana."

As mentioned earlier, the Kings of Muḍgala dynasty ruled Uttara Tosāli, i.e. north Orissa during 6th and 7th centuries A.D. The Soro copper plates (*Epigraphia Indica*, Vol. XXIII, p. 198) records the grant of Mahārāja Shambhujasha, Mahārāja Bhanudatta and Mahāsandhi-vighahika Somadatta, of this dynasty. The Patiākela copper plate (*Inscriptions of Orissa*, Vol. I, part -II, pp. 124 -127) was the grant of Mahārāja Shambhujasha, which speaks of his rule in southern Tosali. At the site of the dilapidated temple of Mohangiri in Kalahandi district, two small inscriptions are found, one is of Sphita Chandra who belonged to Muḍgalakula and the other of Vydha Bhairava, who was probably the presiding Deity. Details about the Muḍgala dynasty, who ruled the north-east portion of Orissa and how they shifted to the west via South Tosali, in the hilly and forest tract of Kalahandi region in medieval period are not yet known. The Muḍgalas were Śiva worshippers and practised Śaiva tantra, as inscription of Vydha Bhairava is found at Mohangiri. On the stone basement of the Śiva temple of Mohangiri, a line of four tortoises are chiseled marching towards the temple in a line, in north-west direction of the Śiva temple, which has Śiva liṅga as the main Deity. These tortoises symbolise Vajroli mudra. In Vajroli Spiritual yogic practice for Spiritual illumination (i.e. rise of Kuṇḍalini), the male should contract and draw back the penis into the abdomen. Tortoise contracts its head, neck and legs inside its shell. Therefore tortoises are chiseled at Śiva temple of Mohangiri, showing that Vajroli tāntric spiritual yogic practice was prevalent there and the site was a Tāntric piṭha. This form of Vajroli is called Kūrmasthiti, according to "Tantraraja Tantra." Kūrma be first known. Kūrma is of four kinds namely Para Kūrma, Desagata Kūrma, Grāmaga Kūrma and Gṛhaga Kūrma. That is just as the Supreme Tortoise supports the whole Universe, the others support particular Countries, villages and dwellings. As observed earlier the Kāpālikas and Kālāmukhas also practiced Vajroli, so it can be supposed that Mohangiri was visited by Kāpālikas and Kālāmukhas in their hey days, when these Tāntric horrid Śaiva cults were popular.

## ADVENT OF ŚAṄKARĀCĀRYA

The visit of Śaṅkarācārya to Orissa, specially to Puri in the early part of ninth century A.D. during ruling period of Bhauma-Kara dynasty might have stimulated the growth of Śaivism.

Spiritual genius Śaṅkarācārya was born in the Chera country about the year 788 A.D. Latest study of S.D.Kulkarni informs: "In determining the period of Ādi Śaṅkarā, as 509 B.C. to 476 B.C. we have collated all possible evidence in favour of this date. The currently held view about Ādi Śaṅkara's period, at 788 A.D. to 820 A.D. is not backed by any record of any of the Peeṭhas (matts) founded by Ādi Śaṅkarā." During his digvijaya he visited Puri, Sṛṅgeri, Dwaraka and Jyotirdham. In order that the great wisdom of the Rishis may not be lost to posterity, Śaṅkara established four Maths and the four disciples at the above mentioned four places.

"ŚRĪ YANTRA," a diagrammatic embodiment of the creative sexual activity of the Universe is placed till today in all the Maths founded by Śaṅkarācārya. It is the most important of all Tāntric yantras, each of the outer triangles is occupied by the Devatas which represent the sub-divided energy-Self of the Goddess. This is the very image of the process of creation, metaphysically Sexual. To a Tāntric, Creation is a continuous process. So the form, the desire (KĀMA) assumes is that of his female identity by making the World for one to enjoy as Bliss, Consciousness and ultimately the Being. So, it can be said that the whole Creation is pleasure garden of the Creator, which operated through the Kāmadeva, the God of Desire.

At Puruṣottama Puri, Śaṅkarācārya defeated the Buddhists and established one of the icon of Buddha as Divinity of Govardhan Maṭha as Lord Vishṇu Jagannāth, and his Śākti is Vimalā. It seems "Jagannāth," established as the male Deity of Govardhan Maṭha at Puruṣottama Puri by Sankara revolutionalised Jagannāth as a Vaishnav Deity. Further Śaṅkara's commentary on the "Prasthānatray," added fuel to the fire of Purushottama Cult, Jagannāth Cult and made them synchronised as Purushottama Jagannāth. Lord Purushottama Jagannāth was made the Presiding Deity of Purushottama Kṣetra during the period of Somavaṁśī King Mahāśivagupta Yayāti -I in early part of 10th century A.D.

With the development of Śākta tantra and Śaiva tantra, about the 9th century A.D. Buddhism in Orissa was suppressed, though its influence in literary works continued in Orissa till 16th century A.D. Sexo-Yogic system of Buddhism and Nāthism had become very popular and had influenced the Social flow. Conversion of one of the image of Buddha, as Lord Viṣṇu Jagannāth Deity by Ādi Śaṅkarācārya was a great blow, a sudden misfortune or calamity to Buddhism. Because of such hostility, gradually there was decline of Buddhism. Even Śaṅkarācārya is known to have founded his Śṛiṅgeri Maṭha on the site of a Buddhist monastery.

## SOMAVAṀŚĪ PERIOD
## (10th century A.D. to 12th century A.D.)

Somavaṁśī period is regarded as the Golden Age of Śaivism in Orissa. Simultaneously there was prevalent of Śaiva tantra and Hari-Hara worship.

Mahāśivagupta Yayāti-I was the first Somavaṁśī King to bring Kōśala and Utkala, i.e. western and eastern Orissa under a single rule. Therefore, he may be regarded as the father of modern Orissa. After the conquest of the coastal tract of Utkala, obviously Yayāti-I visited Ekāmra, which had attained celebrity as a "Siddha Tirṭha." Being inspired by the achievement of his predecessors, naturally he devoted his energy for the construction of a Śaivite temple for which he would be remembered for days to come. This resolve led to the construction of Mukteśvara temple at Ekamara Kṣetra Bhubaneswar. The Jagamohan of Mukteśvara is star-shaped, which shows the influence of "Kōśali style of Rekha temple architecture", and the main deul is pañcaratha in plan. K.C. Panigrahi is of opinion that reference may be made in this connection to the three temples of Baudh, situated in the upper Mahāṇadi valley which was included in the Kōśala country, the original seat of power of the Somavaṁśīs. The three small temples of Baudh are of almost the same height and have identical architectural and sculptural peculiarities. The ground plan in each case is star like, which is most likely necessitated by the Cult practiced in these Shrines. The Śāktis of the Śiva-liṅgas enshrined in them are also Star-like and these shapes indicate that both the temples and Deities were made in the form of maṇḍalas or yantra mystic figures, with the help of which the Tāntrics wanted to attain their Siddhis. Barring these peculiarities in their planning, these three temples are otherwise linked up with the Mukteśvara in respect of other features. All these monuments and the Mukteśvara possess in common the same subdivisions at the base, such as Pada, Khumbha, Pata, Kani and Vasanta with a leaf design in the kumbha linked up with a chaitya arch above: The same form of rounded corners and the same kind of sunken panel marking the transition between the vimana and sikkara. A good number of Tāntric images are found in Mukteśvara. With the Somavaṁśī cultural influence the construction of pancharatha temple style and making of Navagrahas in Orissa temples started.

Under the Bhauma-Karas the Tāntric cult had given rise to the temples of Śiśireśvara and Vaitāl at Bhubaneswar. With the arrival of Somavaṁśīs, the typical Śiva temples inspired by Śaiva Siddhanta school, carried on its body the stamp of Paśupata school as well as the tāntric school. Lakuliśa is found in Somavaṁśī built temple architecture.

The Somavaṁśīs were the staunch Śaivas, as their surnames Mahāśivagupta and Mahābhavagupta indicate. In their copper plate grants, they also style themselves as Paramamāheśvaras, but the type of Śaivism which they professed was not the same as was prevalent in Orissa during the Bhauma period. It seems to have been influenced by the Mattamayura sect of Śaivism. The Somavaṁśīs were typical Hindus, clinging to family Deity of their own, but worshipping all other Deities and extending toleration and patronage to all other sects.

Yayāti-I made Vinitapura, identified with modern Binika, in Subarnapur district his first Capital. Later he made Yayātinagara on the bank of Mahāṇadi, a city named after him, his Capital, which has been identified with modern Jakti near Baud.

In recent years, it has been established that in 10th century A.D. there was a religious revolution and Jagannāth Deity established by Śaṅkarācārya as Male Deity of Govardhan Maṭh was made presiding Deity of Puruṣottama Kṣetra by Yayāti-I and came to be known as

Puruṣottama Jagannāth in 10th century A.D. This shows that there was religious eclecticism during Somavaṁśī period.

The Somavaṁśī Kings in their personal faith were strong followers of Śaivism. Their devotion to the Cult of Śiva is revealed from the verses used in the texts of their epigraphical records.

After the shifting of the Capital to Yayātinagara (i.e. modern Jakti), Yayāti-I issued a charter on his 28th regnal year, where Yayātinagara is described in the following manner :-

". . . where the enjoyment of love is being continually intensified and still more intensified by the close embraces (of lovers), by which fatigue is removed, in which hissing sound often appears and in which hairs often stand on their ends, although such enjoyment suffers interruption as the ardent young couple show their skill in the various processes of conjugal enjoyment with their eyes dilated (with excitement) and with their minds subdued and fascinated by amorous thoughts;

". . . where, even in the midst of quarrels arising from jealousy, lovers, beaten by lotuses from the ears of women who have cast the beauty of the celestial damsels into shade by the greatness of their endless and peculiar charms, have all their mental anguishes roused to action by the entrance of the sharp arrows of Cupid, with their hairs standing on the ends (lit. sprouting up) on account of the sprinkling of the drops of sweet (from the persons of the objects of their love);

". . . where, at the tops of houses beautifully white washed, the places of assignation of unchaste women and their pearl ornaments were whitened by the clusters of rays issuing from the club-like tusks of very lofty elephants—the rays which rendered the autumn moon useless in the matter of dispelling darkness;

". . . (and) where the fatigue of the women enjoying conjugal caresses with ardent attachment is removed by the breezes surcharged with the particles of water sent up by the breaking and swelling of the high waves of the Mahānadi." Such was the town of Yayātinagara.

The sensual description of Yayātinagara on Mahānadi, shows the prevalent of Śaiva tantra. Yayāti's work at Puri was both political and religious. Under Mahābhabagupta II Bhimaratha patronage for Śaivism and Śāktism, these faiths seem to have been extended throughout his empire.

Indraratha, the son of Bhimaratha, continued the policy of munificent patronage for the progress of Śaivism. In his Banpur plates, the Panchākshari mantra "Namah Śivāya," and pays homage to Lord Śiva, in its opening verse :-

"Salutation to Lord Śiva whose matted hair is adorned with the crescent moon, whose three eyes look like the flames, whose threat is blue due to (drinking of) poison, and who is the embodiment of the three qualities of Sattva, Raja and Tama of the whole Universe." Mark the three guṇas (qualities) of Sattva, Raja and Tama, mentioned in the Banpur plates. These three qualities of human being are given importance in Tāntric scriptures.

Like his predecessors Indraratha Mahābhavagupta -III was a devout worshipper of Śiva and as there was political vicissitudes and challenge during his succession, he devoted his whole will to perpetuate his memory by constructing a Śaivite structure at Bhubaneswar, which is known as Indreśvara or Rājārani. In late medieval purāṇic works like Ekāmra purāṇa, Svarṇādri Mahodaya, Ekāmra Candrikā and Kapila Saṁhitā, the so called temple of Mukteśvara is indicated as the temple of Siddheśvara and it is further mentioned in the same work that the temple of Indreśvara is located to the east of Siddheśvarra at a very short distance.

In the light of this Purāṇic evidence it is amply indicated that very close to the famous temple of Siddheśvara or Mukteśvara there was a significant beautiful shrine of Indreśvara or Rājārāṇī in Bhubaneswar, built in the beginning of the 11th century A.D. Lakuliśa images are found in plenty in Mukteśvara and Rājārāṇī temples.

Mahāśivagupta III Yayāti II alias Caṇḍihara shifted the Capital of the Somavaṁśī Kingdom to coastal Orissa and established the new Capital as Abhinava Yayātinagara, identified with present Jajpur, the old Capital Guhadevapāṭaka or Guheśvarapaṭaka of Bhauma-Karas on Vaitarini river. The traditional accounts (Mādalā Pāñji) of Orissa credits Yayāti-II with the performance of a Daśāśvamedha or ten fold horse sacrifice at Jajpur for which purpose he invited ten thousand learned Brahmins from Kānyakubja or Kānauj. Another tradition in same Mādala Pāñji associates him with the starting of the construction of the Liṅgarāja temple at Bhubaneswar and the Candeśvara temple at Candeśvara under Tangi Police station of Puri district. He is credited for constructing stone revetment named Daśāśvamedha Ghāṭa on Vaitaraṇi river at Jajpur also. He was worshipper of Pañcāṁvari Bhadrāmbika, the tutelary Deity of Suvarnapura identified with modern Sonepur. His Queen Kolāvati is compaired with Durgā in verse 11 of the Brahmeśvara temple inscription, which leads to inform that they were Śākti worshippers also.

Liṅgarāja temple at Bhubaneswar,is the most notable temple. Rising to a height of about 180 feet and dominating the entire landscape. It represents the quintessence of Kaliṅga style of temple architecture and is the culminating of the temple architecture activities at Bhubaneswar. Its construction was started by Yayāti-II and completed by his son Mahābhāvagupta IV Udyotakeśarī.

Mahābhavagupta IV Udyotakeśari was responsible to extend his patronage for the excavation and restoration of rock cut chambers at Khandagiri for the Jaina monks and the construction of the temple of Brahmeśvara under the inspiration of his mother Kolāvati. In Brahmeśvara temple inscription of Bhubaneswar, the Deity is designated as "Kirttirāja."

Many Śaiva temples were built by the Somavaṁśis but the notable among them are the Mukteśvara, Indreśvara or Rājārāṇī, Brahmeśvara and Liṅgarāja, all constructed at Bhubaneswar.

It seems that the Pāśupata sect continued its existence during Somavaṁśī period and Śiva was worshipped both in his malevolent and benevolent aspects. Gaṇeśa and Pārvatī as independent Cult Deities were given importance as separate temples were dedicated for them. The Bhuvaneśvarī and Gaurī temples of Bhubaneswar are such examples.

Śaivism reached its highest watermark in the middle of 11th century A.D. In the same time synthesis of Vaiṣṇavism and Śaivism was there and Liṅgaraj came to be worshipped as Hari-Hara. With the completion of the majestic Liṅgarāja temple alias Krittivāsa temple (as known from inscription in Liṅgarāja temple) at Ekāmra Kṣetra, Bhubaneswar became the famous Śaiva centre in India. In the words of L.K. Panda, Śaivism with its various ramifications in Orissa not only resulted in the construction of the majectic and magnificent temples of Mukteśvara, Rājārāṇī, Brahmeśvara and Liṅgarāja, but also in the ultimate analysis contributed its own share to the assimilative character of the Jagannāth Cult.

Udyotakeśari seemed to have inherited from his father Caṇḍihara Yayāti-II, the worship of the Divine Mother Ambikā and Tāntric tradition. From "Bhakti Bhāgavata Mahākavya," a Sanskrit work of Kavi Ḍiṇḍima Jīvadeva of 16th century A.D. it is known that Bhavadeva, a tāntric teacher with Spiritual powers, was the Royal preceptor of Udyotakeśari. Bhavadeva, the Royal preceptor, according to tradition, belonged to Vatsa gotra and devoted himself to Tāntric cult. He is known to have composed a Tāntric work named "Tantrārnava," (and lived at Krittivāsa Kṣeṭra, which is identified as Bhubaneswar). It is probable that Udyotakeśari named the Śaivite structure of Liṅgarāja as Kirttivāsa in memory of the

Deity of Brahmeśvara which was called Kirttirāja. These informations leads to know that Udotakeśarī respected the ideologies of Śaivism, Śāktism and Tāntric cult.

During Somavaṁśī period separate Shrines for Gaṇeśa were erected. Siddha Gaṇeśa temple was built by the side of the river Dayā, at the foot hills of Dhauli, Gaṇeśa shrine in the premises of the Bhava Kuṇḍaleśvara temple of village Tankapani in the Bhārgavi valley, Gaṇeśa temple at Agrahat near Chaudwar, Teraboi in the Daya valley, in Prāci valley at Jajpur and many other places. This was probably the formative period for the cult of Gaṇeśa which later grew into an important Cult with the establishment of the Mahā-Vināyaka Kṣetra at Kapilasa in Orissa.

The idea of the land of Pañca Kṣetras in Orissa, probably took shape during this period. Orissa prides of the Pañca-devatas namely Viṣṇu, Śiva, Sūrya, Gaṇapati and Śākti worshipped in their traditional five pīṭhas in Puri, Bhubaneswar, Koṇārk, Mahā-vināyaka, Kapilāsa and Jājpur. These Pañca Devatās Upāsanās had their relationship in the past ages and Tāntric worship went side by side with the worship of these and other Deities.

## GAṄGA PERIOD
## (12th century A.D. to 15th century A.D.)

The Gaṅga monarch Anantavarma Coḍagaṅgadeva occupied Utkal within 1110 -11 A.D. after inflicting a defeat on Karnadeva, the last king of Somavaṁśī dynasty. As the exact date of the occupation of Orissa by Coḍagaṅga cann't be ascertained, it appears to have taken place about 1110 A.D.

The first epigraphic evidence of the name Kirttivāsa is noticed in the Liṅgarāja temple itself, where an inscription of Anantaverma Coḍagaṅgadeva is found. According to this inscription of the Gaṅgā monarch, Coḍagaṅgadeva visited the Shrine of Kirttivāsa (i.e. Liṅgarāja) in order to worship Lord Śiva in the holy Shrine. The Kirttivāsa is also found in another inscription of 1134 A.D. engraved in the Liṅgarāja temple. So, it seems that in 11th and 12th centuries A.D. the present Liṅgarāja temple was known as Kirttivāsa temple. All the Gaṅga monarchs before Coḍagaṅgadeva were Śaivites and Coḍagaṅgadeva was a Paramamāheśvara before his conquest of Utkala. During this period Rāmānuja, the famous founder of the Viśiṣṭādvaita school of Vedānta philosophy, in course of his journey from Melukote to Delhi, is known to have visited Puri. Being influenced by Rāmānuja, Coḍagaṅga embraced Śrīvaiṣṇavism and constructed the standing temples of Puruṣottama Jagannāth and Lakṣmī at Purī, over the ruin of the Somavaṁśī construction. Although Coḍagaṅga embraced Vaiṣṇava faith, he continued to extend patronage to Śaivism and is known to have visited the temple of Kirttivāsa (Liṅgarāja) many times. The Nāṭamandira and the Bhogamaṇḍapa of the temple of Liṅgarāja at Bhubaneswar were added during Gaṅga period. The Gaṅga Kings extended their benevolent patronage to this temple with their eclectic policy.

There is an inscription of Coḍagaṅgadeva in the Mārkaṇḍeśvara temple of Purī dated 1131 A.D. which refers to the endowment made by the Gaṅga King. The Queens of Choḍagaṅga are known to have richly endowed the temple of Mukteśvara, temples at Krishnagiri and the temple of Bhīmeśvara Mahādeva at Drākṣārama. His brother Parmadi is also known to have donated to the temple of Nilakantheśvara at Bobbili and temple of Kedāreśvara at Bhubaneswar.

Religious aclecticism continued in Orissa and is still continuing. Oḍḍiyāna alias Uḍḍiyāna, identified with Orissa, had attained celebrity as a great centre of Tāntric Śaivism, Tāntric works like Kālikā purāṇa, Brahmayāmāla, Rudrayāmāla and Tantaryāmala written and compiled in medieval period adorn Lord Jagannāth as the Tāntric God of Oḍra.

It has already been known that in 5th century A.D. or thereabout an Asokan pillar was deliberately destroyed and converted into a huge Liṅgam at Bhubaneswar. For this gigantic Śiva liṅga a temple was built during Gaṅga period, which was named Bhāskareśvara temple. According to K.C. Panigrahi it stands about a quarter mile to the west of the Megheśvara temple. The Bhāskareśvara temple contains a huge Śiva liṅgam, nine feet high and twelve feet five inches in circumference, which has characteristically been described in the local sacred texts as Vrihalliṅgam and which, as we have already shown, is in reality the remnant of an Asokan pillar. So far as the shape of the Sikkara is concerned, it is the only one of its type in Orissa and the avowed purpose of its builder has been to shape it like a pagoḍā and to provide a permanent stone model for the wooden pagoḍā (ratha) which is annually used in the Car festival of the place. It is a plain temple, but the images in the side niches and a few chaitya arches carved on the body of the structure indicate that it was most likely built in the Gaṅgā period. The present structure stands on the site of an earlier temple and there are distinct indications of the earlier materials having been used in it.

## ŚIVA AND ŚAKTI IN UNION

The organs of Male God and Mother Goddess have been worshipped since proto-historic period in India. In Orissa, such findings have been done also. Liṅga represents Lord Śiva and Yoni represents Goddess Śākti. As dealt, Sexo - yogic Sādhanās were continuing in Orissa by Śākta and Śaiva tāntrics. Moreover Oḍḍiyāna alias Uḍḍiyāna bandha (abdominal lock) was most probably discovered in Oḍra i.e. Orissa, comprising Mahāṇadi river valley and it was a great gift to Haṭṭa-yoga.

The headquarter of the Tāntric Mattamayūra branch of Śaiva Siddhānta system was established at Amardāka tirṭha, which is identified as modern Amardā of Mayurbhanj district. So, it is natural that lot of Sexo-Yogic practices or Sādhanās were continuing in Orissa. Moreover, the Nāthism has been studied to have been originated in Orissa, in which school of thought Sexo-yogic Sādhanā, i.e. Vajroli was in practice. With this background, it is natural that people round about Amardā, had started worshipping images of Śiva and Śākti in Sexo-yogic posed images or sculptures.

In early fifties of nineteenth century at Devakunda a hill resort, situated on the eastern slope of Similipal mountain of Mayurbhanj district, Kumar Prafulla Chandra Bhañja Deo, the consort of Mahārani Prafulla Kumaru Devī of Bastar, had discovered the broken pieces of the lower portion of abdomen of Śiva and Śākti in Sexual - union, left foot of the Devi and some more pieces of the image. It is known as Jugma Yoni i.e. Yoni and Liṅga in union, locally. A temple named "Ambikā temple," was built by him and these rare pieces of the broken image were installed at Debakunda. It is misfortune that this rare unique image of Śiva-Śākti in union is not yet popularised by Scholars. This image of Śiva-Śākti in union, seems to have been made during early medieval period, when Sexo-Yogic tāntric practice was vogue in this area. The erect penis symbolises Urddhvareta or upward streaming of the reproductive essence for effecting Sexual transformation of consciousness and that is known as Vajroli in Haṭṭayoga.

Śiva has been elucidated in a Śaiva treatise in Oriya vernacular of 16th century A.D. written by Narayanananda named "Rudrasudhānidhi." The Brahmana priests have increased one Svayambhu to eight, known as Aṣṭasambhu. In different places of Orissa, Aṣṭasambhus are worshipped in Liṅga form. The idea of Aṣṭasambhu probably means eight manifestations of Rudra : (1) Śarva, (2) Bhava, (3) Aśani, (4) Paśupati, (5) Iśāna, (6) Rudra, (7) Ugra and (8) Mahādeva. In the 47th chapter of the Ekāmra purāṇa, Ekāmra tirṭha has been described as a "Siddhatirṭha," having aṣṭāyatana Kṣetra, comprising eight holy centres with eight Śiva-liṅgas. An interesting literature is the Sanskrit Gazetteer literature called "Shaṭpanchāsaddeśavibhāga," which forms the 7th Paṭala of the Book III of the "Śāktisaṅgama Tantra," now preserved in the library of the Asiatic Society, Calcutta. This work is assigned to 17th century A.D. and gives an account of fiftysix Countries lying in and on the borders of India, which may be taken as Pilgrim's guide. Śaiva and Śākti shrines with Tāntric influence and the localities are described in this work. In the 2nd and 30th verses, this work refers to Bhubaneswar while describing the extension of Aṅga and Gauḍa countries.

As old Cuttack, Bhadrak and Balasore districts of Orissa are packed up with Buddhist images, ruins of Buddhist establishments and monasteries, the Śaiva Ācāryas seem to have established Śaiva Maṭhas and carried out the spread of Śaiva tantra in Puri, Cuttack, Dhenkanal, Mayurbhanj and Keonjhar districts with much forcefulness. Therefore in Orissa, Lord Śiva is depicted with ūrdhva-liṅga (penis erectus) mostly, signifying Vajroli.

Many Jaina images are found at Subai, Dudhari, Kachela, Suai and Bhairabasingpur of Koraput district. They are now worshipped as Śiva by local people. There is a Śiva temple at the foot of the hills at Bhairabasingpur and the niches in its walls contain many images of Jaina cult. At about four or five miles from this place are located two villages, where one can find number of similar Jain figures.

Borigumma is a village situated midway between Jeypore and Nowarngpur, in Koraput district. It is famous for a temple of Bhairva, which is built at the foot of a hill. Some Liṅgas standing 6 or 7 feet in height have been dug out from there. It seems the spread of Śaivism and Bhairava worship in Koraput district, diminished the influence of Jainism. In recent years lot of Jaina images and sculptures are collected and exhibited at Museum of Jeypore.

## BHAIRAVA WORSHIP IN ORISSA

Historically Bhairava worship began from Vedic Ajaikapada Bhairava. In Śiva purāṇa, Bhairava is regarded as pūrṇarupa of Śaṅkara. Bhairava is protector of Creation and is terrific. It is known from Tāntric texts that Kala-Bhairava is a synonym of Amardāka. Amardāka tirṭha is identified with modern Amardā of Mayurbhanj district, where Tāntric

Śaiva Siddhānta school was popular.

It seems Bhairava worship became popular in Orissan Śaivism from 8th century A.D. It is known from inscriptions that Bhañjas who ruled over Khiñjalimaṇḍala were devout worshippers of Bhairava. "Tad Bhairavam Haravapuh Bhavataḥ prapātu," is the common prayer in the preamble of the charters of Bhañjas of Khiñjalimaṇḍala.

The Bhañjas of Khijjiṅgakoṭṭa were also worshippers of Bhairava. One Ajaikapada Bhairava is found at Museum of Baripada and one Bhairava is found at Museum of Khiching.

Two Bhairavas are found in Vaitāl (Vetāl) temple of Bhubaneswar. In Svarṇādri Mahodaya, chapter XXVII, this temple is called Kāpālinī.

Bhairavas are associated with Yogini Cult. According to Āgamic texts there are sixty-four Bhairavas divided into eight groups and they are the counterparts of the sixty-four Yoginis. At Hirapur the images of Ajaikapada Bhairava, Svacchanda Bhairava and Chanda Bhairava, on the niches of Yogini temple are very fine images. In this Sixty-four Yogini's temple at Hirapur, on the Caṇḍi Maṇḍapa, late Kedarnath Mahāpatra had noticed an image of Ajaikapada Bhairava with four arms and one leg standing on a full-blown lotus. This Bhairava was wearing a garland of Skulls, a tiara over his head and bracelets and armlets. It had a khaḍga in his upper right hand, a shield in upper left hand and the backbone of a fish in the lower left hand. The lower right hand was broken. Now this image is missing.

Bhairava images are found at Jajpur, Ajaikapada Bhairava in Siṃhanātha temple in Baramba ex-state area, Junagarh and Biswanathpur (old Topigaon) of Kalahandi district and many other places in Orissa. One Bhairava image taken from Biswanathpur is installed in a temple of Lanjigarh, which is known as "Bhairav temple." Another Bhairava image taken from Biswanathpur ruins is now worshipped as Danda Bhairava at Ambadola. Hari-Hara with ūrdhva-liṅga (penis erectus) at Sankushgarh is worshipped as Bhairava locally. Two tantra Goddesses and one dancing Bhairava are found at Menda. Prabhat Mukherjee had informed that an image of Bhairava was worshipped along with Jagannāth for a long time at Puri. From documents of the East India Company, it is known that in 19th century A.D. an image was removed from the throne of Lord Jagannāth at Puri, by the priests of the temple, when the Throne was under repair. The priests refused to reinstall the image after the repair of the Throne. It is further reported that the priests destroyed the image into pieces which was thrown into the Sea.

## SKANDA

Śiva and Pārvatī lived in union in their hermitage on Kailāsa. To them a son was born named Skanda or Kumāra who became the leader of the Divine forces. Being nursed in the Six centres of Sushmumṇā, which is symbolised as Agni, he is conceived of, as the Six-headed son of Fire. Skanda is conceived as the fiery God more lustrous and resplendent than even the God (Āditya). He is the very symbol of the prāṇic element within each individual body, which is the Śākti of individual prāṇa (life).

Skanda is but another form of Śiva for all practical purposes in the mythology of Śiva. He is the prominent Deva, the son of Fire and more brilliant than Āditya or Surya. Skanda is the resplendent energy of Śiva who has been nursed from one Cakra to another in a rising order until in the sixth Cakra, the full splendour becomes manifest.

The vehicle of Kumāra alias Skanda is both Peacock and Cock. The Cock is the symbol of Fire or Prāṇic energy. Peacock is a bird that is inimical to vipers or serpents where the pea-fowl is present the serpents are rendered ineffective. The serpent represents poison, that is the sign of death. The birth of Kumāra or Skanda is the signal that the death-conquering aspect of Prāṇic energy has come into full play and will not permit a loophole for the asuras to invade the realm of life. On the one hand there are vipers coiled on the body of Śiva; and on the other hand his son Skanda comes to have the peacock as his vehical and both of them are considered to be reconciled in the family of the great God Śiva, Mahādeva.

Cock is represented as the vehicle of Skanda in some sculptures of Orissa. In Tāntric Śiva temples, Skanda has both cock and peacock as vehicles. An image of Kārttikeya is found under a three, just outside the boundary of Kōśaleśvar temple of Baidyanath with two associated peacock and cock. From the ruin of a Śiva temple of Bhulia-Sikua in Nuapada district, which is studied to have been a Kalachuri structure, one Skanda sculpture is collected and exhibited at Khariar Branch Museum, at Khariar. In this sculpture, both the vehicles are found, which is dated within 12th-13th centuries A.D.

As Skanda is transformation of Śiva's nature and power, he controls the activity of the six cakras of the Kuṇḍalinī Śākti and is conceived as the leader of the Divine forces or activities released by the power of the cakras, nerve centres in the Spinal cord. Therefore Skanda is depicted with six heads. Six-headed Skandas are rarely found, but are located in places of Tāntric-yoga centres. The six heads represent (1) Mūlādhara cakra, (2) Svādhiṣṭhāna cakra, (3) Maṇipūra cakra, (4) Anāhata cakra, (5) Viśuddhi cakra and (6) Ājñā cakra. In Atharva Veda, the body is said to have eight cakras, but the Tantra Yogis regard the six cakras, which are shown as Skanda's six heads to have been the main and important Cakras.

Many Six-headed Skandas may be traced in Orissa, but the author has come across six Six-headed Skandas and they are thus :-

(1) One Six-headed Skanda is found among the images of the old structure, inside the Śiva temple on the embankment of Tirbandha (tank) of Khariar in Nuapada district, dated to Kalachuri period 12th century A.D.
(2) One Six-headed Skanda is found as pārśvadevatā in the Brajeswar Mahādev temple at Dharamsagar village, in Nuapada district.
(3) One Six-headed Skanda is found, made of white marble, inside the Nilahantheswar Śiva temple of Dadpur, in Kalahandi district, dated to Kalachuri period 12th century A.D.
(4) One Six-headed Skanda alias Kārttikeya is found in the west raha niche of a small shrine, on the south compound of Suvarnameru temple at Sonepur, in Suvarṇapur district.
(5) Six-faced (Sanmukha) Kārttikeya is found in the Vimalā temple, at Puri.
(6) Six-headed Kārttikeya is a specimen in the Guteswar temple of Algum.

## VAIṢṆAVA TANTRA

Theistic religion in which Viṣṇu is the object of worship and devotion as the Supreme God, is known as Vaiṣṇavism. In Rigveda, Viṣṇu was recognised as an aspect of Sun and associated in the later Vedic texts more with sacrifice. Therefore it can't be said that Vaiṣṇavism as a theistic sectarian religion flourished in the Vedic age.

"Vāsudevaka," word is used in the sense of "a person whose object of Bhakti is Vāsudeva," is used in Aṣṭādhyāyi of Pāṇini dated to 5th century B.C. Vāsudeva-Kṛṣṇa became associated with Viṣṇu and this process was completed by the 2nd century A.D. because a reference to the founder of this sect can be traced in the Chāndogya Upaniṣad, which refers to sage Kṛṣṇa, son of Devaki, as a disciple of the Risi Ghora of the Aṅgirasa family. Thus the Bhāgavata religion, which was propounded by Vāsudeva and was the parent of later Vaiṣṇavism was probably the development of Sun worship. A further step in the same process was the identification of Vāsudeva Kṛṣṇa Viṣṇu with a deified Sage (or Hero) named Nārāyaṇa. The earliest evidence regarding the identification of Nārāyaṇa with Viṣṇu is probably to be traced in the "Baudhāyana Dharma-sūtra." The tenth Prapāṭhaka of the "Taittiriya Āraṇyaka" contains the formula which regards Nārāyaṇa, Vāsudeva, Viṣṇu and Hari as the same Deity and as the Deity eternal, Supreme Lord.

The earliest Viṣṇu image of Mahāṇadi valley, dated to 2nd century B.C. is found at Burhikhas village in Bilaspur district of Madhya Pradesh. It bears a Brāhmi inscription of 2nd century B.C. and is worshipped in a Viṣṇu-parivāra of the same village.

The Sātavāhanas over ran most part of Orissa in the beginning of 2nd century A.D. The fortune of the Satāvahana family rapidly revived under Gautamiputra Sātakarni who started his reign about 106 A.D. and consolidated his strength in the Deccan by conquering the neighbouring territories. By this period Kaliṅga and South Kōśala were conquered and made a part of the Sātavāhana empire. Gautamiputra apparently climed a sort of suzerainty over the whole of trans-Vindhya India, as he is described as the Lord of the Vindhya (the central and eastern Vindhyas as well as the Satpura), Rikṣavat (portion of the Vindhyan range to the south of Malwa), Pāriyāta (western Vindhyas and the Aravalli), Sahya (Western ghats to the north of the Niligiri hills), Malaya (Tranvancore hills), Mahrndra (Eastern Ghat in Orissa) and other mountain ranges encircling the peninsular of South India. The progress of Vaiṣṇavism during Sātavāhana period might have influenced Orissa to a great extent. The Sātavāhana King of the 2nd century A.D. claimed to be equal to Rāma (Baladeva or Śaṅkarṣaṇa) and Keśava (Vāsudeva-Kṛṣṇa) is also noteworthy, as it shows the growing importance of Vasudevism. The worship of Śiva and Kṛṣṇa was popular and votaries of the different faiths lived in harmony. Sometimes they even gave grants to one another. This shows that assimilation of different faiths was taking place in Society and Vaiṣṇavism seems to have been popular in Orissa.

On the right bank of Udanti river is situated Khalna village in Sinapali Block of Nuapada district. Within Khalna village area, within the rice fields, on the Udanti river bank, a natural patch of Teak plantation is found. The local people have found one stone plaque measuring 10 inches in width and 6 inches in height, from there. Three figures are chiselled on the centre and two figures of monkeys are found on either sides with their hands in Namaskār (Padma mudrā). The whole plaque or stone plate is much mutilated and definitely denotes Laxman, Rāma and Sitā. The local people of Khalna village have installed this finding in a small hut and worshipping it. It seems to belong to pre-Gupta period and Viṣṇu being a prominent Vedic God must have been worshipped by the Brahmaṇical Hindus, in whole of Orissa. This plaque is now shifted to Titilagarh and is kept in one of the temple there and worshipped as side Deity.

Only after Gupta emperor Samudragupta's expedition to Orissa in 4th century A.D. that Vaiṣṇavism received its momentum under Royal patronage.

The Nalas of Puṣkari (identified with Podagarh in Umarkote thana area) of Navrangpur district ruled South Kōśala from later 4th century A.D. till the early part of 6th century A.D. It is known from the Podagarh stone inscription that Nala King Skandavarman installed the footprints of Viṣṇu in a temple, which he built. The inscription was written on a pillar, probably a Garuḍa-stambha in front of the temple. It records the grant of an estate in favour of the Deity, and it is noteworthy that Viṣṇu is called Puruṣa in this connection. This charter was granted in the 12th regnal year of the King and Priti Bhāgavata was the name of one of his officers. In the same inscription the King has offered his prayers to Vāsudeva.

Late Sarat Chandra Behera mentions that the Māṭhara Kings who ruled over Kaliṅga in the 5th century A.D. from the river Mahāṇadi in the north to the mount Mahendragiri in the south in their palmy days, embraced Vaiṣṇavism and extended active patronage for the construction of temples dedicated to Viṣṇu. It is known from the Niṅgondi copper plate grant that Prabhañjanavarma was a worshipper of Lord Nārāyaṇa (Bhagavat Swami Nārāyaṇa Pādanudhyātah). In the Chicasole copper plate Nanda Prabhañjanavarmā declares himself as a Parama Bhāgavata and Caṇḍa Varmā also describes himself as a devotee of Viṣṇu in his Bobili charter. The Māṭhara Kings who ruled over the Mshendra Bhoga Viṣaya, constructed a temple dedicated to Viṣṇu on the top of Mahendragiri. Amidst the ruins of the temple, near the so called Kunti temple a beautiful icon of Nārāyaṇa with four arms is found. It is made of black stone. The image is dressed only in loin cloth and the tiara is truncated. The hallow round the head is plain. It seems that the image was made during the reign of Prabhañjavarmā who was a votary of Lord Nārāyaṇa. Prabhañjanavarmā, who ruled as far as the river Mahāṇadi, in the north also appears to have built a temple for Lord Viṣṇu at

Bhubaneswar, which is essentially a place of Śaiva importance on the bank of the lake Vindusarovara there stands the famous temple of Ananta Vāsudeva which was built by Candrikā, daughter of Anaṅgabhīma -III (Gaṅgā monarch) in the year 1278 A.D. In front of this temple on the very bank of the lake there is a fine image of Viṣṇu, which from its iconographic feature seems to belong to the 5th or 6th century A.D. It is a four-armed image carrying conch, wheel, discus and the palm of lower right hand is shown open without a lotus. The Tiara on the head is cylindrical. Simple loin cloth adorns the waist and the image is in a standing position.

"It appears that this Viṣṇu image was originally worshipped on the spot where the great temple of Ananta Vāsudeva was built in the 13th century A.D. There must have been an old temple where this Viṣṇu image was installed. The Māṭharas, who extended their empire upto the Mahānadī, were probably responsible for constructing the Viṣṇu temple at Bhubaneswar. Probably the temple was destroyed by the vagaries of nature. Thus in the 13th century A.D. Candrikā was prompted to construct a new temple – the temple of Ananta Vāsudeva – in its place."

During this period, the Kings of Śarabhapuriya dynasty, who ruled South Kōśala during 5th and 6th centuries A.D. were Vaiṣṇav. Their Seal bears the figure of Gajalakṣmī. King Narendra was a Paramabhāgavata. In the gold coins of Śrī Mahendrāditya, Śrī Kramaditya and Śrī Prasannamātra, discovered at Maraguda valley, the image of Garuḍa with its spread wings is flanked by a discus on its right and a conch on its left. Mahājayarāja and Mahāsudevaraja are described as Paramabhāgavatas in their grants and these findings definitely show that there was apportunity of spread and establishment of Vaiṣṇavism.

A mutilated Viṣṇu image is discovered at Khariar and preserved at Khariar Branch Museum. The upper portion of this image till the bust is existing. Kiritamukuṭa is worn on the head and the upper two hands are holding conch and discus. Huge ear-rings and ornaments are worn and it seems to be a four-handed Viṣṇu image. One circular Lakṣmī-pada measuring 4 inches in diameter was found at Kortipadar, an adjacent village, near Khariar. These are post Gupta findings and are dated to the Śarabhapuriya period.

The early Somavaṁśīs, known as Pāṇḍuvaṁśī, who ousted the Śarabhapuriyas from South Kōśala were Vaiṣṇav Kings. Tivaradeva had the epithet of Paramavaiṣṇava. Widow-Queen Vāsaṭā, the mother of Mahāśivagupta Bālārjuna, constructed a temple for Viṣṇu (Hari) at the Capital Śrīpur (Sirpur) in 7th century A.D. now known as the

Lakshmana temple. The inscription of this temple reveals that Vāsaṭa's husband, King Harṣagupta (Harṣadeva) was also a worshipper of Viṣṇu. The inscription begins with salutation to Puruṣhottama and continues to invoke this Puruṣhottama as Nṛsiṁha. This shows special emphasis to Nṛsoṁha aspect of Viṣṇu.

About Vaiṣṇavism during the Śailodbhāva period, S.C. Behera narrates that at least a century prior to the rise of the Śailodbhāvas, Vaiṣṇavism was popular and prevalent all over India-Line 24 of the Allahabad pillar inscription indicates that Samudragupta, who conquered Kaliṅga in circa. 350 A.D. was a Bhāgavata. Khoh copper plate points out that Saṁkshobha of the Parivrājaka family of Central India was a devotee of Lord Vāsudeva. Worship of the image of Viṣṇu is also hinted in the Bhilari stone-pillar inscription of Skandagupta. Badagaṅga rock inscription reveals that Bhūtivarman of Assam in Gupta era 253 was a Parama Vaiṣṇava as well as a "Parama Bhāgavata." We know from the Patna Museum plates that Pravarasena-II of the Vākāṭaka family was a devotee of Lord Viṣṇu. And in harmony with the sentiment of the time Orissa also became a stronghold of Bhāgavatism during the Māṭharas and the Nalas. But Śailodbhavas, who arose in Koṅgoda after the decline of the Māṭharas, at once appeared as devotees of Lord Śiva. But it is to be noted that although they became "Parama Maheśvara," Vaiṣṇavism had its strong influence in Koṅgoda. This is known to us from the Khurda plates of Mādhavarāja-II, which suggest that "Lord Mādhava with discus in his hands," was worshipped with great devotion by the people, although the Royal house accepted Śaivism. The prevalence of the worship of Mādhava in Koṅgoda is very significant in the history of Vaiṣṇavism faith. From the use of the name "Mādhava" by three princes of this dynasty we understand that "Mādhava" was a popular Deity in Koṅgoda. Mahābhārata gives an important place to Mādhava. It says that because of his Mauna, Dhyāna and Yoga, the Deity is so named. Thus, it is obvious that Mādhava, famous in Mahābhārata occupied an important place in the religious ideology of Koṅgoda.

"It was during this period that in Kaliṅga Vaiṣṇavism had its strong hold. The Eastern Gaṅga King Hastivarman in Gaṅga era 79 prayed for the graces of Lord Nārāyaṇa in his Narasiṅhapalli charter. The Chālukyas of Piṣṭapura, as known from Timapuram plates, declared themselves as "Parama Brāhmaṇya Parama Bhāgavata." Thus we find that in the south of Koṅgoda, Gaṅgas and Cālukyas accepted Vaiṣṇavism for sometime. In the northern side of Koṅgoda, Utkala also accepted Vaiṣṇavism. Somadatta, king of Utkala and Daṇḍabhukti, refers to Lord Viṣṇu and

Seṣa in the first verse of the Midnapore charter of the time of Śaśāṅka. This seems to be corroborated by the tradition that Liṅgarāja, who according to Purāṇic source, was established at Tribhuvaneśvara, represents the worship of Hari-Hara a synthesis beteen Śaivism and Vaiṣṇavism. Again various synonyous of Lord Viṣṇu namely Mādhava, Śrīnivāsa, Madhusūdana, Hari and Nārāyaṇa - are very often referred to in the copper plate grants of the Śailodbhava Kings of Koṅgoda. This is a clear indication of the strong influence of Vaiṣṇavism. The image of Mādhava in Kōśaleśvara temple at Keonjhar bears testimony to the worship of Mādhava in Orissa. The twin temples of Mādhava and Śiva at Baud of a later period represents the synthesis of Vaiṣṇavism and Śaivism. Thus epigraphic, purāṇic and monumental evidences lead us to believe that a synthesis of Vaiṣṇavism and Śaivism in Koṅgoda in the seventh century A.D."

It is usually regarded that under Śailodbhavas, Bhaumakaras and Somavaṁśīs, Śaivism thrived in Orissa under Imperial patronage. The climax of Śaivism in Orissa was reached in the construction of the great temples of Liṅgaraj and Brahmeśvara at Bhubaneswar. There was temporary set-back in the Vaiṣṇav movement in Orissa.

Vaiṣṇavism, like Śaivism, was not a popular faith of Orissa during the Bhauma-Kara rule, as not a single Viṣṇu temple is known to have been built during their time. Two Queens of the dynasty, Tribhuvana-mahādevi-I and Prithvimahādevi alias Tribhuvanamahādevi-II, were however, the devotees of Lord Viṣṇu, as is indicated by the epithet "Paramavaiṣṇavī" or "one intensely devoted to Lord Viṣṇu," which they assumed in their copper plate charters. Besides, we find occasional references to Lord Viṣṇu and his consort Śrī or Lakṣmī in the records of the dynasty. The huge images of Viṣṇu in Śayana (recumbent) posture found at Serang and Bhimkand, on the rock bed of Brahmāṇī river in Dhenkanal district have been assigned to the Bhauma period.

During circa. 850 A.D. -1050 A.D. the Bhañjas ruled Khijjiṅgakotta empire consisting of Keonjhar, Mayurbhanj and parts of Balasore districts of Orissa and Midnapore area of Bengal, till ancient Tamluk. About the prevalent of Vaiṣṇavism in that empire, Arjun Joshi informs that although the Bhañjas of Khijjiṅga were Śaivas or Śāktas, they allowed Vaiṣṇavism to thrive side by side with Śaivism in Khijjiṅga. This is testified by the existence of the Shrine of Viṣṇu near a mound towards the west of Khijjiṅga. Among the ruins of this mound are the pedestals of two figures of Vaiṣṇavite origin. This indicates the existence of a Viṣṇu temple. The Viṣṇu Cakra (1'.3" dia x 2' height) with

Navagrahas with Sculpted Deities on either side, is now preserved in the Site Museum at Khijjiṅga. This Cakra has an original pedestal to be fixed at the top of a temple. Besides this emblem of the Viṣṇu temple at Khijjiṅga there are figures of Viṣṇu in the Site Museum at Khijjiṅga.

Vaiṣṇavism was popular during the later medieval period and the temples of Budha Jagannāth at Baripada and Rasikaraja at Haripur were built by Raja Vaidyanath Bhañja (A.D. 1575). The temples of Rādhāmohana and Lakṣmī-narayāna at Haripur and Gundicha temple at Vṛndāvanapur were constructed by Raja Vikramāditya Bhañja of the later period. The figure of Vāsudeva discovered in the village of Badasahi with the figures of Lakṣmī on its left and that of Vasumati on its right is a specimen of a high order of workmanship datable to the 16th century A.D. The figures of Lakṣmī - nārāyana, Garuḍa, Varāha and Narasiṁha and incarnations of Viṣṇu are ample evidence of Viṣṇu worship in the Khijjiṅga Kingdom during the later medieval period."

One Vaiṣṇavi sculpture is found at Khijjiṅga, dated to 10th century A.D. This shows that with the Tantra influence on Vaiṣṇavism, the Śākti of Viṣṇu came to be worshipped as Vaiṣṇavi. The earliest trace of Vaiṣṇavi in Orissa is found as a Saptamatrika in 7th century A.D. as already stated and it represents the mental quality lobha or covteousness. With the spread of Tantraism, Vaiṣṇavism could not remain aloof from Tāntric influence.

Yogāviṣṇu is found at Baripada Museum, dated to 10th century A.D. The hair of Viṣṇu is carved like the curly hair of Buddha. The Yogāsana form of Viṣṇu has been described in "Siddhārtha Saṁhitā," "Baikhana Sagama" and "Caturvarga Cintamaṇi (II. 114)." This form of Viṣṇu is regarded as the composite from of Viṣṇu and Buddha. Yoga-Viṣṇu are noticed at Deori, Marh Piparia, Bina and Baleha in Sagar district of Madhya Pradesh, Indian Museum at Calcutta (exhibit No. 2592), Mathura Museum (exhibit No. 379), Khajuraho, Kalleśvara temple at Bagali (Billary district) and one collected from Karitalie, Jabalpur district and exhibited at Mahanta Ghasidas Museum of Raipur. The purpose of development of Yogeśvara Viṣṇu was that, as Buddha was accepted as an incamation of Viṣṇu by Hinduism and as lot of Dhyāni Buddha images were made throughout the Country, to keep equilibrium Yoga-Viṣṇu or Yoga-Nārāyana were made. Lalmani Joshi, very rightly informs that the acceptance of Buddha as an incarnation of Viṣṇu by Hinduism was a "well conceived and bold stroke of policy (which) cut the ground from under the feet of Buddhism."

Mādhava worship had already started in Orissa from Sailodbhava period. Kausalyarani Raghavan informs that according to Śrī Sathya Sai Baba, the word "MĀDHAVA" contains two syllables, "MA" and "DHAVA." "MĀ" can be interpreted to mean "Māyā" or illusion; "MA" means Prakṛti, or nature; "MĀ" also stands for Goddess of Wealth or Lakṣmī. "DHAVA" means Master. One who is the owner of "MĀYĀ" or "Prakṛiti" or Lakshmi. He is "Mādhava." He is also the Paramathma.

Mādhava worship is very popular in Orissa. The oldest of the Mādhava image is that of Nīlamādhava of Gandharadi at Boud area. In Prachi valley there are traces of Mādhava worship at Mudgala Mādhava, when the antiquarian remains of the site is assigned from circa. 8th century A.D. to 12th century A.D. and Mādhava; where the unique Deity of Viṣṇu is worshipped inside a temple of 13th century A.D. as Madhavānanda. Nilamādhava is worshipped at Kantilo, on the right bank of Mahāṇadi, in Khandapara area. The present temple does not seem to be ancient, but the Deity apparently represents an earlier figure of medieval period. Mādhava worship is still apparent in most of the places of coastal Orissa.

An image of Kṛṣṇa, discovered from the Mahānadi river bank of Sambalpur town is preserved at "Dr. N.K.Sahu Museum," of Sambalpur University. It is made of greenish chlorite stone with crude workmanship. Kṛṣṇa stands in tribhanga pose at the centre. It is standing with the left leg resting on the floor. Kṛṣṇa is flanked on two sides by two female figures standing gracefully in tribhanga attitude. Two hands of the main image are resting on the shoulders of the two female figures on both the sides, with an attitude of embrace. The head portion of Kṛṣṇa is broken from the chest upwards. There is no Cow in the lower or side portion of the sculpture. The possibility of the earlier date may not be ruled out, but it is tentatively assigned to 10th - 11th century A.D.

The advent of Śaṅkarācārya to Puri, establishment of Jagannāth Deity, finally the installation of Puruṣottama - Jagannāth Deity and construction of its temple in early 10th century A.D. by the Somavaṁśī King Mahāśivagupta Yayāti -I gave fresh impact to the rise of Vaiṣṇav pantheon. The Cult of Jagannāth, the symbolic representation of all religions, the quintessence of all religious creed and philosophies became prominent in Vaiṣṇavism with the centre of its eminence at Puri. In the whole Country of India, when wide wrath of Tāntrism was prevalent,Vaiṣṇavism could not remain unaffected and developed Vaiṣṇav tantra. The composition of "Lakṣmitantra," between the 9th and 12th centuries A.D. became the most useful work of Vaiṣṇav tantra. Lakṣmītantra literature has two objectives in view – to establish the supremacy of Lakṣmī as a philosophical principle, ranking if not higher than Viṣṇu; then at least equal to Him, and to set down a full record of exclusive Śākta - upāsanā. Here Lakṣmī is explained in terms of Lakṣmī as the Supreme Being.

## THE GREAT TĀNTRIC PĪṬHA PURUṢOTTAMA - PURI

The reigning period of Anantavarma Coḍagaṅga is within 1078 A.D. to 1150 A.D. according to K.C. Panigrahi. The exact date of the occupation of Orissa by Coḍagaṅga can't be ascertained, but it appears to have taken place about 1110 A.D. Coḍagaṅga's ancestral Capital was at Kaliṅganagara identified with Mukhaliṅgam, situated in the Shricakol district of Andhra Pradesh, but after his occupation of Orissa, he transferred his Capital to Cuttack which was more centrally situated in his vast kingdom. Here the Gaṅgās ruled for fourteen generations and gradually became Oriyas and lost their former identity.

With this conquest of Utkala by Coḍagaṅga there began the Golden age in the history of Vaiṣṇavism in Orissa. His empire extended from Gaṅga to Godāvari. He was a devout worshipper of Śiva, but after his conquest of Utkala, he is known to have embraced Vaiṣṇavism. It was during this period that Śrī Rāmānuja in course of his journey from Melukote to Delhi between 1107 A.D. and 1117 A.D. visited and stayed at Puri. His disciple Govinda established the Maṭh called "Em-permanur" or Emar Maṭh. With the influence of Rāmānuja, Coḍagaṅga embraced Vaiṣṇavism and constructed the standing temple of Jagannāth and the temple of Lakṣmī at Puri, over the old Somavaṁśī constructed site.

The mode of worship at Jagannāth temple are partly Vedic, partly Tāntric and partly Purāṇic. According to "Paraśurāma Kalpasūtra," and "Śrīmad Bhāgavata," the worship should be performed in three different ways such as Vedic, Tāntric and Miśra (mixed) mode. The Bhāgavata (Chapter -VIII, 6, 19) further notes that those who are desirous of attaining mokṣa should worship the Lord in both ways, Vedic and Tāntric.

Pañcamakāra mode of ritualistic worship is done at Jagannāth temple. In present day understanding Pañcamakāras are (1) Matsya (fish), (2) Māṁsa (meat), (3) Madya (wine), (4) Mudrā (money) and (5) Maithuna (sexual intercourse). The first Matsya is substituted for green vegetables cooked with Hingu (asafoetida). The second i.e. Māṁsa consists of the preparation of Adā Pacidi (Ginger). The third i.e. "Madya" substituted for green cocoanut water offered in the bellmetal vessel. The fourth i.e.

"Mudrā" consists of a pudding prepared with sugar and flour (mixture) named as Kānti. The fifth i.e. Maithuna which consists of peculiar kind of dancing by Devadāsīs (utkacanṛtya). But according to some this Maithuna aspect is represented by the Aparājita flower. This flower is conceived as Yoni. This shows that the Tāntric features are sublimated in the pure form at Jagannāth worship with the help of these Anukalpas (substitutes). The theology of Jagannāth Yoga system is based upon the Haṭhayoga.

It is interesting that the Śākta mode of sacrifice of Ram etc. before the Goddess Vimalā is also made. It is only thrice in a year during the Mahāṣṭami tithi of the autumnal worship of the Goddess Vimalā, the animal sacrifice is made for three days. She is also offered fish from the Saptamī tithi upto Navamī as She is conceived as Durgā. Goddess Vimalā is made of stone. It is in the standing posture and is four-armed. The upper right hand holds Akṣamālā (rosary) and lower right is shown in the Varadā pose. The upper left hand holds a beautiful mermaid (Matsya Kanyā). The lower left hand holds a Pānapātra (drinking vessel). Vimalā is three-eyed and is wearing Kiriṭa (Crown) and other ornaments. There are two female attendants, naked and fierce-looking, on either side.

The Shrine of Vimalā inside the temple of Puruṣottama - Jagannāth is of importance. According to the Tāntric tradition, She is Bhairavi, the consort of Jagannāth who is also regarded as Bhairava (Vimalā Bhairavī yatra Jagannāthastubharivah - Tantra Cūḍāmaṇi). The famous Mahāprasāda of this temple is only efficacious after the final offering made to the Goddess Vimalā, who is established in the form of Bhairavi within the precincts of the Shrine. It is on this principal and practice of the well-known communion, that the temple is regarded as the Bhairavī - cakra or the circle of the Goddess Bhairavi - Durgā and hence no caste restrictions are observed according to the Tāntric dictum.

Goddess four-armed Bhuvaneśvarī is found inside Jagannāth temple, seated on a white lotus in Padmāsana pose. She holds aṅkuśa in the upper right hand and lower right being shown in Varada pose. She holds a nāgapāśa in the upper left, the lower one being in abhaya mudrā. She is also three-eyed and has the crescent moon in her crest.

The four-armed Goddess Lakṣmī inside this Jagannāth temple is seated on a white lotus in the padmāsana posture, holding lotuses in her two upper hands, the lower hands being in the Varada and Abhaya poses. A few other images of Lakṣmī are shown holding Śaṅkha and Cakra in their upper hands inside the campus of this temple.

In the Bhogamaṇḍapa of this temple all the Dikpāla (the guardian deities of directions) images are carved along with their Vāhanas and Śāktis. The Śāktis are placed above the Dikpālas. The sculpture of Mahiṣāmardinī Durgā is also found in the Bhoga Maṇḍapa.

According to "Nīlādri Mahodaya" the image of Jagannāth is based on "Cakrayantra," the image of Balabhadra is based on "Śaṅkhayantra," and Subhadrā's image is based on "Padmayantra."

The most significant sculpture engraved on the Bhogamaṇḍapa at its northern side is that of "Durgā Mādhava." Here Jagannāth is shown along with Śiva and Durgā. This shows a definite syncretic tendency. This motif is found in the Sun temple of Kornārka also.

Maithuna assumed an important place in Tāntric world and they were worshipped. The females practising Maithuna are called Yoginīs. The "Tantrarāja tantra and Keulāvali tantra," mention that offerings should be made to fifty Maithunas. On the Anaṅgatrayodaśī day, the Maithuna images on the temple of Jagannāth are worshipped. The first Maithuna image that is worshipped is Anaṅgāturā carved on the outer northern wall of the Jagamohana of Jagannāth temple.

Lord Jagannāth is all pervading and He combines in Himself all the main five Hindu Deities namely Nārāyaṇa, Rudra, Gaṇeśa, Sūrya and Durgā. When He is on the Ratna Siṁhāsana of His temple, He is Nārāyaṇa; during the Nabakalevara ceremony, he is considered as Rudra; during the Snāna yatra, he is conceived as Gajānan (Gaṇeśa); at the time of Car-festival, he is taken to be Sūryanārāyana; while enjoying the Divine slumber (Sayana yātrā), he becomes a Durgā. Thus all the main Deities of Hinduism are considered to have been merged in Him. Thus, He is represented as a Supreme God to Śaivites, Śāktas, Gāṇapatyas, Sauras and Vaiṣṇavas. So Pañcadevatās are represented within Lord Jagannāth. With this background in Jagannāth Yoga, Haṭha yoga is practised. The upward journey of the Kuṇḍalini towards the Sahasrāra is considered as the march of the finite towards the infinite and their union is taken to be the delliance of Śiva-Śākti by the Śāktas and Śaiva tantras and Rādhā and Kṛṣṇa in eternal Rasa arena by the Vaiṣṇav tantra.

Puruṣottama Puri is given importance as a Śākta Kṣetra in Tāntric literature. In the words of B.C. Pradhan, in the Tāntric lore Jagannāth is considered to be a Bhairava and Vimalā is worshiped as Mahādevī. In "Devī Bhāgavata," Vimalā is considered to be the Kṣetra Śākti. Matsya purāṇa chapter-XXIII refers to Puruṣottama Kṣetra as a Śākta pīṭha with its presiding Goddess Vimalā. Vāmana purāṇa refers to Puruṣottama along with Virajā as a sacred pilgrimage centre. "Rudra Yāmalā," a famous work on Tantra composed in circa. 950 A.D. glorifies Jagannāth as adoring the Mahāpīṭha. "Kalika purāṇa," refers to Oddra pīṭha as a famous Śākta pīṭha which was the celebrated seat of the Goddess Kaityayani and God Jagannāth. "Tāntra Yāmalā," another old tāntric work of Brahminical Hinduism refers to Jagannāth as the presiding Deity of Puruṣottama Kṣetra in Utkala. In the last list of 108 Pīṭhas found in the "Prana Tosini Tantra," refers to Vimalā as the presiding Goddess of Puruṣottama Kṣetra. The "Brihan Nila Tantra," also gives a similar references to Puruṣottama Kṣetra as a Śākta Kṣetra. In the Purāṇic list of 100 names of the Mother Goddess, "Namastottara Sata (Vr.9)," there is expression, "Vimalā Puruṣottama." In the list of Mahāpīṭhas and Upapīṭhas given by the author of "Śiva carita" (quoted by D.C. Sircar in "Śākta Piṭhas") there is also the mention of Nila Parvata or Nīlācala as an Upapīṭha where Vimalā is the Presiding Devi and Jagannāth is Bhairava.

"Mahāpīṭha Nirūpaṇaṁ," in verse 13, refers to Jagannāth as Bhairava and Vimalā as Mahādevi. Subhadra is daily worshipped in the Mantra of "Bhubaneśvari," one of the Goddess of Daśa-mahāvidyā.

An illuminating suggestion revealing the mystery of Pranava was made by Acyuṭānanda Das, in his "Sayantra Śūnya Saṁhitā" (palm leaf manuscript discovered by K.C. Mishra and preserved at Orissa State Museum, Bhubaneswar). According to him the Ratnavedi (Siṁhasana), Sudarśana and the three icons, Jagannāth, Balabhadra and Subhadra all are mounted in the figure called "Oṁkār-yantra." This Yantra is constituted of five Māntrās or marks which have been termed by the poet as Nāda, Vindu, Daṇḍaka, Tūraka and Kuṇḍali. K.C. Mishra further remarks that when these marks are conjoined, they form the letter "OM" of the Indian especially alphabet of Oriya which again is the outline of the image of Jagannāth Himself. The five Māntrās symbolise the original Divine principles, their image forms in the Jagannāth Cult and also the bija Mātrās as shown in the table below.

| *Mātrās* | *Divine principles* | *Image* | *Bīja mantras* |
|---|---|---|---|
| 1. Nāda | Mūla Prakṛti (Basic principle) | Siṁhāsana | Pḷim |
| 2. Vindu | Mūḷa Brahma | Sudarśana | Dhḷiṁ |
| 3. Daṇḍaka | Viṣṇu | Jagannāth | Kḷiṁ |
| 4. Tāraka | Brahmā | Subhadrā | Sḷiṁ |
| 5. Kuṇḍali | Śiva | Baḷabhadra | Hḷiṁ |

Further the following diagramatic presentation of "OM" in five Mātrās will show that five is an elemental number and the five Mātrās symbolise the entire World of existence resolved in terms of five. Thus Jagannāth as manifested in the form of Oṁkāra, stands for the summation of all things and the Oṁkāra yantra is the most befitting form for the image of Jagannāth. In this tradition it is worth noting that Jagannāth is represented by a part of Yāntra (Daṇḍaka) and also as the entire Yantra itself. This accounts for the predominance of Jagannāth.

Prafulla Chandra Bhanja Deo, in his unpublished manuscript, "The Mysticism of the Tantras," informs that the sacred diagram of "Mahāvidyā Tripurā," is buried in the Vedi or altar on which the images of Jagannāth, Subhadra and Balabhadra are installed and daily worship of the temple is carried out with Tāntric formulae and formalities.

Tripurā yāntra brings all round success and wealth. The Great Śaṅkarācārya has composed "Tripurā Sundar Stotra," whose English translation has been done by Arthur Avalon (pen name of Sir John Woodroffe), which goes thus :-

(1)

"I seek refuge with Tripura Sundari
Who wonders in the Kadamba forest,
The Spouse of the Three-eyed one,
Bank of cloud (in the Sky of the heart) of a number of Sages;
Whose hips defeat the mountains of their greatness,
Who is served by celestial Women,
Whose eyes like new-blown lotus
And who is dark as the colour of a freshly formed rain-cloud.

(2)

I seek refuge with Tripura Sundari,
The spouse of Three-eyed one,
Who dwells in the Kadamba forest,
And who is ever wandering.
The large-eyed one who holds a golden Vīṉā,
Wearing a necklace of priceless gem,
Whose face is glowing with wine,
And who of Her mercy grants prosperity to Her devotees.

(3)

Ever are we protected by Her whose abode is the Kadamba forest,
The weight of whose breasts are garlanded with glittering gems,
Whose breasts are rising,
And excel the mountain in greatness,
Whose cheeks are flushed with wine,
Ever singing sweet songs, the playful one, dark as a cloud,
Even compassionate to all.

(4)

I seek refuge with Tripura Sundari,
The Spouse of the Three-eyed one,
Who stays in the Kadamba forest.
Who is seated in the golden circle,
Dwells in the Sic lotuses,
Even revealing like lightning the great power (of devotees),
Whose beauty is like that of java flower,
And whose brow is adorned with the full moon.

(5)

I take refuge with Her, the sweet speaker,
Daughter of the Sage Mātaṅga,
Whose breast is adorned with Viṇā,
And whose head is beauteous with locks of curling hair,
Who dwells in the lotus,
The destroyer of the wicked,
Whose eyes are reddened with wine,
The charmer of the enemy of the God of love.

(6)

I take refuge with Tripura Sundari,
The Spouse of the Three-eyed one,
Who should be meditated upon,
As in the first flush of her mobile youth,
Her blue garment stained with drops of blood,
Holding the wine Cup;
Her eyes rolling with wine,

With heavy, high and close-set breasts,
Dark of colour and with dishevelled hair.

(7)

At time of recitation, I remember the Mother.
Lustrous as the scarlet hibiscus,
Her body pasted with saffron and sandal,
Her hair kissed my musk.
The mother with smiling eyes,
With red garlands, ornaments and raiment,
Who hold the arrow, bow, noose and goad,
The charmer of countless men.

(8)

I worship the World-Mother
Who is served by celestial Women,
The Spouse of Indra,
Skilful in plaiting,
The devoted Spouse of Brahma,
Anointed with Sandal - paste.
The Spouse of Viṣṇu
Adorned with pleasing ornaments."

-Arthur Avelon's translation

This Tripurā Sundari Stotra of Śaṅkarācārya has mystic phrases of deep metaphysical significance. D.N. Bose and Hiralal Haldar have tried and given elaborate exposition of only twenty three expressions thus:-

(1) *Tripurā*- The body of Śiva became triple in the form of Brahmā, Viṣṇu and Maheśvara. The Devī is then (the Spouse) the Śākti of the Parama Śiva, i.e. Divine energy of Brahmā.
(2) *Kadamba forest*, i.e. the Universe which the Devas permeate. Śrī Kṛṣṇa too has been represented to stand under a Kadamba tree and playing upon His Divine flute, calling all to his fold of love.
(3) *Three-eyed* - We are two-eyed; the central eye is the eye of Wisdom which Śiva possesses.
(4) *Sages* - Like a ruin-cloud, She quenches the Spiritual thirst of the Sages and Devotees.
(5) *Greatness* - Obviously refers to the Cosmic image of Śākti, like that of the Viśvarūpa in the Gītā and of the Puruṣa Sūkta in the

Rigveda, and this has been referred to in verses 8, 9 and 15. Priceless gems refer to Stars and other heavenly bodies of the sky. Breasts refer to that in her Viśvarūpa; fullmoon also to that of Viśvarūpa, her brow in the Sky.

(6) *Ever-wandering* - Dynamic forces of the Universe, the Divine energy that is ever working in the Universe. There is indeed nothing stationary in nature, but everything is in motion, even the door nail is ever in motion. The word 'rest' is a misnomer (vide : the restless Universe).

(7) *Vīṇā* - Lyre which stands for harmony. Harmony is the expression of the Cosmos, the order of the Universe. Out of harmony rose the World and in harmony does it exist. (Pythagoras)

(8) *Wine* - Ambrosia.

(9) *Glowing with Wine* - the Spirit of gladness that pervades the Creation. She is the fountain -head gladness and joy.

(10) *Sweet Songs* - reeling in her own joy of self-contentment.

(11) *Playful one* - her play in her Creation.

(12) *Circle* - nebula of light.

(13) *Six lotuses* - six cakras of the human body, viz. (1) Mūlādhāra, (2) Svādhiṣṭhāna, (3) Maṇipūra, (4) Anāhata, (5) Viśuddha and (6) Ājñā cakras.

(14) *Great power* - awakening the great potentialities of Yogic powers of her devotee.

(15) *Daughter of Mataṅga* - another name of Kāli is Mataṅgini.

(16) *Hair* - the Clouds.

(17) *Destroyer of the wicked*- So Śrī Kṛṣṇa speaks of himself in the Gīta, Vināśahetu duṣkṛtām.

(18) *Enemy of the God of Love* - Śiva, who reduced Kāma into ashes by the fire of his anger.

(19) *Blue garment* - Obviously the vast space designated by the blue sky.

(20) *Drops of blood* - At the fluorescent period of youth, garment stained with drops of blood shows that the woman is ready to bear. Her signs are seen which herald her creation.

(21) *Paragraph 7* is the Dhyāna Mūrti of Śākti, i.e. the image which the devotee has formed about Śākti in his mind for meditation.

(22) *Charmer of countless men*- She deludes the people with Māyā.

(23) *Spouse of Indra* - Śākti or energy of Indra.
*Spouse of Brahmā* - Śākti or energy of Brahmā.
*Spouse of Viṣṇu* - Śākti or energy of Viṣṇu.

She is the Śākti of every God; in other words, she manifests herself as Śākti, power, force or energy in every thing and in every being. The Universe is the manifestation of Śākti. At the top level of Ratna Siṁhāsana three Yantras are chiseled and the three Deities of the Temple are seated on these Yantras.

All these indicate that Puruṣottama Puri is the great Tantra pīṭha. Śaṅkarācārya the founder of Jagannāth Deity, in his commentary of "Prasṭhānatrayī," has established that Iśvara or the Puruṣottama stands for akṣara. Akṣara is the Brāhman, the Supreme Being. "He does not perish when all beings perish."

## AFTERMATH OF VAIṢṆAV TANTRA

"Śrī Cakra Yantra," was installed by Śaṅkarācārya in each of the Maths, which were founded by him and still they are thriving. "Śrī Cakra Yantra", or "Śrī Yantra", is a Vaiṣṇava Yantra, because Śrī is one of the names of Lakṣmī. As stated earlier Śrī Yantra is a diagrammatic embodiment of the Creative Sexual activity of the Universe.

Grace E. Cairns states that the Central feature of the Śrī Cakra is the series of symbolic interlocking triangles in the centre. These are surrounded by two circles of lotus petals bordered by three circular lines. Outside these is a square with four gateways, one at each of the cardinal points. The interlocking triangles are composed of five inverted triangles, the Śākti triangles, and four upright triangles, the Śiva triangles. The center triangle formed by interlocking Śākti triangles, called the Kāmakalā triangle, is the core of the diagram whence the entire Universe symbolised by the Śrī Cakra emanates. In its center is the Mahābindu, the Sarvānandamaya Cakra. This is the first, beginning from the center, of the total of nine cakras of this Yantra. Its function is in its use by the aspirant for enlightenment in his Spiritual journey towards Mokṣa. The Cakra clearly delineates the identity between the form-body of the Great Goddess and that of the devotee in all aspects, material, vital, mental and Spiritual. . . . Thus the primary Tāntric method of Self-realization involving the Cakras with the individual that together correspond with the macrocosmic Śrī Cakra in Kuṇḍalini Yoga.

In the initial stage the Yantra worship is performed on constructed symbols. In an advanced stage the Sādhaka contemplates his own body as Naba Cakra or Śrī Cakra yantra and realises one's identity with the Absolute Self of the Universal Mother, the Ever effulgent Light of Consciousness.

From Regolu stone inscription, it is known that Coḍagaṅgadeva was a student of great Tāntric teacher Nidhiniskaraja and his son presented a lamp to Candika. "Bhaktibhāgavata Mahākāvya," mentions that Coḍagaṅga mastered mantras from Gouri Guru and he was blessed by Śākti. There is mentioned in Madalapanji that Coḍagaṅga was well versed in Tantra. It is known that He had donated a village in the Varaha Vishaya to Goddess Bhāgavati Jathiśrī.

It will be suffice to mention that in 1907 M.M. Haraparasad Sastri discovered as many as fifty songs composed by different Siddhācāryas belonging to Sahajayāna and these were published in 1917 under the caption "Bauddha Gāṇa O Dohā." Subsequently P.C. Bagchi was able to discover in the Tanjur collection the Tibetan translation of all these Songs. Investigations show that these Buddhist Sahajiya dohā and caryā songs were popular in a very wide area during a period roughly from 8th to the 12th century A.D. P.C. Bagchi discovered and published more dohās composed by Sarahapāda and Kānhupāda and also number of dohās composed by Tillopāda. Rahula Samkrityayāna too had discovered and published many more dohās of Sarahapāda and also published the Tibetan translation of many dohās of Saraha, the originals of which are still missing. S.B. Dasgupta has thrown much light on the Buddhist Sahajiyā Cult, in his work "Obscure Religious Cults," while on Vaiṣṇava Sahajiyā movement of Bengal, M.M. Bose has dealt in his work, "Post-Caitanya Sahajiyā Cult."

The philosophical standpoint of the Sahajiyā Buddhists is revealed in the verses of Sarahapāda thus:-

"Do not meditate on the inanimate. Do not wish Selfhood. The illusory phenomena enter into (i.e. disappear in) the great Bliss (Mahāsukha) as salt disappears in water. Saraha says : So many are the merits of the Jina. Such is the way, such is verily the ultimate reality. The immorable circle is without success (i.e. fails). The (rush of) wind breaks down in the grasp of one's own mind. Even the Citta disappears, the acitta comes into existence. (The real state) dawns clear through the instruction of the excellent teacher. There is no peace in muttering mantras. Can the fallen wall rise up? Looking at the fruit the tree is not smelling it. Does the disease fly away at the sight of the physician."

The names like Caṇḍāli, Ḍombī, Śabarī etc. in these dohās are suggestive of untouchable castes. Śākti transcends all sense perception of human beings. As woman of the Doma caste can't be touched by orthodox Brāhmanas, her true nature can't be realised. She s available only to the unprejudice, who can give up all feelings of egoism, disobey scriptural injunctions and disregard public scandal or opinion.Therefore Kānhapāda says :-

"Outside the city, O Ḍombi, is thy cottage; thou goest just touching the Brāhmanas and the shaven-headed (and never reveal thyself to them). O. Ḍombi, I shall keep company with thee and it is for the purpose that I have become a naked Kāpāli without aversions. There is one lotus and sixty-four are the petals—the dear Ḍombi climbs on it and dances there. Honestly do I ask thee, on whose beat dost thou come and go? The Ḍombi sells the loom and also the flat basket (made of bamboo). For thee have I done away with the drama of life. Thou art the Ḍombi and I am the Kāpāli, for thee I have put on a garland of bones. The Ḍombi destroys the lake and eats up the lotus stalk. I shall kill thee, Ḍombi and take thy life.

"Of what nature, O. Ḍombi, they cleverness hair? The aristocrate are outside thee and the Kāpālis are within. Thou hast spoiled everything, through the law of cause and effect, thou hast destroyed the moon. Some speak ill of thee, but the learned never cast thee off from the neck. Thou are Kāmacaṇḍāli—there is no woman more cunning and unfaithful than the Ḍomb."

Buddhist Sahajiyās maintained that "Prajñā pāramita," is a pure transcendental entity, but in the disguise of a woman She is everywhere. That is why Sexual union with a female partner or mudrā is necessary as a means to realise the great Bliss of non-duality. It is only through union with the female partner than an individual can realise the true nature of one's Self and have what is known as Sahaja mahāsukha.

In Sexo-yogic process of Śaiva tantra, Buddhist Sahajayāna and other tantras seems to be the same.

Patnagarh of Balangir district, is long since known as Kaunri Patna or Kumari Patna after the Seven Tāntric maidens, who lived in this township for some time and practised esoteric rites. These maidens were popularly known as their assumed names Gāṅgi Gauḍuṇi, Suā Teluni, Jñanadei Māluni, Netāi Dhobani, Luhakuṭi Luhuruni, Sukuṭi Camārni and Patrapindhi Sabaruni. There are popular tales and traditions in Western Orissa depicting the occult practices and tāntric activities of these maidens. They seem to be the followers of Lakṣmīkarā, who propounded Sahajayāna Buddhism in Western Orissa in the 9th century A.D.

Though Lakṣmīkarā belonged to 9th century A.D. the mentioned Tāntric maidens seems to be of 11th-12th centuries A.D. All of them might not have survived in some period but Netāi Dobani had survived in 12th century A.D. Late Anirudha Das informed that it is known from the Mādalā pāñji that due to the treachery of Vāsudeva Brāhmin, Coḍagaṅga Deva conquered Orissa. Coḍagaṅgadeva learnt witch-craft from Netāi Dobaṇi to whom he was devoted as a disciple and God-son. There are two images of Stone, installed in a small miniature temple in Cuḍanga Sai of Puri, one is a male and another of a female. Anirudha Das identified them as images of Anantavarma Coḍagaṅga Deva and Netāi Dhovani.

In the words of Anirudha Das, "It will not be out of place here to give a little introduction of Netāi Dhovani. The name Netāi Dhovani is well known in the folk-tales, stories of Withcraft etc., in many parts of Orissa. People still believe that many people and specially children are influenced by evil Spirit as a result of which they are diseased and sometimes they die also. So, one adept in Witchcraft is called and one recites, "Nahebāra boli kāhāra Ājñā, Kitai Ma, Patra Saurupi, Natāi Dhovani, Sidha Sauruñi Ājñādai Mālunira, Koṭi Koṭi Ājñā." So, in the names of all these ladies, such as Kitāi Ma, Patra Sauruṇi, Netāi Dhovaṇi, Sidha Sauruni and Ājñādei Māluni, the person well versed with the Mantra to cure possession of evil Spirit, cures the patient. In many parts of Western Orissa, Natai Dhovaṇi is worshipped by certain classes of people. She has been described in the Mādalā pāñji as the Nagara Devī or the Deity of the Capital."

From the time of Coḍagaṅga the Vaiṣṇavism of the Rāmanuja school pushed its way to Orissa and ultimately the Vaiṣṇava's of Mādhava Sect received Royal patronage in the time of the Imperial Gaṅgās. Twelfth century A.D. indeed is significant with history of Vaiṣṇavism in Orissa. Middle of this century witnessed the rise of Jayadeva as a great saintly luminary in the horizon of Orissa. Jayadeva conceived the Supreme God in the form of Mādhava. It was Jayadeva who emphasised the importance of the worship of Rādhā along with Kṛṣṇa in the Vaiṣṇava pantheon in his immortal lyric "Gīta Govinda." This conception of "Gīta Govinda," influenced the later Sahajiya Vaiṣṇava sect. Like the worship of Lakṣmī - Nārāyaṇa and Rādhā - Krishna, worship of Sītā - Rāma had also started and it had attained celebrity during the reign of the Imperial Gaṅgās.

With the conception of Gīta Govinda and Vaiṣṇava tantra, Lakṣhmī-Nārāyaṇa images like Umā-Maheśvara were made during Gaṅga period in Orissa, which traces can be found in Lakṣmī-Nārāyan images at (1) Inside Liṅgaraj temple of Bhubaneswer, (2) Lakṣmī-Nārāyana temple at Lakṣmisagar, in the vicinity of Bhubaneswar, (3) Lakṣmī-Nārāyana temple at Chaurasi, (4) Lakṣmī-Nārāyaṇa in the Math of Thakur-patna in Prachi valley, (5) Pratapnagari, (6) Konduli, (7) Cuttack town and (8) Belkhandi.

In the words of Sarat Chandra Behera, we learn from "Narahari Yati Stotra," which forms a portion of "Stotra Mahodadhi," that Mādhva, the Ācārya of the Dvaita school of Vedānta philosophy, had deputed his disciple Narahari Tirtha to Kaliṅga to obtain the image of Rāma and Sitā from the Gaṅgā monarch. Śrīkurmam temple inscription of s. 1203 proves that Narahari Tirṭha had really exerted preponderating influence over the Gaṅgā monarch. We learn from the two sources cited above that Narahari Tirṭha came to Orissa during the reign of Bhānu - I (1264 A.D. - 1278 A.D.) and acted as the Spiritual guardian to the young prince Narasiṁha. When Narasiṁha-II succeeded to the Throne after the death of his father, he became the Governor of Kaliṅga and had strong hold over the Monarch. His presence in Orissa as tutor-guardian of the Crown Prince and subsequently as Governeor of Kaliṅga must have resulted in the tremendous growth of Vaiṣṇavism in Orissa. It was during this period that the famous temple of Anantavāsudeva was completed by Candrikā, daughter of Anaṅgabhīma-III, in the year 1278 A.D. at Bhubaneswar.

With this background the Cult of Kṛṣṇa Gopivallabha and the form of Viṣṇu with Rādhā as his consort as described in the Gītagovinda of Jayadeva, which represents the Vaiṣṇav Sahajiyā Sect.

Sun cult finally merged into the Vaiṣṇav Cult in Orissa and Sun was conceived as an aspect of Viṣṇu (Sūrya-Nārāyaṇa) and was called Vīrañci - Nārāyaṇa also. Traces of Saura Cult and Sun temples are found at Ayodhya, Purnagaon, Kunisahi and Domagandara in Balasore district. At Kaupur and Palia of Bhadrak districit; Sun temples are existing. The great beautiful Sun temple of Konarka is very popular, in its ruin condition, which was built by Gajapati Narasimha-I of Gaṅga dynasty in 13th century A.D.

The Sūryavaṁśī Gajapatis started their rule in Orissa in 15th century. During Suravaṁśī period no new features were introduced and Religious culturally the Sūryavaṁśī period merged into Gaṅgā period. They followed the same pattern of the Gaṅgas. This was the period when Sexo-Yoga practice, Tantra and Kāmaśāstra had come to mix up with one another and formed a queer amalgam. The secrets of Sexo-yogic practice, rising of Kuṇḍalini through Vajroli was forgotten and Sahajiyā Vaiṣṇava had taken to Sensual pleasure. It was the time when Buddhist Vajrayāna and Sahajayāna had just gone through the periods of their glorification and flourishment and were very much in the air.

At this juncture Sāralādās was born in 15th century A.D. He is the writer of the Oriya Mahābhārata and is acclaimed as the Ādikabi of Oriya literature. During his period the Sahajiyās were an extreme class of Tāntrics who advocated free indulgence of Sexual acts and sometimes they themselves acted as free lances. Sāralādās has shown respect to all Sects in his writings but has ridiculed the tenets of the Sahajiyā sect as prepounded in the "Gītagovida," The Sahajiyā's religious philosophy was based on Jayadeva's love lyric "Gītagovinda," Sāralādās abhorred this faith and other great poets like Balarāma Dās, Jagannāth Dās, Ananta Dās and Yasovanta Dās, who followed Sāralādās, had anything to do with the religious philosophy expounded by Jayadeva in his "Gītagovinda." Still then, traces of Tantra are found in the three writings (1) Vilaṅkā Rāmāyaṇa, (2) Caṇḍī purāṇa and (3) Mahābhārata of Sāralādās. Till 16th century A.D. these poets and Yogis followed a pattern of Vaiṣṇavism which was very different from the one to be found in "Gītagovinda." These five Saint poets, who are usually known as Five Associates had absorbed in their writings the essence of Tantra, Buddhism, Vedanta and the Cult of Prema-Bhakti.

The literatures of Pañcasakhā or Five Associates in Orissa are very vast. Their call was to undertake an inner voyage and to explore within, assuming that what one has to live by outside has first to be felt and found out within. For them, a way was not the primary thing; what was primary was an enquiry, an enquiry into as far as one could go in order that one could find the real centre. Chittaranjan Das is of the opinion that the Pañcasakhā made no distinction between what have been known in the vocabulary of Indian Sādhanā as Pinda and Brahmāṇda, the individual microcosm and the universal macrocosm. They made no distinction between the Upanisadic conception of the Brahma, the Supreme Truth and the Buddhist conception of Śūnya. And what was more, like many of the medieval mystics in the Country, they gave the whole concept a sense of palpability and proximity by calling it the Śūnya - puruṣa.

It will be befitting to quote Sarat Chandra Behera, when he states that before the arrival of Śrī Caitanya, Bhakti movement had already dawned over Orissa. Jagannāth, Balarāma, Ācyutānanda, Yaśovanta and Ananta were the five associates who had absorbed in their writings the essence of Tantra, Buddhism, Vedānta and the Cult of Prema - Bhakti. The most famous of these Five Associates, Jagannāth Das had composed "Śrīmad -Bhāgavata," which is considered to be the most representative work of Oriya literature. In this magnum opus he incorporated all the different faiths which evolved in Orissa and identified Śrī Kṛṣṇa with Lord Jagannāth. Śrī Kṛṣṇa of the five associates is the Personal God of Purāṇas as well as the Impersonal Being of the Upanishads. Rāi Rāmānanda, who was the Governor of Rajhmahendri under Pratāprudra, was an exponent of the Prema Bhakti Cult. Before the arrival of Śrī Caitanya he had expounded the Chief tenets of this Cult and composed the great work "Jagannāth Vallabha." When Śrī Caitanya came to Orissa in 1510 A.D. he was anxious to meet Rāi Rāmanada. The meeting of these two Stalwarts of Neo-Vaiṣṇavism has been graphically narrated by Krishnadas Kaviraj in his famous Bengali book *Caitanya Caritāmrta*. In course of the dialogue Śrī Caitanya is reported to have commented that Rāi Rāmānanda was already well versed in Prema-Bhakti Cult. After this meeting Rāi Rāmānanda relinquished his Services and devoted the rest of his life in the service of the Lord. Śrī Caitanya in the company of the Five Associates, Rāi Rāmānada and Śarva Bhauma spent eighteen years at Puri. He identified Śrī Kṛṣṇa with Jagannāth and consequently Kṛṣṇa consciousness and Jagannāth consciousness were rolled into one. In the words of Sir Jadunath Sarkar, "The diverse religions of Orissa in all ages have tended to gravitate towards and finally merged into the Jagannāth worship, at least in theory."

J.V. Boulton has expressed, "So, to be blunt, Caitanya came to Orissa not to teach, but to be taught."

Sāralādāsa in the Sabhāparva of his Mahābhārata prays : "Jagannāth, you are present here as the Buddha for the deliverance of the people of the World." In Ādi, Vana, Musali and Salya parvas of the same Mahābhārata, the same devotional expression is found. Jagannāth Dasa, in his "Dārubrahma Gīta" and "Deuḷatoḷā" narrates the legendary origin of Lord Jagannāth and identifies the Deity with Buddha. Acyutānanda Dāsa in many places of his "Śūnya-Saṁhitā", declares that Jagannāth is no other than the Buddha. Pratapa Ray in his composition "Śaśisenā", declares, "Hari Himself is present in the Sanctuary of Śrī Nīḷagiri (the Jagannāth temple, Puri) in the form of the Buddha."

Caitanyadāsa, the Saint poet, was born at Salebarat near Shindhekela in Balangir district of Orissa province in early part of 18th century A.D. and had lived mostly at Badamula in the vicinity of Khariar, while Raja Prataprudra Singh Deo was ruling from his Capital, then at Komna. It seems the settlement with the name "Kharial," which later became "Khariar," during British period, had emerged into prominence during the ruling period of Raja Prataprudra Singh Deo, whose ruling period was within 1793 A.D. - 1818 A.D. Caitanyadāsa sings the names of

"Rājā Pratāprudra," "Bhagirathi Babu," "Badamula-grama" and "Khariala," in his poetry, "Nirguṇa Mahatmya." The theory of five Dhyāni Buddhas, expounded in Tāntric Buddhism, has found striking exposition in his "Viṣṇugarbha purāṇa," where it has been given a novel Vaiṣṇavite setting. The great philosopher conceives of Six Viṣṇus, one of which known as Nirā Kāra Viṣṇu is characterised as the shapeless and figureless Śūnya and hence, is the same as Vajrasattva, while the other five who are emanations of Alekha Puruṣa, do undoubtedly resemble the five Dhyani Buddhas, Vairpcana, Akṣobha, Ratnasaṁbhava, Amitābha and Amogha Siddhi.

The assimilation of Buddhism and establishment of one of Buddha's image; as Lord Jagannāth by Śaṅkarācārya had already taken place in 9th century A.D. and in 10th century A.D. Lord Jagannāth was established or installed as Puruṣottama-Jagannāth, the presiding Deity. So, the view of N.K.Sahu that Buddhism was prevalent in Kaliṅga, Jhārkhanda and in the territory round about Jagannāth as late as the 16th century A.D. can't be accepted. The literatures of Saraladas and Panchasakhās shows the assimilation of Buddha with Jagannāth Culture. What they truely preached was pure Vedānta. In this process, it has been observed that TANTRA and NĀTHISM which originated in Orissa, played a great role in assimilating Buddha as Lord Jagannāth.

Great God Lord Jagannāth is the epitome of Tāntric worship and Sādhanā in Orissa. There was rise and decline of Tantra in India, i.e., Bharat, but in Orissa, Tantra is the living religion in the Cult of Lord Jagannāth.

According to Tāntric thought, "Every Human Being is a temple of God," and this gave a fillip to the art of religious edifices.

## CHAPTER IV

# Tāntric Art of Orissa

The Ring stones of neolithic period are associated with the Mother Goddess Cult, which found continuation to the early historical period. Varieties of Ring stones and of different sizes are found throughout Orissa, abundantly.

Stone YONI, which is of quartzite stone and is of ferruginous colour was discovered at Maraguda valley, in Nuapada district and preserved at the private possession of the author. Such a Stone YONI is also discovered at Soseng village, situated on Sunabeda plateau of the same district and preserved in the private possession of the author. The Centre of the YONI, found at Soseng village is hoofed out, because of local vandalism.

Yoni worship which probably started in proto-historical period, is still continuing at foothill of Guru donger near Boden in Nuapada district and at Sindhekela in Balangir district of Orissa. In both the places the YONI Deities are worshipped as "DUARSANI."

One natural shaped Liṅga was discovered at Bargaon village, situated to the west of Khariar and is preserved in private possession of the author.

Regarding the conception of Liṅga and Yoni, D.C. Sircar states that the worship of the Liṅga of the Great God Śiva originated from the conception of the God as the father or procreater. But in the matter of the procreation of beings of YONI (pudendum muliebre) of the Mother Goddess should naturally be regarded as much important is the Liṅga of the father God. Both the Father God and the Mother Goddess were worshipped by the Pre-Aryan Peoples of India. The objects discovered at Mohenjodaro show that Śiva and Śākti were worshipped not only in the human form but also in the symbolic form of the Liṅga and the YONI, the former representing procreation and virility and the latter motherhood and fertility. (Marshall, J. *Mohenjodaro and Indus Civilization*, Vol. I, London, 1931, p. 52 ff.).

Worship of YONI of the Divine Mother is referred as certain Tirṭhas, containing Yoni tanks in the Mahābhārata, but the worship of YONI is prescribed only in the late - medieval Tantra works like Yonitantra, Bṛhaddharma and others. One Yoni temple, which is a Kalachuri structure attached with a Śākta Maṭha is excavated at Māraguda valley, which is the only Śākta Maṭha, discovered in Orissa province so far and is dated to 12th century A.D. because the plan of YONI temple is exactly similar with the plan of Pataleswara temple at Amarkantak in Shahdol district of Madhya Pradesh.

Neolithic rock shelter painting of Yogimath Donger of Nuapada district is interesting, because it shows the paintings of bulls, triangles, rings and triple strokes. These show the prevalence of Phallism, since remote past. In ancient days BULL was the representation of Sun-God.

These show that there is no dearth of Pre-historic and Proto-historic Tāntric art in Orissa.

The Great tradition of India and Orissa province, is the Vedic culture, which is the Summon bonum of Spirituality. Bṛhadāraṇyaka Upaniṣad, which forms a part of Śukla Yajurveda symbolises Woman as a medium of sacrifice, her lap as sacrificial altar, her hairs as sacrificial grass, her skin as Soma-Press and copulation, as the act of sacrifice. It proclaims a series of rules and advises its followers to observe them unmistakably for a choicable progeny. Chāndogya Upaniṣad, which forms a part of Samaveda also illustrates woman as sacrificial fire and the generative organs as fuels. The Kauṣitaki Upaniṣad suggests sacrificial rites for the expiation of Sin for prosperity, for the increasing longevity and for the fascination of man and woman. Source of Tantra is found in the Atharva-veda also. From the Vedic background, it is known that Creation is the outcome of Divine Desire or KĀMA or WILL (icchā). Sarbeswar Satpathy remarks, "therefore Divine is Kāmamayi or icchāmayī in its ultimate consciousness." Yogic process is the path to conquor KĀMA and Yogis and Rishis have discovered the path to Blessedness. The quintessence of which is found in the Ashtanga Yoga of Sage Maharshi Patanjali's work "MAHĀBHĀṢYA," dated second century B.C. All the Yoga is centralised and channelised through discipleship and Guru (Master), whose Grace acts like a fortress. These analysis indicate that mystical belief was already in existence in pre-Buddhistic days in India.

Tāntric tradition in India was in existent from dawn of Civilization, from the early Vedic time onwards, to its development by the time of the Purāṇas and to the actual Hindu, Jaina and Buddhist Tantras.

About Tāntric pūjā, Avalon, in his "Principles of Tantra," gives a fine narration thus : "Meditation, worship, japa and homa are the four hands of the Yajña or worship; Mātṛkā, Soḍhā and other Nyāsas form its body; knowledge of the real truth as to Iṣṭadevatā is its Ātmā, devotion is its head, reverence is its heart, and the act of performing is its eye. Knowing the body of Yajña to be composed in this manner, a good Sādhaka should perform it in all its limbs, and not divide and make it limbless — It is by His union with the Supreme Śākti which arises out of the effort to accomplish all those limbs that the Yajña-Puruṣa produces Siddhi." And here is the culminating phase of external worship with flowers: "The knowing ones regard the following as the ten flowers to be used to worship : non-ignorance (amāyā), non-egoity or non-appropriation (anahaṁkāra), non-attachment (arāga), non-vanity (amada), non-delusion (amoha), non-pride (adambha), non-culmination (anindā), non-perturbation (akṣobha), non-jealousy (amūtsarya) and non-greed (alobha). But better than these are the five virtues which make up the other group of flowers : non-injury or non-violence (ahiṁsā), self-control or subjugation of the senses (indriya-nigrāha), charity or kindness (dayā), forgiveness (kṣamā) and knowledge (jñāna)."

In Orissa province and India in general, art has been closely related to religion. Because of this reason proper understanding is necessary to have knowledge of various forms and symbols representing the Supernatural powers. According to Yoga, the mystery of Creation is that the entire Creation is present within the human body. With this edify Temples were built and Human being is regarded as Microcosm in Tāntric Hinduism. From about the 5th or 6th century A.D. Tantra as a special religious concept gradually came into use.

## TĀNTRIC BUDDHIST ART

Prabhat Mukherjee under the heading "Orissa, early medieval Buddhist Art," stated that Buddhist art in Orissa developed from the 5th century A.D. The main Stupa at Ratnagiri was constructed over an earlier edifice belonging to the Gupta period in the midst of the debris, of a stone slab inscribed with the "Pratiya-Samutpada Sutra," in the characters of the Gupta period.

"The images at Lalitagiri, Udayagiri and Ratnagiri reveal strong influence of the Gupta art of the Saranath school. The Orissan artists of this period introduced not only Gupta sensuousness and sublimity, but also infused an element of forceful vigour and it is rather this rare combination that attaches greater importance to these Sculptures.

"But the early medieval Buddhist art of Orissa was not an imitation of the Gupta art. The Sculptures introduced Tri-bhaṅga (three bends) pose and the modelling of the torso was not always realistic. But the images are characterized by dignified composure which added grace to the figures. The austere simplicity of some of the images, contrasted by decorative background, is another point of departure.

"Other typical Orissan features are the absence of any clear indication of drapery, absolutely plain elliptical nimbus in high relief and long tapering pointed halo, either plain or fringed with flamboyant scrolls.

"The Bodhisattva figures of Lalitagiri indicate a high standard of plastic art. A spirit of passive contemplation and spiritual fervour has been successfully depicted on the faces of these images. But even if the Spiritual significance of these image is ignored, no connoisseur will hesitate to include the Bodhisattvas found on the Naltigiri (Lalitagiri) among the most lovely things shaped by the hand of man."

In the words of D.R. Das, "It is more than a mere coincidence that two very strong centres of Buddhism emerged almost simultaneously in Kōśala and Orissa respectively. Connected as they were by a well - travelled route along the Mahānadi, the possibility of their isolation from one another seems unlikely. The existence of some form of link between them becomes almost a certainty when images found at Sirpur in Kōśala and Ratnagiri and other sites in Orissa suggest that at both the places, like Vajrayāna form of Buddhism was in practice. As the evidence stands, Ratnagiri comes to view a few decades after Buddhism first appeared at Sirpur. The conclusion, therefore, becomes inevitable that Buddhism spread to the lower Mahānadī valley from Kōśala. This fact goes a long way to explain the Lalitagiri - Ratnagiri sculptures whose Gupta flavour has no precedence in Orissa. The identity is visual representation of images between Ratnagiri and Sirpur shows that the Gupta plastic tradition travelled from Magadha to Orissa via Kōśala. The flowing grace imported through a sensitive and summary modelling endows the Lalitagiri-Ratnagiri figures with a liveliness and linear freedom with the sculpture certainly derived from Sirpur. The smoothness of the surface and the supple roundness of the colossal Buddhas of Sirpur became the prevailing note of the images in the lower Mahāṇadī valley. The long tapering halo characterising the Divine images of Orissa has its origin in the elliptical nimbus of Sirpur."

The unfoldment of Tāntric Buddhism in Orissa may be first attributed to Gūhyasamāja Tantra by Guhyasiddhi of Padmavajra, which is the first work of the Buddhist Tantra school in Orissa ; Jñānasiddhi of King Indrabhuti, Sādhanāmāla and Advayasiddhi of Lakṣmīṅkarā in the 8th century A.D.

In Guhyasamāja tantra, it is recommended that Sexual intercourse with young Cāṇḍālī girls and beautiful women is to be indulged in for the sake of Buddha worship and where Buddha declares that even the most wicked men — murderers, thieves, libertines and even those who have incestuous intercourse with mothers, sisters and daughters may reach perfection. So, it seems that by 8th century A.D. Sāndhyabhaṣā was used in literatures of Orissa. Sāndhyabhaṣā (intentional language) is used in the Tantras of India in general. Sāndhyabhaṣā can be considered to be a particular type of symbolic language. Mother is the base center of the Yoga body, while Sister and Daughter signifies the heart and the throat of the Yogi.

Gūhyasamāja tantra seems to have been mostly popularised at Gahadevapāṭāka or Guheśvarapāṭāka, the Capital of the Kings of Bhaumakara dynasty in 8th century A.D. in the vicinity of Jajpur.

In "Jñānasiddhi," of King Indrabhuti of Sambhala (identified with Sambalpur region) in Uḍḍiyāna, Cāṇḍālī, Ḍombī, Brahmāṇī are considered as Mahāmudrā and the doctrine of the five Dhyāni Buddhas has been expounded and throws light on the various esoteric rites of Vajrayāna. The Sambhala was most probably a province of Kōśala and was known as Samvaravāḍi Maṇḍala during the reign of Somavaṁśī ruling house in South Kōśala. It was a Citadel of Kālacakrayāna from where Ācārya Pitopāda introduced this Tāntric system into the monastic University of Ratnagiri in Orissa. Kālacakrayāna tantra is a system of Yoga which rolls up the Universe in the body of man and introverts the macrocosmic forces of time in the process of the human organism. The system of Yoga in both Kālacakrayāna and Tantraloka of Abhinava Gupta are the same. In Sekoddeśatīkā, a tāntric text of Kālacakrayāna, Karmamudrā means a woman with exuberent breasts and a rich display of hair.

Sarahapāda was the founder advocate of Sahajayāna, but most of the Scholars believe that Lakṣmīṅkarā, the sister of King Indrabhūti, played the initial role in the evolution of Sahajayāna. R.P. Mishra informs that although Lakṣmīṅkarā was primarily a follower of Vajrayana because of her relation with Indrabhuti and other teachers of tāntric Buddhism, She discouraged the Scholastic sophistry and elaborate rites and rituals followed in different religious system including Vajrayāna. As She professes in Advayasiddhi, there is no need of physical torture, fasting, ritual, ceremonial bathing, purification, going away from the village — living, worship of image made up of woods, stones and clay, consideration of the auspicious nature of the place, time, tiṭhi, days and nakṣatras, reading of religious texts and erecting Caityas. The doctrines professes by Lakṣmiṅkarā thus differ from those of Vajrayāna in respect to later's encouragement to the elaborate rites and rituals and religious formalities.

Lakṣmīnkarā married Prince Sevola, the son of King Jalendra of Laṅkāpuri, identified with Sonepur region. She probably died in Laṅkāpuri alias Sonepur in the first quarter of 9th century A.D.

Goddess Laṅkeśvarī is depicted as a Tāntric Goddess in one of the Sādhanās of Sādhanāmala. Goddess Laṅkeśvarī is now worshipped at Laṅkeśvarīdarha of Mahāṇadī river near Sonepur and in Hindu garb at Junagarh. The name of "Laṅkeśvarī", now survives as Laṅkagarh in Baliguda Sub-division of Khondmal district and "Laṅkeśvarī forest," in Nuapada district of Western Orissa.

There are many other Tantra texts in Tāntric Buddhism. About the Tāntric art of Buddhism in Orissa, it can be mentioned that Buddhists paid greater care and attention to modelling their images, as the beauty of the monuments are unknown, because they are all fallen and forming mounds. The Buddhist tāntric arts are reflected in the Stupas, Monasteries, Caityas, Temples, Sculptures and Bronzes.

With the vagaries of nature and vicissitude of time, many Buddhist monuments have been destroyed by the intolerant people of Brahmaṇical religion and later on by the iconoclast Muslims. Still then, from the ruins of the existing monuments, the hey-day of Tāntric Buddhist art are enlightened.

The earliest Tāntric Buddhist temple of Orissa is the ruined temple of Tārā, found at Bāṅkaḍa, the capital of the Koṅgada maṇḍala, which was ruled by Śailodbhava dynasty within circa. 550 A.D. to 736 A.D. Tāntric scenes are found on a portion of the doorway. N.K. Sahu is of opinion that the Buddhist temples of Ratnagiri, Lalitgiri and Udayagiri near Jajapura were, to all probability plain and simple in design and excepting their highly ornamental doorways. On the large niches were fixed superb images of the Mahāyānic Gods and Goddesses, in the art of which the Buddhists undoubtedly excelled.... The evolution of Tantra led to the canonisation of the mode of icon making as a result of which the Buddhist art became mystic but stereotyped and the primary aims of the artists degenerated into serving the purpose of the innumerable devotees rather than that of the art connoisseurs. Nevertheless, Tāntric sculptures could also achieve a high order of excellence, as attested by the exquisite images of Chaudwar, Ayodhya, Khiching and some other art centres.

**Ratnagiri**

The works carried out by Archaeological Survey of India, through excavation at Ratnagiri on the bank of river Kelua, has exposed monasteries, colossal stupas, temples and sculptures. The Tāntric Buddhist establishment of this site is from 5th century A.D. to 12th century A.D. From Tibetan sources it is known that Ratnagiri was famous for pursuit of Kālacakrayāna in the later part of 10th century A.D. which was popularised by Naropa there.

Eight brick temples have been excavated so far there. These temples were of Rekha type and are assigned to 10th century A.D. One of the temples in front of Monastery 2, contains a two armed standing images of Mānjuśrī (9th century A.D.), another temple contains the images of Vajraraga, Raktalokeśvara and Vajrasattva of artistic variety. One temple contains a four armed image of Lokeswara seated in Lalitasana with an inscription of Dharani (dated within 9th-10th century A.D.).

The inscribed Seals discovered in this site has the popular epithey of Puspagiri futile, which goes thus "Śrī Ratnagiri - Mahavihara Aryabhaiksha Sanghasya. "Large number of Sealing bearing inscriptions, "Ratnagiri Mahāvihāra," have also been found. Excavations have established that imposing quardrangular monasteries were rebuilt more than once. Many of the Divinities found in the locality are of Vajrayāna pantheon. One of the manastery, as known from excavation was reconstructed after 11th century A.D.

Excavation of a small monastery at Ratnagiri yielded three copper plates of Somavaṁśī King Karṇa (11th-12th century A.D.), which records the grant of a village to Rani Karpuraśrī, held from the Solanapur Mahāvihara, near Jajapura. It seems Rani Karpuraśrī passed her last days at Ratnagiri. Many images are recovered from the site by excavation and mention may be made of standing and seated images of Buddha, Lokeśvara, Maitreya, Mānjuśrī, Tārā, Jambhala and stone sculptures of Dhyani Buddhas, Padmapani, Vajrapani, Mānjuśrī, Vajraraga, Heruka, Sambara, Hariti, various forms of Tārā, Vasudhara, Aryasarasvatī, Aparājitā etc. Vajrāsana Buddha images found at Ratnagiri in early part of 20th century A.D. are not to be found now and seems to be removed.

The Tārā images of Ratnagiri are found in graceful tribhaṅga poses and the largest one among them, is preserved in Patna museum.

According to N.K. Sahu, "Among the Tāntric images found at Ratnagiri, mention may be made of a two-armed Heruka, which measures 5'2" by 2'6". It wears a long garland of human skulls and holding a

Khaṭvāṅga in its left arm dances with intoxication over a corpse in ardhaparyanka pose. Heruka, an emanation of Akṣobhya, is one of the most popular deities of Tāntric Buddhism and he is generally found with his consort Vajra Vārāhī in Yāb - Yum pose; but he is also often worshipped singly, and the Ratnagiri image is one of the most successful representations of him.

"Close to the temple of Mahākāla an interesting image of a Tāntric Deity is found in good state of preservation, although some of the hands of the image are broken. It appears to be a representation of a variety of Vajrajvālānalārka, whose Sādhanā is narrated as follows:- "The worshipper should conceive himself as Vajrajvālānalārka of blue complexion round whose person radiate fiery flames, who is four-faced and eight-armed whose four faces display the sentiments of amour, heroism, disgust and compassion; who carries in his four right hands the Vajra, the Sword, the Cakra and the arrow; and in the four left the Ghaṇṭā, the Bow, Noose and the Khaṭvāṅga surmounted by the banner of variegated colours : whose brown hair resembles a burning flame; who is decked in ornaments of bracelet, armlet, girdle, nūpura, torque, earring and tiara consisting of the (eight) great Lords of frightful serpents; who stands in the Ālidha attitude and tramples upon Viṣṇu with his consort who are expert in choosing the discus of Mahāmāya."

The image referred to above, conforms to this Sādhanā to a great extent. Three of its heads are visible in the front and the fourth head is supposed to be at the back which is not visible. Out of the three heads the middle one displays compassion, the right one heroism and the left one the sentiment of amour. The image is represented in the Ālidha attitude, but instead of trampling upon Viṣṇu and his consort, it stands on a running tiger placing his right foot on its head and the left foot on its tail.

"Sri R.P. Chanda saw in 1928 another image of this type, close to the Mahākāla temple, but it is now found nowhere in Ratnagiri, it being probably carried away by some curio-hunters. The photo plate of the image has, however, been preserved and it indicates that the image is the representation not of Vajrajvālānalārka but of a variety of Trailokya Vijaya. It has four faces and twelve arms, two of which carrying the Ghaṇṭā and the Vajra, are placed against the breast exhibiting the Vajrahuṁkara attitude. The two upper most hands carry a long piece of cloth, which bends above its heads in the shape of a an arch, while a Khaṭvāṅga, tipped with human skull, passes through the left shoulder, and is held by one of the left hands. Many of the ayudhas in other hands have been damaged but the bejewelled ornaments and the long garland are in tact. The front face expresses the sentiment of passion, and the right and the left ones display disgust and rage respectively, while the fourth face displaying the spirit of heroism is represented at the back and is not seen in the front. The image exhibits the attitude of Yoga, all the eyes being half closed, and standing in the Pratyālidha pose it tramples down with its heavy feet the tiny figures of Maheśvara and Gauri."

The above description of the images of Vajrajvālānalārka, shows the rivalry between Tāntric Buddhism and Tāntric Hinduism. The images of different periods of this site, shows divergent styles and are of artistic merit.

## Lalitagiri

Three small hills, the Clāsuni, the Laṇḍā and the Pārābhadi combinedly known as Lalitagiri or Nalatigiri is a Tāntric Buddhist site. The ruins of Lalitagiri is more extensive than Ratnagiri site and covers a vast area. The whole area is overflowing with extensive ruins of brick monuments and medieval ruins.

Carved doorjamb with Mahāyānic images of two-armed Padmapāni and four-armed Tārā is found there. Large number of Buddhist images of magnificent grace and beauty are found there. Caturbhuja Sitā Tārā, Maitreya, Buddha in Bhūmiśparśa mudrā, Aparājita Tārā goddess, Sthira Cakra Māñjuśrī, different varieties of Padmapani Avalokiteśvara, Tārā and Vaiśravana are found there. Many of the images are preserved in a Museum at that place. Still then many ruins and images are hewn here and there. Hatikhal a cave of Pārābhadi peak yielded several life size images of Padmapani Avalokiteśvara. Several other images of this place are shifted to Mahānga, Indian Museum at Calcutta and to various places.

Just above the pass between the Laṇda and the Parabhādi hills, there is a temple of Tāntric goddess BASULI, built on the ruins of a Buddhist site, because the ruins of older shrine containing few Bodhisattva images are there.

The hill Olāsuni is famous in Orissa, as the seat of the great Yogi Arakṣita Dasa, who lived there during the later half of the 18th century A.D.

**Udayagiri**

Udayagiri is situated at the north of Virūpa river, at a distance of 10 kms. from Lalitagiri. It forms a triangle of Tāntric Buddhist monuments with Ratnagiri and Lalitagiri.

A colossal inscribed image of Lokeśvara, carved out of a single piece of chlorite stone is a beautiful specimen at Udayagiri. It has an inscription in the character of 8th century A.D. and records the name of the donor, Kesavagupta alias Subhagupta.

A large rock cut Well, 24 ft. square, containing a flight of 31 steps is seen at Udayagiri. The well contains an inscription, in the characters of 10th-11th century A.D. and declares that the Well was excavated by a Chief named Vajranāga, who was probably a feudatory chief under the Somavaṁśīs and was a local patron of Vajrayāna.

Seated image of Dhyāni Bhddha Amitābha, Jaṭāmukuṭa Lakeśvara, twelve armed seated Prajñāpāramitā, Dhāyani Buddha, Vaisravaṇa, Avalokiteśvara, pot-bellied Hayagrāva, Tārā, well carved doorway, carved figures of Bhṛkuti and Hayagriva and many colossal images are found there.

An image of Lokeśvara with Dhyāni Buddhas over the head is found and on its back an inscription of 25 lines (in the character of 8th century A.D.) records the invocation of Tārā, Padmasambhava, other Deities and Tathagata adhisthita Dhatugarbha Stupa. The images of Mārici and Vaiśravana, found at Udayagiri are now preserved in the collection of Indian Museum, Calcutta.

The figure of Kurukullā with her Dhārani inscribed just below her seat, is the most precious Buddhist Tāntric Goddess, found at Udayagiri. She is represented in Lalita-kṣepa pose holding the red lotus and the bow in her two left hands and exhibiting the club and the varadā attitude in two right hands. She may thus be called a variety of Tārodbhāva Kurukullā.

N.K. Sahu informs that there is a small village named Kurukurā, which is probably so named after the Goddess Kurukullā, in Cuttack district. On our suggestion, Kumar Prafulla Chandra Bhañja Deo of Baripada, Tāntric Scholar, visited the village Kurukurā to examine the iconographic features of the images of Kurukullā. Two images of this Deity Kurukullā were found. He took away one of the images to his residence at Baripada, while the other one highly mutilated condition is lying uncared for in the village. In tāntric Buddhist literature "Sādhanāmālā II, intro. p. xxvii," it is said that the Goddesses Kurukullā and Vajravārāhi who are described in the Tāntric literature as the presiding Deities of Uḍḍiyāna, are found only in Orissa and nowhere else in India. When Tāntric Goddess Kurukullā is worshipped with her Mantra and propitiated, She benefits great merits. Indrabhuti was the author of "Jñānasiddhi," and "Kurukullā Sādhanā." As image of Kurukullā is not found anywhere in India, it definitely shows Indrabhuti to have been King of Sambhala in Uḍḍiyāna, situated within modern Orissa province.

At a distance of this site, there is a temple of Mahākala (a Śaivite temple). The original Buddhist temple was later on converted to a Śiva temple. The figures of Gaṅgā and Yamunā originally carved in the doorjamb of the Buddhist temple are seen in the present shrine. The Goddess Gaṅgā from Udayagiri, which is now preserved in the Patna Museum, is a remarkable specimen of fine art.

As Ratnagiri, Lalitagiri and Udayagiri sites are situated around the Asia hills, mention may be made of other Sculptures scattered around the hills and they are : Vajrapāṇi, Sthira Cakra Mānjuśri, four-armed Tārā which is identified as Durgottarini Tārā who is a variety of Green Tārā, Aṣṭabhuja Mārici called Samkṣipta Mārici, two-armed Avalokiteśvara etc.

## Langudi

Further north of these three sites, there is an unique Buddhist site Langudi, which is a picturesque hillock, situated in Salipur village, in Mirzapur Grampanchayet of Jājatinagar district. This site is inexhaustible art centre of Mahāyāna-Vajrayāna Cult of Tāntric Buddhism, which is not yet fully explored.

## Khiching

Khiching, the ancient Khijiñgakotta, situated in Mayurbhanj district was the early Capital of the Bhañjas and was flourishing centre of Buddhism and later on Brāhmanism. The sculptures unearthed here belong to Buddhist, Jaina, Śākta, Śaiva nd Vaiṣṇava pantheons. Buddhist icons found from this place are Bodhisattva Avalokiteśvara, Arapachana, Mānjuśri, Vasudhara, Jambhala, Tārā, Lokeśvara and Vajrasattva. Most of these images are preserved at Khiching museum and two tāntric Sculptures of this site, Apaarachana Mañjuśrī and Aśokakāntā Mārici are preserved at Bāripada Museum.

N.K. Sahu informs that two important images from Khiching are now preserved in the small museum at Bāripada, one of which is the figure of Mānjuśri and the other one that of Mārici. The image of Mānjuśri sits cross-legged on the lotus throne and brandishes a sword in its right hand over the head, while in its left it carries a lotus, on which has been placed a book, presumably one of the Prajñāpāramitā works. The smile of the face is now slightly damaged, but in spite of it the entire figure decked in princely ornaments looks graceful and vivacious. The image undoubtedly represents Aparachana, who is sometimes known as Sadyonubhava Aparachana or Sadyonubhava Mānjuśrī.

"The image of Mārici carved out of the granite scist is exquisitely fine and appears to be endowed with the warmth of life. It stands in Āliḍha attitude on the car drawn by seven sows, and the head of Rāhu occupies the position of the charioteer, which in either end of the car is visible a kneeling devotee and the moving wheel. Its three faces of which the left one is like that of a Sow, display the usual emotions and the middle one possesses the glow of a Divine virgin. It has eight arms, and in the four left hands it holds the Vajra, the goad, the quick arrows and the needle, while the four right hands display the Tarjani and Noose, the bunch of Aśoka flowers, the bow and the thread. An Aśoka tree is visible behind it in the background, and thus the image may be supposed to be that of a variety of Aśokakāntā Mārici. The popular Buddhist creed : "Ye dharma hetu" etc. are incised on the slab to the left side of it and on palaeographical consideration the image may be placed not earlier than the 10th century A.D.

**Ayodhya**

Ayodhya situated about 14 kms. from Nilgiri town in Balasore district surrounded by Ghaghara, Sona and Sindhu rivers to the east, north and west and hill ranges to the south; was a flourishing Tāntric Buddhist centre.

N.K.Sahu records that once this Ayodhya site had more than one hundred shrines whose ruins and images are found strewn all over the area and considerable number of them are buried inside the debris.

The presiding Goddess of this place is three-faced, eight-armed Mārici, standing in āliḍha pose on the chariot drawn by seven pigs. She is worshipped by the Hindus as Goddess Durga at present. Mārici image contains a Buddhist Dharani in the character of 10th century A.D. Her original Shrine of worship was situated about 2 kms. to the west of the present temple. Many fine pieces of Sculptures and images of this place are taken away, some are kept in modern temples of the villages round about and some are found in the compound of Fakir Mohan College, Balasore. The images worth attention of this area are Mārici, Avalokiteśvara, Tārā, Vajra Tārā, Lokeśvara and Mañjuśrī.

Goddess Tārā of exquisite art had a separate temple dedicated to her, in this place. This shows that Tārā occupied a prominent place, next to Mārici at this centre.

## Solampur

Solampur is recorded in the Neulpur copper plate grant of Śubhākaradeva I (790 A.D.) of Bhaumakara dynasty. A vast monastic establishment of Tāntric Buddhism was at Solampur, situated to the north-west of Jājapura, on the other side of the river Vaitaraṇi and most probably formed a part of Jajapura culture complex. Few of the Buddhist images found in this area are fixed to the outer walls of the Raghunathjee temple. The sculpture of Buddha representing the eight great events (eight miracles) of his life, found in this collection, is of importance. The miraculous events depicted in the panel are Buddha's birth from Mayadevi, turning the Wheel of Law in the Deer Park, his descent at Sankisa with Brahmā, Indra and thirty-three other Gods to expound his doctrine to his decrased mother, receiving the bowl of honey from the monkey at Vaisali, deliverance at Sravasti after performing a great miracle, overpowering the madden elephant Nalagiri, the topmost figure illustrating the Mahapari-nirvaṇa of the enlightened and representation of Six Manusi Buddha below the last scene of Buddha's life.

A two-handed Avalokiteśvara of this place, sitting at ease on a lotus throne betrays the influence of the Ratnagiri school. Two-armed Tārā standing in tribhanga style, a standing figure of Avalokiteśvar flanked by two miniature image of Tārā, the chlorite image of Vajrasattva (now preserved in Indian Museum, Calcutta) are Sculptures of remarkable artistic grandeur.

## Khaḍipada

Khaḍipada is not far from the river Vaitaraṇi, but within the environ of Jajpur; about 14 kms. to the north of Solampur. The Khaḍipada image inscriptions of Śubhākaradeva I's time, who belonged to Bhaumakara dynasty refers to a Buddhist monk named Rahularuci, styled as

Mahāmandulācārya Paramaguru or "the teacher of the great division and the Supreme preceptor." The title indicates that he was a famous Buddhist monk holding the high position of the State pentiff during Śubhākaradeva I's time. The image on which this inscription is found is two-armed Avalokiteśvara Padmapani, now preserved at Orissa State Museum.

Few colossal and life size images of Buddha and Bodhisattavas have been recovered from this site and preserved in Orissa State Museum, Bhubaneswar. Buddha in Dharma Chakra Mudra of this site, made of three carved stones is of interest. Buddha in Bhūmisparśa mudrā of this site, is also made of three carved stones.

This site had a monastic institution. Many images of this place are preserved in State Museum and a number of Tāntric Buddhist images are kept in the village Shrine. The artistic grandeur of this place; is that the carving of images were done in pieces.

**Kupari**

Situated at a distance 20 kms. from Bhadrak, is Kupari. There is early reference of this place, in the writing of John Beam, which indicate that there was a Buddhist monastery and a temple, wherein one colossal image of Buddha with the image of Mayadevi the mother of Gautam Buddha were found. The temple exists no more and the images are missing.

Kupari as Kumparakugrāma finds mention in the Neulpur copper plate Bhaumakara King Śubhākaradeva. The Caves in the hills running to the north of Kupari are supposed to have been used by the Buddhist recluses. There are remains of two narrow pillared halls, one inside Kupari and the other in its outskirt. These indicate two monastic establishment. There are octagonal monolithic pillars, made of chlorite stone.

**Kuṇḍeśvara**

Kuṇḍeśvara village is situated in Balikuda Police Station area of old Cuttack district boundary. One two-armed Tārā image seated on the lotus throne in Lalita pose exhibits masculine vigour. N.K.Sahu informs that as this Deity has prominent busts, it might pass for a representation of Padmapāṇi Avalokoteśvara. A broken image of Tārā found there, has feminine grace, beauty and has full of life. According to N.K. Sahu, the lower half of the image is missing and the remaining portion indicates that it is four-armed and is probably a seated figure. Two small representations of Tārā standing in tribhaṅga pose are seen on both sides of the Goddess paralled to her head and the top portion of the slab is occupied by five Dhayāni Buddhas, Vajrasattva and the Mānuṣi Buddha.

Another tāntric Buddhist deity found at Kaṇḍeśvara is of interest. While describing its details, N.K. Sahu states, "The noteworthy image in the Kuṇḍeśvara group is that of a God, seated in Lalita pose on a lotus throne, placing his right foot on the back of a naked girl, who lies on her breast, but looks upward with amorous face, decked with nose ring and ear rings. The left hand of the God is damaged, but in the right hand he carries a Skull cup (Karoṭa) full of blood and his face, possessed of youthful vigour, is bloomed with a smile of contentment. The garland of skull hangs prominently on his neck and almost teaches the lotus throne, while the tiger skin is visible round his loins. It is, however, difficult to identify the image with our present knowledge of iconography; very possibly, it represents the Tāntric Buddhist God Sambara.

## Bāṇeśvarṇāsi

Bāṇeśvarṇāsi is a hillock island in the bed of Mahāṇadi river in Narasimhapur area. This area once formed part of old Airāvatta Maṇḍala. K.G.Gupta, the then Commissioner of Orissa, brought this site to limelight in February 1902. Images of Buddhistic, Jain and Brahmāṇical faiths are found there. Prajñāpāramitā Tārā and Padmapāni Avalokiteśvara are the prominent images of Buddhist pantheon, which are carved with artistic care and iconographic accuracy. Buddha in bhūmiasparsa mudrā is of inferior workmanship. Brahmāṇīcal deities like Varuṇa, Kuvera, Indra and Īśāna are also found there.

Many images of this place have found their way to different places and some are lying buried under the ground and worshipped in Hinduised alias Brahmāṇical form as Mahākāli, Bhaṭṭārika, Rāmacaṇḍī, Chuṭiāśuni, Baḍarāullā etc. The Siṁhanāda Avalokiteśvara is worshipped by the local people of Purukuṭiā as Goddess Sumaiśuni and animals are sacrificed.

## Chauduar

Chauduar is situated on the northern bank of Virūpa, a distributary of Mahāṇadi river, about 9 kms. to the north of Cuttack. It was occupied by Janamejaya Mahābhāvagupta, the founder of Somavaṁśī power and was Capital for a long time. The antiquities of this place are both Buddhistic and Śaivite, dated within 9th and 10th centuries A.D. Chaudar has been denuded of its art treasures by curio-hunters and icon seekers and beautiful images seen by R.P. Chanda in 1928 are now missing.

The most prominent image of Tāntric Buddhist pantheon found at this place, which is now missing is Prajñāpāramitā.

Vajravārāhi and Khadiravaṇi Tārā images noticed by R.P. Chanda in 1928 in a modern Vaiṣṇavite temple are also not to be found now. In Tāntric Buddhist literature "Sādhanāmālā," Vajravārāhi is described as the presiding Deity of Uḍḍiyāna. Vajravārāhi is characterised as the Queen of Śrī Heruka and the Yāb Yuṁ (Yuganaddha) form of these two Deities, is the cult of the celebrated Cakrasaṁbara Tantra and Vajravārāhi Tantra. These two forms of Tantra seems to have been popular in Coastal Orissa, which were rare Tāntric Buddhist Cults.

The image of Vajravārāhi is missing, but N.K. Sahu gives its description from the available photograph, which goes thus: "Goddess Vajravārāhi is represented is nude and amorous form, dancing with dishevelled hair on two fierce looking corpses in the Ālidha attitude. She is two-armed and one-faced, and displays Vajra and Tarjani in her right and holds a Kapāla in her left hand, while a Khaṭvāṅga tipped with Vajra passes across her left thigh, bust and shoulder. She is worshipped by a female devotee, who kneels down before her, and just above the devotee a Lāmā is represented offering homage in a mustic way, standing on a lotus and holding a small human figure in his añjali, whereas behind the Goddess is found the figure of Vajrasattva, which appears like a miniature form of the Salaṁpur image. Two celestial figures are hovering in the Sky playing gracefully on musical instrumeṇts, while a full blown lotus decorates the top most part of the slab. H.C. Das informs that he had come across another image of Vajravārāhi at Badagaon near Bahanaga, worshipped as Baseli by the Brahmin priests.

Two-armed Khadiravaṇi Tārā of Chauduar is missing. Two-armed Avalokiteśvara and a bronze mask of Buddha were also noticed by R.P.Chanda in 1928, at Chauduar, which are now preserved at Indian Museum, Calcutta. The image of Tārā from Chauduar is now missing, but photograph available. Two images of Buddha, one in Dharmacakra-pravartana mudra and the other in Bhūmisparśa mudra are from Chauduar, which are found in the collection of late Laxminarayan Acharya at Chauduar.

Chaudaur was surrounded by eight Śiva temples, known as Aṣṭa

Sambhu. Out of these temples, Uttareśvar Śiva temple and Buddhaliṅga temple have been conserved by Orissa State Archaeology department.

## Kuruma

On the Sea shore near Koṇārk is situated Kuruma, an ancient Buddhist site. Over a mound images of Buddha in Bhumisparsa mudra, Avalokiteśvara in lalitāsana pose, Yamari and Trivikrama Viṣṇu are collectively worshipped. Excavation has revealed ancient brick walls, Vihāra or monastry and stupa. Local collections of terra-cotta ornaments, beads, miniature terra-cotta image, pottery of redware, black ware and a terra-cota Seal inscription, dated to circa, 9th century A.D. are found from there.

From excavation it is known that the original monastery flourished during c. 7th-8th centuy A.D. at Kuruma, which collapsed after a decade and followed by reconstruction during c. 9th-10th century A.D. Kuruma site has been identified with Che-li-ta-lo, as mentioned in Hiuen Tsang's account.

## Baud

Baud is probably a name derived from the enshrined Colossal Buddha in Bhūmisparśa-mudrā, seated on a lotus pedestal. During clearance of debris during Darbar administration the structure of a Buddhist Vihāra and several images were found.

The image of Buddha at Baud is built in sections like the Khaḍipadā and Udayagiri images but is larger in size than either of them. The plastic treatment, is more crude and warrants a later date than the 8th century A.D.

Buddhist figures, both Mahāyānic and Tāntric, are found in compound of the Rāmeśvara temple. At present the Rāmeśvara group of images are regarded as Hindu Deities, although a number of them carry the usual Buddhist creed "Ye dharme hetu — etc." One among them; a seated image of grace, is worshipped as Ugra Tārā, but R.D. Banerji has identified it with Mahattar Tārā and the same Scholar also points out that the big image leaning against the back wall of the Rāmeśvara temple is that of "the Lokeśvara class.'

Two exquisite bronze images have also been discovered from Baud. One of them is richly ornamental figure of two-armed Maitreya, seated gracefully in lalita pose on the throne, holding in the left hand a bunch of Nāgakeśara flowers and in the right the nector vase. The other image is that of a variety of Lokeśvara, which has been identified as Śaṅkhanātha Lokeśvara by N.K. Sahu. Such a variety of Lokeśvara is rarely found.

This Śaṅkhanātha Lokeśvara sits erect on a lotus throne and places its right foot on a foot stool (pāda pīṭha). It is four armed and one-faced. It carries in the upper right hand a conch shell and in the upper left hand a lotus, while the lower right hand is in Varada pose and the lower left is placed on the throne. It is in Lalita attitude. These bronze images with their exquisite workmanship are comparable with the bronze images of Achyutarajpur, near Banpur.

## Stray Buddhist figures

This study of Tāntric Buddhist art has been done from the discovered famous centres of Orissa and is not exhaustive one, as Buddhist images are found in almost all parts of Orissa.

The Colossal image of Amoghasiddi preserved at Orissa State Museum was found at G.Udayagiri. The conception of Amoghasiddhi belongs to Vajrayāna.

The Goddess worshipped as Tāriṇi in Bānapura is Goddess Tārā, originally brought from Bānkāḍa. Khadiravaṇi Tārā is found in the compound of Banpur High School. Avalokiteśvara with an inscribed Buddhist Dharani is at Lataharan. Samkhapani Avalokiteśvara is in village Mudgala, seated image of Trailokyavijaya is near Amar-prasadgarh, Mārici is found at Aṣṭaranga and Buddhist images are seen at Sisireśvar temple and many temples of Bhubaneswar. Headless Lokeśvara found in Orissa State Museum was recovered from Badagada area and footless image of Lokeśvara kept in Orissa State Museum was unearthed in Jhārpada, a northern suburb of Bhubaneswar.

N.K.Sahu rightly states that Śaivism had its fluorescence and Buddhism its decline in Bhubaneswar and a number of Śiva temples with magnificent carvings and highly aesthetic decorations, raised their curvilinear heads in many places of this area. Śaivism naturally appropriated to itself the Buddhist art-tradition that had developed there and the Buddhist artists have also left the impress of Buddhism in the midst of the artistic exuberance of Śaivism.

"On the walls of some of the early temples of Bhubaneswar, Buddhist images are engraved in bold relief, while some of the Śaivite figures are found there endowed with the Buddhistic attributes.—At the Yupa pillar of Vaitāl temple of Bhubaneswar two images of Buddha seated in Dharmachakra mudra are carved, on the body of the sacrificial post. It seems to suggest the clash between the Buddhists and the Śāktas in this region about the 8th century A.D. when the Vaitāl temple was built."

Among other Buddhist arts mention may be made of Vajraghaṇṭi near Amareswar, the images of Jaṭāmukuta Lokeśvara and Amitābha in the Solopua Ma temple of Cuttack, Chunda worshipped as Basuli Thakurani at Bania Sahi of Cuttack, image of Maitreya in Baleswar town, Avalokiteśvara in the compound of Fakir Mohan College, Baleswar, Avalokiteśvara and Buddha in Baleswar Museum, Tārā, Avalokiteśvara with inscribed terra-cotta sealing with Buddhist Dharani from Avana, Buddhist images of Sora, Orasahi and in the collection of Lakshmannath Roy Mohanty in Baleswar district, Ārya Tārā and Khasarpanā Lokeśvara from Rabibandha, Janguli Tārā from Hariharpur, figures of Mārici from Udala in Mayurbhanj district. Jambbala in the Jagannāth temple of Baripada, Tārā image of Binika, two Muchalinda Nagaraja Buddhas of Ganiapali and Buddhist traces at Nagraj in Bargarh district, Stupa ruin and Buddha image at Maraguda valley in Nuapada district, Muchalinda Buddha at Biswanathpur in Kalahandi district and unknown scattered images in the known and unknown places of Orissa, indicate the efflorescence of Tāntric Buddhist art in Orissa.

## Buddhist Bronzes

Earliest bronze image of Buddha is Bhūmisparśa mudrā was collected by H.C. Das from Jayrampur in Baleswar district in 1964. H.C. Das collected the image and a copper plate grant of Achyuta, a feudatory chief under the overlord Maharajadhiraja Gopachandra belonging to 5th-6th century A.D. This grant was issued for maintenance of the Svetavalika vihāra and the presiding God Bhagaban Śrī Avalokiteśvara was recovered from the site while removing old bricks. A bronze image of Tārā was discovered from the same village, which is dated within 10th-11th century A.D. These findings shows that once bronze industry survived in Jayrampur area for considerable period.

## Achutarajpur Bronze Hoard

Achutarajpur is situated near Banpur. While foundation excavation work was going on to lay the foundation of Godavarish Mahavidyalaya in 1963, two huge earthen ware pots containing hoard of bronzes and a set of copper plates of Somavaṁśī King Indrarath were found. With the help of D.P. Dash, I.A.S., the then Collector of Puri, the entire hoard of bronzes was shifted to Orissa State Museum, where the entire hoard is preserved. Devala Mitra has done extensive detail study of this Bronze hoard in a volume named, "Bronzes from Achutarajpur, Orissa." The Bronze images are assigned inbetween the period 8th-11th century A.D.

In this Bronze Hoard; Brahmaṇical icons are five (Mahiṣamardinī-one, Umā-Maheśvara - one, Viṣṇu - one and Gaṇesa - two), Jaina icons-ten (Amba - four, Riṣavanath - one, Candraprabha - two, Vasupujya - one and two other Tirthaṅkaras) and the rest belong to Buddhist pantheon.

In total 50 Buddhist icons are known from this Bronze hoard. Out of these Buddha - sixteen, Manjushree - four, Avalokiteśvara - ten, Vajrasattva - five, Maitreya - three, Jambhala - one, Heruka - one, Trailokyavijaya - one, Tārā - seventeen, Bhrukuti - two, Pandara - one, Mārici - one, Cunda - five and Kurukullā - one. The Bronzes prove that Achutarajpur was a flourishing centre of Vajrayāna form of Tāntric Buddhism.

**Trailokyavijaya**

Among this bronze hoard, the single Trailokyavijaya meaning conqueror of the three Worlds is very interesting, because this shows superiority and preponderence over the Hindu Gods and Goddesses. This bronze image is the biggest in the hoard (42.3 cm.) and is dated to last part of 10th century A.D. The Iconographic feature of this Tāntric Buddhist Deity is found in "Sādhanāmālā."

The icon of this figure is that it has strong built body with broad shoulders, strong chest, long arms and wrathful facial expression. It stands in the pratyālịdha pose with the two forearms against the chest in the gesture of Vajra-humkara and trampling under his feet the prostrate figures of Śiva and Pārvatī who are holding trident in their hands. The Deity here wears a garland of miniature Buddha figures.

This icon of Trailokyavijaya represents the strength and vigour of Buddhism and its triumph over Brāhmaṇism. The trampling under the feet, the two major Cult divinities of Brāhmaṇical pantheon are indicative of the rivalry between Buddhism and Hinduism, and an attempt to triumph over Hinduism. Devala Mitra describes this icon thus, "It appears that the Buddhists of this establishment, being apprehensive of the mastering strength of the followers of the Brāhmaṇical cults, particularly Śaiva and Śākta, at this place created and installed this icon, a flagrant example of ill-feeling towards the Brāhmaṇical faith, with the object of combating with the all absorbing forces of Brahmāṇīsm which was, apparently, in the ascendancy and of drawing the people to the Buddhist fold by showing the importance of the Brāhmaṇical Deities fallen under the feet of the Buddhist God. The overcoming power of this two-armed Buddhist Deity is emphasized in a dramatic way by the depiction of the scattered weapons of the multi-armed Brāhmaṇical God and Goddess."

Single Jambhala image of this hoard is the Buddhist God of Wealth, which is regarded as the counterpart of the Hindu God Kuvera (the God of Wealth). This art is assigned not later than 9th centuryA.D. It has pot-belly. Its association with Mangoose is an interesting story. Mangoose, the natural enemy of the serpents is considered the guardian of Wealth lying hidden beneath the earth. It took away the treasures from the Serpents and concealed it in its stomach. Thus, the Mongoose as the repositor of Wealth is associated with Jambhala to distinguish him from Kuvera, the Hindu counterparts having purse as his symbol. Laxicon Meaning nakula, means a kind of purse and in "Divyavadra," a Buddhist work; it finds prominent place.

Buddhists bronzes have been found from Jayrampur, Ratnagiri, Chauduar, Boud and Prachi valley. Brāhmaṇical, Buddhist and Jaina icons in bronzes are also found from Kakatpur, Bheradupatna, Charchika and Nijagada Tailapur. Brāhmaṇical bronzes are found in plenty in Orissan temples and as household Deities in every village and town. This bear evidence that traditional metal casting and metal art in Orissa is of grand style.

## ART OF NĀTHA DHARMA

The founder father of Nāthism was Matsyendranātha, who was born in Orissa. So, it is but natural that traces of the art tradition of Nāthism should be traced in Orissa. At this juncture, the narration of H.K.Mahatab comes to help, when he states that the philosophy of Nātha Dharma as propounded by Gorakṣanātha and his Divine Master Matsyendranātha is absorbed in theory and practice, in the Nirguṇa Bhakti Cult. Almost all the Ācāryas of the present day, Yoga practice follow, practise and propagate one or some aspects of the practical Yogic methods of Gorakṣanātha and his successors which they have treasured in their books, "Siddha Siddhānta Paddhati," "Gorakṣa Paddhati," "Amanaska Yoga," "Gorakṣa Śatakam," "Gorakṣa Sidhānta Sangraha," "Satkarma Sangraha," etc. But it is a matter of curiosity that none mentions the name of the Nāth-Siddhas to whom they are so much indebted for their achievements, whereas historical datas give ample evidence of the influence of Nātha Dharma since eighth century A.D. towards the end of eighteenth century A.D.

"Evidences of Nātha Dharma in Orissa can be traced since the last quarter of the eights century A.D. A statue of Matsyendranātha in the form of Padmapāni Avalokiteśvara at forest of Rajnagar under Deravisi Block of Kendrapara district is still worshipped by the Nāthas of the surrounding villages. The inscription on both sides of the Statue is in Kuṭila-lipi or proto-Uḍralipi. The present Oriya script was not evolved by then and the period of that Script is accepted to be inbetween sixth and eleventh century A.D. The proto-type of the same Statue is seen at Kendrapara bus stand with the same inscription and another at Trilochanpur village under Mahajajpur Gram Panchayat near Bahugram, is also worshipped by the Nāthas of the surrounding villages. This proves that towards the last quarter of ninth century, Matsyendranātha and Gorakṣanātha were worshipped in Orissa as the incarnations of Viṣṇu and Śiva respectively. The most ancient specimens of Oriya prose and poetry are ascribed to be the works of Gorakṣanātha and other Nātha-Siddhas.

"The theory of Piṇḍa-Brahmāṇda (Cosmos in microcosm) of Gorakṣanātha serves as the backbone of Orissan Vaisnava philosophy of the Pañcasakhā literature as in the case of Nirguṇa Santh Kāvyas of Hindi, Punjabi and Gujarati literatures of the ancient and medieval periods.

"Since the dates of Sāralā Dasa, the Nāthas of Orissa found to be mentioned as Rudraja and Sisuvedi Brahmana (Śiśuvedi hoive pañcaviṁśa sathasra Brāhmana, Madhya parva; Śiśumana Vedenaye Lakṣekas dvija-Sabhā Prava). They observe most of the Vedic Brāhmaṇical rites so far as Social customs are concerned with some variations. The Sacred thread are according to the Nāthas, is ever pure (Pavitra) even during the period of an cleanliness due to birth or death. The dead body is buried seated in Yogasana in a compound specially preserved in the premises of Maṭha or homestead land. The Samādhis are treated as sacred shrines. Śiśuveda of the Nāthas is regarded as the fifth Veda. A person from any caste or religious Sects can accept Nātha-Dharma, but he must use the title of "Nātha", after his name after due initiation. Hundreds of Nātha Pīṭhas and Gādis are scattered all over Orissa. Although idolatry is forbidden in Nātha Dharma, it came to be mixed up first with Buddhism then with Hinduism. Buddhist and Brāhman idols were accepted by the Nāthas as theirs. It is the Nātha-Dharma which made Yoga popular in Orissa."

The religious discipline of Nāthas was that of Haṭhayoga. So, "Haṭha Yoga Pradipikā," where the classical description of Vajroli mudra is found, was followed by the Nāthas.

The reliable texts on Haṭha Yoga written by Nātha Yogis are "Goraksha Saṁhita" by Yogi Gorakṣanātha," Haṭha Yoga Pradipika" by Yogi Swatmarama, "Gherand Saṁhitā" by Yogi Gherand and "Haṭharatanavali" which was written by Śrinivasabhaṭṭa Mahāyogīndra. All these texts are considered to have been written between 6th and 15th centuries A.D.

## SIGNIFICANCE OF HINDU TEMPLE

Hinduism is a way of life, rather than a religion, which has observed several concepts and practices of different Sects into its fold. A Hindu, regards the temple as Art and Science of enclosing or cladding space created by nature. Temples are found everywhere.

Temples are the meeting place of Art and Religon. Art extends immense scope for freedom of expression, but with the disciplinarian traits of Religion, religious art developed, where rituals, rites, which necessitated inventions of objects, places and equipments for worship, could be done. This satisfied the aesthetic aspirations of the population, besides of course their intuitive and imaginary needs.

Temple structures remained not just the embodiments of faith, they were also conceived with a view to perpetuate the human adherence to faith, so that the succeeding generations do not go astray from the ideals originally conceived, adorned and believed in by the Yogis and Rishies of India.

Temples are also symbols, which effectively employed for communication with common man who otherwise had no access to the great intellectual treatises on ethics, philosophy and metaphysics. These ideals were interpreted and re-interpreted by the devotees in an endless fashion as one could see in the Religous developmental process in India.

The Hindu temple is believed to represent a human body. This reflects the old and almost Universal doctrine of basic correspondence between man and cosmos - man as microcosmos and cosmos an macro-anthropes, which was also found expressed both in theoretical expression and practical application in Tāntric Yoga. A popular Sanskrit saying "Kṣetraṁ Śarīra prastaram," also conveys that temples were made in the form of human body.

## TEMPLE ARCHITECTURE IN INDIA

India has a long narration of its temple architecture, which may be grouped as (1) Pre-Vedic architecture, (2) Vedic architecutre, (3) Architecture of the post-Vedic age, (4) Architecture as described by Pāṇini, (5) Architecture of Epic age, (6) Architecture as mentioned by Viśvakarmā, (7) Architecture as described or stated by Maya, Purāṇas, Āgama Tāntric literatures, Kauṭilya's Architecture and Varāhamihira, (8) Architecture as described by Bharata, Bhatta Lollita, Bhaṭṭa Nāyaka and Abhinavagupta.

Architecture is the sign of Civilization. There is lot of Truth in this statement, because architecture is the best material and visible source which gives us an ideal of human beings intellectual development. It is through the art of building that one can have a clear picture of the Social, Political and Spiritual life of the people in different ages.

The Hindu temple evolved from the remotest antiquity of a platform or a Vedi, open to sky with some kind of representation or symbol of the Deity. The earliest Vedi, may be noticed in the Fire altar of Vedic period. The second stage was reached when railings were provided round the platform or Vedi. At first bamboo and wood railings were used and later railing of stone.

The Buddhist and Jaina school of architecture also followed the same footsteps of a central platform surrounded by a railing. A time was reached when the railing and monumental gateways (the best example of the gateway is at the Stupa of Sanchi) fell inro disfavour.

The Brāhmaṇical temple now came into the field, retained the platform or Vedi which now served as the high plinth if the temple and the pillars of the railing were assimilated into the full size of the high plinth. The temple or shrine was placed in the centre, on this high terrace. Evolution of Temple, developed with its Garbhagriha and Sikhara.

The third stage of evolution begins from about the 4th century A.D. in the Gupta period, when there was a parallel development of the Buddhist and Brāhmāṇical Shrines. The earliest example is found in the Gupta temple at Sanchi. Its characteristic features are : (1) There is a small square sanctum or garbhagriha in which the image was placed, (2) there is a flat top and no Śikhara, (3) the walls of the Sanctum are plain both on the inside and the outside as was in the case of the proceding gandhakutis, (4) there was provided a small maṇḍapa or pavilion on pillars but open on the three sides most probably to provide some shelter to the worshippers, (5) a moderately high plinth was provided both for the garbhagriha and maṇḍapa.

As was natural each one of these features underwent an evolution which may be seen in temples built during the 4th, 5th, 6th and 7th centureis A.D., that is, mainly in the architectural complex of Gupta civilization.

Next to the "Arthaśāstra," of Kauṭilya, an equally remarkable work and record of ancient Indian life, the "Kāmasūtra" of Vātsyayāna Mallanāga might be noticed. The evidence of Vātsyayāna shows that the knowledge of mechanics was considered as forming part of the general equipment and accomplishment of people. In the sixty-four arts, which Vātsyayāna Mallanāga gives at the beginning of his work and which form a syllabus of general education that men and women underwent, an art named yantra - mātṛkā is mentioned. The valuable gloss Jayamaṅgala on the Kāmasūtras explains Yantra-matṛkā as the Science of making different kinds of Yantras and in this connection refers to the Treatise of the architect Viśvakarmān, where they are dealt.

The "Sulba Sūtra", describe methods for taking a rope and stake to locate corners and how to make a square. The square reflected Vedic cosmology, which saw the World as square. A ritual diagram prescribed for Temples in the 6th century A.D. "Bṛhat Saṁhitā," of Varāhamihira is Vāstupuruṣamaṇḍala. Vāstu plan made out of 8x8=64 small squares for a temple plan, is for worship of Brāhmanas and Vāstu plan made out of 9 x 9 = 81 small squares for a temple plan is for worship of Kings alias Ketriyas. The "Īśānaśivagumdeva - paddhati," make it clear that a Vāstu of 64 squares is for worship by Brāhmanas and one of the 81 squares for worship by Kings.

With the popularisation of Tantra within 5th - 8th centuries A.D. in India, temple plans were mostly based on Yantra based or Vāstu plan. Yantra is the design for the requisite disposition, adjustment and control of power which Mantra has set in operation. So, it is the means, instrument of apparatus Spiritually. Because of the Yantras of different worship the next stage of the Hindu (Brāhmaṇical) temple began with the more elaborate development of the plinth, the Garbhagriha (Sanctum) and the Tower (Sikhara), accompanied with the elaboration of the Image itself. This work began about the beginning of the Gupta period and continued right upto the medieval period, that is, from the 4th to the 13th century A.D. when the grand monuments of the Hindu temple attained their fullest splendour.

With the Iconic sculptural art, the temples have Sculptures of social topic then; like Women enjoying scenes of toilet, dance, music and past times with birds and garden sports under asoka and kadamba trees and alasakanyās. Another feature which attracts frequent notice is the presence of series of different erotic postures - figures or ratibandhas, as described in different texts of Śilpa-śāstras and Kamasūtra. The "Bṛhat Saṁhitā" of Varāhmihira (6th century A.D.) mentions that door jambs of temples should be decorated with several auspicious objects including amorous couples. In the "Agni purāṇa," it is mentioned that doorways should be decorated with Maithunas. The "Samarangana - sūtradhara," enjoins that women should be represented as engaged in Sexual activity. "Skanda purāṇa," recommends the depiction of erotic sculptures as device to evert horror and protect the temple from thunderbolt. "Kāmikāgama," consists of several chapters on architecture. This took place because of the influence of the prevailing religious conception of Tantra worship. A temple is convinced to the plan of Human body. Sex is found in the outer zone of Human body and in similar manner, erotic sculptures were given at the erotic zones. Śilpa-texts mention that the symbolic representation of Sex scenes and Śrngāra should be camouflaged by the portrayal of erotic figures on Temple architecture.

The Śilpaśāstras of India recognise three main styles of temples, known as the Nāgara, the Drāviḍa and the Vesara. There were regional or provincial styles of Temple Architecture also. The descriptions given are however, vague and inadequate, and it is not possible to equate the description of the texts with any of the extant examples of Indian temple architecture. The origin of the styles have been expounded in mythical manner.

## TEMPLES OF ORISSA

The present province of Orissa mainly comprises the territory of ancient Kaliṅga, Utkala and South Kōśala. Alround influence from all directions developed and influenced the monuments, temples and Religious faiths of Orissa.

Orissa has rich heritage of beautiful temples, which are full of Sculptural motifs and excellent work, which shows the carving in their facial expression and sensuousness. James Fergusson was of the opinion, "There are more temples now in Orissa than in all the rest of Hindusthan put together."

The Orissan group of temples are regarded as of Nāgara style, but the regional manifestation with the modifications and transformations in course of evolution has beautifield the Orissa temples to such an extent that the temples of Orissa earned a name as "Kaliṅga Style," because of its distinguishing peculiarities. An inscription on the Capital of a pillar in the mukhamaṇḍapa of Amṛteśvara temple at Holal (Bellary district) mentions the "Kaliṅga Style," type, along with the Nāgara, Dravida and Vesara styles.

In South Kōśala portion, comprising western part of Orissa, i.e. the upper Mahāṇadi river valley, "Kōśali Style," of rekhā temple and "Kōśali Style," of Khakhara temples are found. From literatures like Āgama, Mayamata, Mānasāra and Bhuvanapradipa, two varieties of "Kōśali Styles," of Temple architectures are known.

The Rasikaraya brick temple at Haripada in Mayurbhanj district, Chandaneswar temple at Chandaneswar in Balesore district and few other temples in the north-east portion of Orissa, have Curvilinear roof, belonging to late medieval period, which are of Gauḍīya Style of Temple architecture.

Orissa had its own Canons of architecture, "Bhuvanapradipa," and "Śilpa Prakāśa." Bhuvanapradipa seems to be the earliest, whose exact period is not known, but "Śilpa Prakāśa," belong to the date of the ruling period of Anantavarman Chodagaṅgadeva (1077-1147 A.D.) of Gaṅga dynasty. "Viṣṇu Dhamottara (III, chapter 43, stanzas, 1-15)," and "Śilpa Prakāśa," mentions that the symbolic representation of Sex, love scenes and Sṛṅgara should be camouflages by the portrayal of erotic figures on it. Bhuvanapradipa and Śilpa Prakāśa were Manuals for the architects of Temples in Orissa. The active Tāntric architectural remains of Orissa, broadly covered the period from 6th century A.D. to 13th century A.D. but in ritual the influence of Tāntric form of worship, still continues.

The Śilpa texts of Orissa, mention three types of temples as Rekhā, Piḍhā and Khākharā. The Rekhā and Piḍhā form two component parts of one architecture set up. Rekhā temple forms the main Sanctum, while the porch having pyramidal roof in front of the Sanctum is made of Piḍhā. The Khākharā order is noted by its surmounting semi-cylindrical roof and such temple was meant for Tāntric Śākti worship.

Orissa temple consists of the Sanctum and the Porch, the two together make a temple, a complete whole. The main temple meant for the presiding Deity is called Deul or Vimāna, is of Rekhā order and has a carvilinear super-structure with its vertical ascent, symbolizing the human being's quest for the Divine. The Orissan craftmen considered the temple as the body of the Cosmic Being. Therefore the Rekhā temple has four divisions named pishta, bāda, gaṇḍi and māstaka. The piṣhṭa is not a compulsory element, but is generally found in temples of the latest phase. Piṣhṭa means pedestal.

The constituent elements of the bāḍa are pābhāga, jāṅgha and baranda. In later temples the bāḍa is composed of five elements, pabhaga, tala-jāṅgha, bāndhanā, upar-jaṅgha and barand. This type of trianga bāḍa is found in temples of the earlier period. In later temples the bāḍa is composed of five elements, pābhaga, tala-jāṅgha, bāndhanā, upar-jāṅgha and barand. The bāḍa is thus pañcāṅga type, the jāṅgha being divided by a set of moundings called bāndhanā into two register known as lower jāṅgha and upper jāṅgha. The pābhāga (foot part) denotes the bottom part of the wall and is composed of mouldings called khura, kumbhapata kani and basanta. The baranda, forming the top most part of the bāḍa, is generally composed of a series of seven or ten mouldings.

There is no difference between the Deula and the Jagamohana in the treatment of the bāḍa, but they differ in the disposition of the gaṇḍi. The gaṇḍi of the Jagamohana is of pyramidal shape, whereas the gaṇḍi of the deul has a curvilinear outline. Both, however, underwent modifications in the course of the evolution of temple architecture in Orissa. Sometimes the gaṇḍi of the main temple is decorated with anga sikharas which add to the grandeour of the temple.

The mastaka of the rekhā deul consists of the beki, the amla, the khapuri, the kalasa and the āyudha. The main Sanctum has only one door and is not lighted by windows. But, in the Jagamohana, sometimes there are four pillars to provide additional support to its roof. In the earlier phase of the style, the Jagamonana is provided with latticed windows at the sides in addition to the main entrance. In case of Jagannāth temple of Puri and Sun temple of Konarak, their Jagamohanas are provided with three entrance doors.

It is also to be noted that the interior walls of the temples are generally plain, but the exterior is fully decorated. It is interesting to know that the Jagamohana of Konarak has sculptural art in its inner walls.

At the bottom of the door-jambs of Orissan temples, generally figures of dvārapālas, Gaṅgā and Yamunā are found. In the centre of the door lintel, the figure of Gaja-lakṣmi is depicted. The earlier temples of Coastal Orissa had eight planets, but from Somavaṁśī period (9th to 12th centuries A.D.) nine grahas were depicted and eight Digpālas were carved on the walls in their respective directions in the temples of mature stage in Orissa.

The Kōśali style of Rekhā temple which developed in South Kōśala region, influenced the construction of three Tāntric temples at Baud and developed pañcaratha temple plan in coastal Orissa, during Somavaṁśī period.

## TĀNTRIC TEMPLE OF SOUTH KŌŚALA

In between 7th-9th centuries A.D. there was rise of "Kōśali Style," of temple architecture, based on Tāntric Śaivism at South Kōśala area, which comprised upper Mahāṇadi river valley. From Ādhabhara plates of Mahā Nannarāja (*Epigraphia Indica*, Vol. XXXI, pp. 219-222 ff.), it is known that Ādhabhara, situated in modern Bilaspur district of Madhya Pradesh was known then as Aṣṭadvara vishaya. The ruling period of Mahānannarāja is assigned within circa 570-595 A.D. This synonym "Aṣṭadvāra," probably helped in development of temple plan of two squares placed diagonally and intersecting each other at angles of 45 degrees. This plan is based on Yantra, based on Śaiva tantra, as mentioned in the Mantras of "Ānanda Lahari, verse 20," and "Saundarya Lahari, verses 20 and 42," of Ādi Śankarācārya, and temples based on this plan are found at (1) Ādhabhara in Bilaspur district, Madhya Pradesh, (2) Chitawari Devi temple at Dhobni, near Damakeda village in Raipur district, Madhya Pradesh, (3) Pātāleśvar Śiva temple at Bodhi Komna in Nuapada district, Orissa and (4) A temple in ruin at Kansil village area, in Ranipur-Jharial complex in Balangir district, Orissa. As four temples with the same plan are found in South Kōśala region, it seems, it will be proper for the temples of this plan of two squares placed diagonally and intersecting each other at angles of 45 degrees, to be identified as "Kōśali Style of Rekha temples."

The author accompanied with Nrusingha Prasad Tripathi had the opportunity to visit Dhobni village on 22nd Februāry 1986. Visited Chitawaṛi Dẹvi temple of Dhobni, but to all surprise, the author found that the Śiva Liṅga Deity was painted red by vandalism, the Śākti of the Liṅga removed and kept near the back wall of the Sanctum and worshipped as Chitawari Devi. Originally this temple is a Śiva temple. Same thing has happened at Ādbhara also. In "Bilaspur District Gazetteer, 1978," it is mentioned that there are two ornamental doorways of an old ruined temple of a Devi, in the Ādbhara village. The ruined temple of Ādbhara was a Śiva temple, which was visited and have been recorded by Prof. Nirmal Kumar Bose of Calcutta University, during the early part of 20th century A.D. and reported in his work, "Indian Temple Designs, 1981."

It will be suffice to mention that Mahāśivagupta Bālārjuna, whose reigning period was (circa. 595 -655 A.D.), the Pāṇḍuvaṁśī alias Somavaṁśī King of South Kōśala was a devout Śaiva. S.R. Nema informs that Mahāśivagupta being a great devotee of Śiva, enjoyed the epithet "Parama-Māheśvara" in his charters and also had the Śaivite emblem of the Bull on his Seal, while the Seal of his ancestor (grandfather's brother) Tivara who was a "Parama Vaiṣṇava," bore the Vaiṣṇava emblem of Garuḍa. He, as well as his subordinate Chiefs gave patronage to Śaivism. We know from the Senakapat inscription that "Durgaraṣita, son of Devarakshita, was a bee at the foot," i.e. a Servant of Mahāśivagupta Bālārjuna. He, being a worshipper of Śambhu, constructed a temple of Śiva at the village (modern) Senakapat and made it over to an ascetic, Sadāśivācārya who was probably the Spiritual successor of Sadyahśivācārya, hailing from the penance grove, entitled Amaradeka. In Lodhia plates, the donee Śūlapāṇi was a disciple of Pramathācārya who is said to be an inhabitant of Pāncayajña - tapovana in Dvaitavana. Here it is sufficient to say that these Śaiva-ācāryas probably belonged to a Sect of tāntric-Śaivism which later came to be called Mattamayūra and as such, it may be assumed that Mahāśivagupta may have accepted the doctrine of Paśupata-dharma.

The essence of the teaching of Śaiva tantra is that the so called individual Soul (Jīva) that is the enjoyer, the Universe which is the object enjoyed, the Supreme Lord Śiva who is the giver of enjoyment and the Guru (Master) who grants release, are absolutely non-different (i.e. One). By a devoted study on the Śaiva hymns, by reflecting on its teaching and by meditating on the Truth taught, one will gain the Supreme and which is release.

In "Śivānandalahari (verse 42)," Śankarācārya informs that Śiva likes to reside in Fortresses, which is impregnable, well guarded and provided with every convenience. Plans of temple architecture based on Śaiva Yantra and sometimes with variations of plans in South Kōśala, shows that they were built to guard Śiva's extreme meditation.

With the influence of Tāntric Śaivism named "Mattamāyūra," a school of temple architecture developed in South Kōśala, which came to be recorded as "Kōśali Style" of Rekha and "Kōśali Style" of Khākharā temple architectures. Bhuvanapradipa, a treatise on temple architecture of Orissa, describes three types of temples; the Rekhā, Bhadra and the Khākharā. Much emphasis is placed in this text on the exact proportions and height of different parts of the Walls. The text details 36 types of Rekhā temples, five varieties of Bhadra temples and three types of Khākharā temples with detailed measurements of each type. In this architectural treatise "Kōśali Style" of Rekhā temple and "Kōśali Style" of Khākharā temple is mentioned. The detail description of the "Kōśali Style of Rekhā temple" is not yet found, but Nirmal Kumar Bose of

Calcutta University, in his works "Orissa Architecture, Calcutta 1931, pp. 124 and 172-173", and "Canons of Orissan Architecture, Calcutta, 1932, pp. 172-173," gives measurement narration of "Kōśali Khākharā temple Style."

In the newly published work "Fragments of Indian Culture, Calcutta, 1995", Ram Prasad Mishra has done an error, while describing the plan of the ruined brick temple in Ranipur-Jharial complex, whose plan is of two squares placed diagonally and intersecting each other at angles of 45 degrees. Ram Prasad Mishra states, "On the left side of the approach road leading to the main temple site of Ranipur-Jharial the ruins of a damaged brick temple is found. This brick temple does not show at the present day the Mukhaśālā, antarala and garbhagriha. It shows only the piḍha on which the temple had been built. In the midst of the relics of this temple few large stone pillars basement built of bricks and the Star-shaped layout are clearly observed. The Garbhagriha being evidently a square shape is measured 6 feet and 4 inches both in length and breadth. The damaged doorway of the temple is 3 feet and 5 inches in breadth and 6 feet and one inch in height. A lotus carved on a stone was found here. This is perhaps the part of a celling of this temple. Brick used in the erection of this temple is one foot and two inches in length, 8 inches in breadth and 3 inches in height. The people of Ranipur-Jharial call it Chheliya temple. In a Tāntric Buddhist manuscript called "Vajritoṣana Tantra," the Tāntric Buddhists or Vajrayānists are instructed to adore the primal Buddha Vajrasattva with Tāntric rites in a Star-shaped edifice."

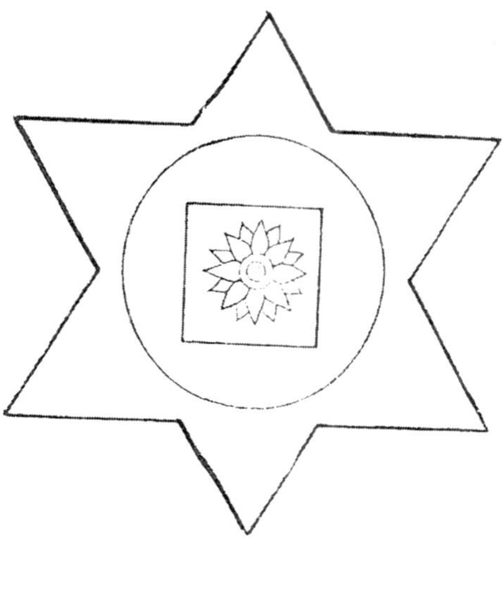

As this Tantra suggests the Tāntric Buddhists should enshrine Vajrasattva in association with his consert Vajranāri or Prajñā and other members of Vajra family on a pedestal shaped as conjoint double lotus. This double lotus pedestal should be erected on a square-shaped pavilion encompassed by a circle of perfect tranquility. This circular space of tranquility should be located in a Star-shaped. As so called Chheliya temple is a Star-shaped edifice and as in a reliable proximity of this temple an image of Lord Buddha is found, it is reasonable to believe that this Chheliya temple was originally a Shrine for worship of the Supremest Tāntric Buddhist God, Vajrasattva along with his Śākti and Vajrakula."

It is interesting to mention that what R.P. Mishra thinks to be Six-pointed Star-shaped temple, is in reality a plan of two square placed diagonally and intersecting each other at angles of 45 degrees. Thereby making an arial view of eight pointed Star. (Vide: Sketch photo).

When only one wall of this Brick temple was existing, in early part of 20th century, N.K. Bose of Calcutta University had visited Rāṇipur-Jharial and had reported (Vide: *The History and Culture of the Indian People*, Vol. V, *The Struggle for Empire*, ed. R.C. Majumdar, Bharatiya Vidya Bhavan, Bombay, 1966, p. 556).

In recent years American Scholar Thomas E.Donaldson had visited Ranipur-Jharial and had recorded the plan and measurement of the ruined Brick temple of Rāṇipur-Jharial and states, "A similar brick temple composed of intersecting squares producing an eight pointed Stellate ground plan existed at Kausuli near Rāṇipur-Jharial though only the foundation of the deul and antarala has survived along with the pīṭha, the jagamohana being completely destroyed. The Temple faces east and the intersecting squares measure 14 feet in each side. The antarala has a large pillar on either side of its door opening but nothing of the frame has survived whereas the jambs of the Sanctum door, also of stone, are partly intact but relatively plain. A Stone slab, 42 inches square, is decorated with a lotus rosette and probably served as a Celining ornament for the antarala. The Sanctum, seven feet square, has a stone pillar set into the brick foundation at each corner. A water spout pierces the north wall. Only the lower two mouldings of the pābhāga of the exterior have survived, a Khura at the base and a Kumbha above. The outlines of a Kiriṭa are visible on the Khura moulding while three Campaka-leaves hang down from the Kumbha. There are no surviving Sculptures. Stylistically the temple is closely aligned to the Pātāleśv temple (of Bodhi Komna) and can likewise be dated to the late 9th or early

10th century A.D." These studies shows the opinion of R.P. Mishra wrong.

## TĀNTRIC TEMPLES OF ORISSA

The Tāntric Cult had a very long and popular career in Orissa, very vehemently, forcibly and impetuously within the period 6th-13th centuries A.D. and is still continuing in ritual worship. As observed, the Tāntric influence gave an impetus to the development of Art and Architecture in different parts of Orissa province and evocated kineshthetic sensation and emotions and finally enabled the Tāntric practitioners to grow and expand to realize the consciousness of the Absolute reality.

The Pātāleśvar Śiva temple of Bodhi Komna in Nuapada district and Chheliya temple at Kansil in Rāṇipur-Jharial complex in Balangir district are early Tāntric Śiva temples of Orissa, which influenced the development of temples in Orissa. With the influence of the Tāntric Śaiva temples of South Kōśala, which earned the name of "Kōśali Style of Rekhā temple," the three Tāntric Śaiva temples at Baud developed.

In Baud town there are three small temples, within the compound of Rameśvar temple. The last Ruling Chief Raja Narayan Prasad Bhanja Deo of Baud had started the construction of Rameśvar temple during British period, but; because of Second World War, its construction stopped and it remained uncompleted. The three Tāntric Śiva temples inside Rameśvar temple compound of Baud are standing in a triangular formation. The triangle is pointed to the east and this triangle forms a Yantra and signifies Liṅga, which is known as Vajra also. So, the location of these three stone temples represent the Sexo-Yogic practice of Vajroli, practised by the Śaiva tāntrics. The temple standing at the southern end is named Bhubaneśvar and the temple standing on northern end is Kapileśvara. Both of them are facing east. The name of the temple at the apex of the triangle is Paścima Somanātha and faces west. The dhvaja of Paścima Somanātha is a Cakra, which signifies Hari-Hara Cult, where Śaiva tantra and Vaiṣṇav tantra were practised. The plan of the garbhagriha of these three temples of Baud are in the plan of two squares placed diagonally and intersecting each other at angles of 45 degrees. The presiding Śiva liṅga Deities of these three temples have their Śāktis alias arghyas made in stellate on the principal of intersecting two squares places diagonally and intersecting each other at angles of 45 degrees. These three Śaiva tāntric temples were built over a Buddhist establishment, because remains of Buddhistic images are still found in its compound.

J.D. Beglar visited this site in 1874-75 and has left a concise account of these temples thus: "Each of these temples stand by itself on a raised platform and each consists of a Cell and its attached portice only. The plan will show the minute recesses and angularities in plan, which produce so charming an effect in the variety of light and shade and confer an appearance of greater height from the continued cluster of vertical lines they really possess." Navagraha slabs are found in these temples. These are profusely ornamental, therefore Beglar had remarked that though small they are Gems of art in their humble way. These three Śaiva tāntric temples seems to have been built during the early period of Somavaṁśī rule in Orissa and had influenced in many features, the Mukteśvara temple at Bhubaneswar, where dream is realised in Standstone. With the influence of Somavaṁśī rule, new elements were added like pancharatha temples and in econography of Cult Deities in Coastal Orissa temple architecture and the addition of Ketu, to the planet slab became permanent and Navagraha slabs became an indispensable feature in later phases.

Khākharā type of temple is mentioned in Śilpa Śāstras of Orissa. This type of temple was meant specifically for the Śākta tāntric Goddesses. Khākharā means Pumpkin shaped or having the shape of a boat. The shape of the Khākharā variety of temple has a semi-cylindrical roof. This can be told Wagon-vault roof also, which seems to have been derived from the Caitya halls of the Buddhists. This order of temples were meant for Śākti worship, they are dark inside, as this variety of temples was specifically for Śākta tāntric practice or worship. The Sanctum of the Khākharā temple is intensely dark creating a grim atmosphere. The terrible dark atmosphere were suitable for esoteric practices. The seriousness of awful esoteric rites was heightened by the darkness of the main temple and by the presence of several terrific images.

The Khākharā-muṇḍi is a very common decorative motif on Orissan temples of both the Rekhā and Pīḍha orders. Because of the secret esoteric practices of Śākti tantra worship, selective places were chosen for constructing Khākharā temples. Hence this type of temples are not much found. Mention of Khākharā temples of Orissa, may be done serially thus:-

(1) Vaitāla temple at Bhubaneswar, is the best preserved and best

specimen of Khākharā order in Orissa. Its presiding Deity is Cāmuṇḍā associated with Saptamatrikās and images of some Yoginis. It has a rectangular jagamohan. It is assigned to Bhaumakara period, 8th century A.D.

(2) Varahi temple at Chaurasi stands with its sanctum and rectangular jagamohan. It is 27 feet high. The presiding deity is Varahi in colossal size, striking features and in good state of preservation. Varahi is two armed, holding a Skull in the left hand and fish in the right hand. She is seated in the lalitasana on the back of a buffalo. This temple is the sole surviving member of group of Seven temples in that region, each dedicated to one of the Matrikas. Each Matrika had separate temple and separate Cult of the seven Matrikas had developed round about Chaurasi. Of the pārśvadevatās, Sūrya on the west and Gaṇeśa in the south are still to be seen. The temple is later than the Paraśurameśvara temple (7th century A.D.) but seems earlier than the Mukteśvara temple (10th century A.D.).

(3) Mahiṣamardinī temple at Sergada is a Khākharā temple. Sergada in Baleswar district was a flourishing site containing the remains of many temples of Rekhā order and numerous images of Gaṇeśa, Kārtikeya, Sūrya, Pārvatī, Ajaikapāda, Gaṅgā, Yamunā, Viṣṇu, Vārāhi, Tārā and figures of Tirthaṅkaras. These indicate that there was fluorescence of Buddhism, Jainism, Vaiṣṇavism, Śaivism, Śāktism and Saura Cult.

The Mahiṣamardinī temple at Sergada is of Khākharā type and its Deity is eight-armed Mahiṣamardinī. This small temple is of 13 ft. in height with mastaka. The door jamb is richly decorated with scroll works and floral motifs and Gaja-Lakṣmī at the central part of the lintel. The Caitya window, which is detached from the temple contains a four-armed Śiva in lalitāsana, with his two-armed consort Umā, associated with their Vāhanas Bull and Lion. Saptamatrikas with Birabhadra and Gaṇeśa are also found in a panel. The temple is dated within 9th-10th century A.D.

(4) Khākharā style of Mahiṣamardinī Durgā temple stands at Baideśvar on Mahāṇadi in Cuttack district, very near the Singhanath temple of Baramba area. The temple is made of Khandalite stones. The presiding Deity of this temple is eight-handed Mahiṣamardinī which can be dated within 8th-9th century A.D. The niches of this temple contain images of eight-armed Mahiṣāmardinī, a two-armed female figure flanked by a female attendant, a two-armed Kārtikeya, four armed Gaṇeśa and four-armed Ajaikapāda Bhairava.

(5) Brahmaṇi temple at Avana is of Khākharā style. Avana is situated at a distance of 22 kms. to the south of Bahanaga railway station. In 1981, the N.S.S. Volunteers of Belabhumi college, Avana through excavation brought to light the entire structure of Brahmaṇi temple. The Brahmaṇi temple of Avana, is in dilapidated condition, made of laterite stone and is standing. It is about 12 ft. in height. The presiding Deity is locally known as Brahmaṇi and is a four-armed Cāmuṇḍā with Ḍambaru, Triśūla and a Bell in three of her hands, while the other is at the mouth, in biting position. Its body is skeleton like, with sunken belly, wide open mouth and drooping breasts. This temple faces west with a small passage, which gives dark atmosphere, suitable for esoteric practices.

(6) There is Caṇḍī temple at Kishorepur situated in Betnati Police station area of Mayurbhanj district. The Caṇḍī temple of this area is of Khākharā order. The presiding Deity is a ten armed Cāmuṇḍā seated in Mahārajalilasana pose, on the back of a prostrate male. From architectural view, this temple is very akin with the Gopālini and Śavitri Khākharā temples at Bhubaneswar. This temple is later than Vaital temple and can be dated to late 8th century A.D.

(7) Gaṅgeśvarī temple of Bayalisbati is situated near Gope in Puri district, is of Khākharā style and is about 34 feet in height. The presiding Deity of this sanctum known as Gaṅgeśvarī, has a crude head. The original image of this temple is worshipped at a distance of the village as Grāma Devī, which is a four-armed Mahiṣāsuramardinī. This four-handed Mahiṣāsuramardinī was probably the main Deity, enshrined in the Sanctum. This temple has a Jagamohana, built in fully developed pīḍha style, which can be dated to 13th century A.D. There are images of Śiva and Śākta (side) pantheons like Ajaikapāda, eight-armed Cāmuṇḍā, four-armed Mahiṣāsuramardinī and Varāhi in this temple.

(8) Small Durgā temple at Rameśvar in Cuttack district, which is of Khākharā style, on ground of style, it can be assigned to the period of Vaital temple at Bhubaneswar.

(9) Durgā temple at Baulapur, near Tapang of Puri district, is also of Khākharā style of temple architecture.

(10-13) Mention can be made of four more temples of Khākharā variety, found at Bhubaneswar. Gouri temple, Gopalini temple, Savitri shrine on the north of the Liṅgaraj temple compound and a miniature shrine; on the terrace in front of Mukteśvara temple.

(14-15) Two Khākharā temples are found at Ranipur-Jharial of Balangir district. Lahiri temple of Khākharā style stands towards the left of Someśvara Śiva temple and faces east. There is a miniature

Khākharā temple in front of Circular sixty-four Yogini temple, facing north. Both the Khākharā temples are made of stone and are empty of Deities.

(16) Triveniśvara temple at Madhipur, near Konarak was also of Khākharā style. The mastaka of this temple has been throughly restored, so that the original character can't be ascertained with certainty.

Few Khākharā temples are found outside Orissa also. Mention may be made of Barrel-vaulted Sanctuary, Bharhut (now kept in Indian Museum, Calcutta), Bhimaratha temple at Mahabalipuram, City-gateway of Sanchi, Monolithic Shrine now kept in the Mathura museum, Caṇḍikā temple, Nava Durgā temple, Kalipa temple and Pushti-Devī temple at Jagesvar. One temple of Khākharā style is found at Palace of Gwalior.

As more temples of Khākharā style of temples are found in Orissa, it can be said that Khākharā variety of temple architecture originated in Orissa, because in this region Sexo-Yogic tāntric practice called Vajroli developed and esoteric practical worship and practices were continuing. The Nātha Dharma was first founded in Orissa and its Religious Scriptures taught Vajroii (Spiritual practice of rechannelling Sexual energy), for which Uḍḍiyāna bandha (abdominal lock) is necessary. As Uḍḍiyāna was the territory located in Mahānadi river valley, it proves that eastern part of Madhya Pradesh, presently known as Chattisgarh and Orissa province areas made a great gift to Mankind by teaching the Yogic Vajroli i.e. Sexual transformation Yoga. The detail of Vajroli is found in "Haṭha-Yoga Pradipikā," and other Śākta Dharma Scriptures.

## YOGINI TEMPLES

Yogini worship basically is an integral part of the Śākta tāntric pantheon. With the influence of Purāṇas, mythology. Tāntric Buddhism and sectarian religions, there was growth of many Goddesses. According to H.C. Das, "The literature of the Vedic and post-Vedic period often mentions the name of Yoginis as manifestations of female principle. But Yoginis in the shape of a Śākta tāntric Cult came into existence in the 6th-7th century A.D. when the efflorescences of Śāktism, Tāntricism and Śaivism either in individual form or in combination swayed the religious realm of India. Whatever might be the time of origin of this Cult, it continued to flourish as an important manifestation of Śākta-tāntricism and the propitiators acquired magical and supernatural faculties, through the help of Yoginas with a view to the destruction of enemies. Through the process of transformation over the ages the Yoginis finally multiplying into sixty-four gained supremacy particularly in the eastern zone of India. Matsyendranatha in view of popularity of the Cult gained over the period, systematised and expounded it, in his famous work "Kaulayānanirṇaya," which has become the authoritative text of the Cult."

Matsyendranātha was born at Chandhali-Dhamra area of Orissa. He was the founder of Nātha Dharma and equally he can be claimed as the propounder of Sixty-four Yogini Cult from Orissa, which spread to other parts of India and abroad gradually. The lists of Yoginis are found in Kālikā purāṇa, Skanda purāṇa, Bṛhada-Nandikeśvara Purāṇokta Durgāpūjā Paddhati, Caunsaṭha Yogini Nāmāvali, Caṇḍī purāṇa or Caṇḍī Yudha by Sāralādāsa of Orissa. Durgā pūjā (a palmleaf manuscript, Orissa State Museum, Dh.No. 345, folio 22-23) and Briha Nila Tantra.

Nine Yogini temples are discovered so far; distributed in Orissa, Madhya Pradesh, Uttar Pradesh and in Coimbatore district of Tamil Nadu. Of these five were discovered before 1875 A.D. by foreign archaeologists-Cunningham, Beglar and Col. Macferson. Bherāghat and Khajurāho in Madhya Pradesh, Ranipur-Jharial in Orissa and Coimbatore in the south. The remains of other five Yogini temples are found at Shahdol in Madhya Pradesh (images now preserved in the Dhubela museum in Chhatrapur district), at Mitauli and Dudahi in Lalitpur district of Uttar Pradesh and at Hirapur near Bhubaneswar in Orissa, discovered by Kedarnath Mahapatra. All these temples except that at Khajurāho are hypaethral in appearance and are open to the Sky. The Caushat-Yogini temple at Khajurāho is rectangular and open to sky.

It may be mentioned that there was a Caushat-Yogini temple at Suruda in Kalahandi district (The Indian Antiquary-A Journal of Oriental Research, 1878 A.D.), which was noticed by Major General John Campbell on 28th January 1853. This Yogini temple was in a very deplorable dilapidated condition, when Campbell saw it, as known from Campbell's "Operations in the Hill Tracts of Orissa, printed for private circulation (London, Hurst and Blarkett, 1861)." It is unfortunate that no effort has yet been made to survey SURUDA village area of Madanpur-Rampur area in Kalahandi district of Orissa, so far.

Two Caushat-Yogini temples have been known so far in Orissa and they are at Ranipur-Jharial and Hirapur. Mystic esoteric Tāntric worship and practices were going on these Yogini temples as systematised by Matsyendranāth. According to "Haṭha Yoga Pradipika," a Yogini is one who practises Vajroli. In Chapter 3, verse 99 of the same text, it mentions,

"If a Woman practises Vajroli and saves her rajas and the man's bindu by thorough contraction, She is a Yogini." This proves that the Yoga of transforming the Sexual energy to rise of Kuṇḍalini was very popular in Mahāṇadi river valley, through Yogini Cult. Kuṇḍalini is the name of a sleeping dormant potential force in the Human organism and it is situated at the root of the spinal column. In the masculine body it is in the perineum, between the urinary and excretory organs. In the female body its location is at the root of the uterus, in cervix. This centre is known as Moolādhara Cakra.

## SCULPTURAL ART

Recent excavation carried out by Orissa State Archaeology department at Chandan Mahal mound of Maraguda valley in Nuapada district has exposed a huge Śiva Liṅga and an inscribed stone slab. The inscription is a Śaiva Mantra on a fragmentary slab and the letters are of 4th century A.D. in Gupta character. So, it can be claimed that the earliest inscribed Śiva temple of Orissa, is found at Maraguda valley.

The Naṭarāja image of Asanapat dated within 5th-6th century A.D. may be the earliest image of Naṭarāja in Orissa. This Naṭarāja has Ūrdhva-liṅga (penis erectus), because Lord Śiva is the Master of Yoga in Vedic tradition and he never ejaculates. He is regarded to be in Vajroli Haṭha Yoga always, in perpetual Samādhi. Haṭha Yoga is the means for Rāja-yoga, the highest state of Yoga. Once a Sadhaka of Haṭha Yoga reaches the stage of Raja-yoga, Haṭha-yoga ceases to be necessary for that individual.

Siṁhanātha temple is located in an island of river Mahāṇadi in the ex-state of Baramba. An interesting relief of this temple depicts the Liṅgodbhavamūrtti. Śiva is said to have appeared in the form of a blazing pillar of immeasurable size to quell the pride of Brahmā and Viṣṇu. This story is almost identically given in the Liṅga purāṇa, the Kumra purāṇa, Vāyu purāṇa and Śiva purāṇa.

In Sitabinji of Keonjhar district the Liṅgadbhava form of image which is locally called Mukhaliṅga is also found. These show the early popularity of Śiva Liṅga worship.

A series of temples were constructed in Orissa from the 8th to 13th century A.D., the most important of them being Paraśurāmeśvara (750 A.D.), Mukteśvar (950 A.D.), Liṅgarāja (1000 A.D.) and Rājārāṇi (1150 A.D.) at Bhubaneswar. The Jagannāth temple of Puri (12th century A.D.) and the gigantic sun temple at Konarak (13th century A.D.).

With the arrival of the boroque C.L.Fabri states, mannerism has been left behind, and in these magnificent works of art, among the best in India, the artist turns to that full luscious romanticism that boroque means, rich, ornate, lush, a delight in excess, a love of profusion and multiplication, a passion for the beauty of the female form, a sensuous delight in the loveliness of the World.

Before dealing with the Sculptural tāntric art of Orissa, it is worth knowing the comments of Charles Louis Fabri that there has never been a copyist in this country (Orissa), never a mere immitation of other master's work. I know of no artist of ancient Orissa whoever followed Śilpaśāstras. K.C. Panigrahi had also stated that in fact Orissan Sculptures particularly the Hindu icons seldom conform to the peculiarities and descriptions given by the Tāntric texts. This shows that Orissan artists and sculptors followed the instructions of the maker of temples more than the texts.

Sculpture of a Tāntric seated Yogi wearing a Yogapaṭṭa is found on a Caitya niche, on the jagamohana of Paraśurāmeśvara temple of Bhubaneswar. He is bearded, has matted hair and holds a rosary. Few images of Gaṇeśa wearing Yogapaṭṭa are found from Bhubaneswar and exhibited at Orissa State Museum.

The Sculptural Tāntric scene of hair cutting ritual in association with copulation is found at Bhubaneswar, Puri, Koṇark and Ratnagiri.

In tradition of Sculptures in Orissa, mention may be made of decorative female figures, secular scenes with figures, animal figures, decorative motifs like Kirttimukha, Chaitya window and scroll works. Even bestiality is depicted. Cult images are found in plenty. The most remarkable are the Erotic figures.

The erotic depictions of India are of many types and they are classified by Devangana Desai thus:-

I–A. A man with two partners.
I–B. Two men with one woman in subdued relationship.
II–A. A man with two -women in sexual relationship.
II–B. Two men having sexual relation with one woman.
III–A. Attendants present near an amorous non-coital couple.
III–B. Attendants present near a copulating couple.
III–C. Attendants helping the copulating couple.
III–D. One of the partners while copulating touching the sexual parts of the attendents—who are also shown in excited conditions—with their own hands on the sexual parts.

IV–A. A man in company of many women.
IV–B. Many men in sexual relationship with one woman.
V. Many men and women in a promiscuous orgy.
VI. A number of couples simultaneously involved in sexual relations.

In Orissa specially III-C variety are represented. Devangana Desai concludes by remarking. "Our study of Sexual representation in Indian Culture convinces us that there is no philosophical or rational motivation behind it. Its presence in religious art is a pointer to the continuity and persistence of primitive and popular cultural elements in a Civilized Society. Far from being an anomaly in Hindu culture, erotic motifs were in harmony with the religious environment to which they belonged and with the majestic courtly and artistic temples they decorated. They were alaṅkāras."

All the erotic depictions mentioned are not related to Tāntrism, only few are. Most of the varieties show erotic sports (Krida).

Divergent views are held by critics about erotic sculptures. But, it shouldn't be forgotten that during Tantra period, the philosophy of Bhoga as Yoga was not an easy path. The Hindu temples are no idle work of idle hands. The temples were made in the shape of a Human body, representing symbolically the Cosmic Body or the Universe. It is, as a microcosm, a replica, of every detail of the macrocosm or the Universe. So, every detail of human life and its influence are given.

In the words of Kanwar Lal, "Finally, we have the view that this union of man and woman is symbolic of the union of the individual Soul and God, that this completes the circle beginning with the point when one was divided into two, male and female, to afford Him delight through reunion later; or to create the vale of illusion, to beguile us into a sense of duality though, in fact, man and woman were not two separate beings but were essentially one. And this Buddhist, who had at one time seen a conflict between Saṁsāra and Nirvāṇa, between Sex and Salvation, was now, like the Hindu who had earlier created the antithesis of Yoga and Sex, equating these two as identical. Though the high reaches of philosophy and subtle and intricate reasoning and theorization, the Hindus as well as the Buddhist had brought about a total reversal, and regarded Kāma no longer as an enemy but as the instrument and vehicle of our Salvation. These new philosophies offered liberation, not through sorrow and suffering and hard penance, but through enjoyment, through Mahāsukha, through Bliss which had the nature and character of God himself. Many were the ways and we find Śākti pūjā and Sahajayāna and the Vajrayāna and all the Tāntric schools putting forth seemingly different views and practices, but basically all these religious and philosophies were aimed at the synthesis of elements which were earlier regarded as opposites and as antithetic."

Through Sexo-yogic practice of Yoga called Vajroli, sex ceased to be an obstacle; woman ceased to be a hindrance. While practicing Vajroli each man is Śiva and each woman Pārvatī, because all are engaged in the Cosmic romance where Kāma (desire) is no longer an enemy but is an ally. Therefore Umā-Maheśvara image signifies Śiva Lata Mudrā.

Robert E.Svoboda and his teacher (Guru) Vimalānanda define Śivalata mudrā thus : "When a man and a woman come together for Śivalata mudrā the woman must sit on the man's left thigh and hold his penis with her right hand. He must cup her left breast with his left hand. Like a creeper She drapes herself around him, clinging tightly like a delicate vine; and he permits himself to be clung to, offering her support.

"There are three types of Śivalata mudrā : Mundane, Spiritual and one which is beyond both the mundane and the Spiritual. The mundane gives maximum sexual excitement, the Spiritual is for Sadhana and "beyond" is to advanced to be dealt with here. In all types the female counts japa with her left hand, the male with his right. The Mantras are specific for each type. He forgets who he is, and she forgets who she is. He thinks, "I am Lord Śiva, my Bhairavi." She thinks, "This is my Lord Śiva and I am his Grand consort, His Bhairavi (the Fearful Goddess)."

"If the couple is doing it for mundane purposes they must concentrate on exciting each other. Without realizing it She will begin to breathe through her left nostril and will direct that Śākti to him. His right nostril will be working and that Śākti of his will be directed to her. Hypersecretion of all the glands will result, and at the moment of greatest excitation cessation of breathing occurs for a moment. Then the male mounts and discharges his semen convulsively. Because of hypersecretion he will now eject three teaspoonsful of semen as opposed to his normal one teaspoonful. Because the vagina and cervix have become utterly loose and dilated the sperm will go directly to the mount of the cervix. The result is a child, if this is done at the right time of the month. This is the Brahmacharya appropriate to the ordinary householder because by such sex, satiation occurs for a month or more and ojas is not wasted by frequent orgasms.

"The Spiritual Śivalata Mudrā is quite different. The Śiva must control his Śākti very carefully to ensure that She does not become sexually excited. The couple should be able to sit together for atleast three hours without the least excitation, not twitching or oozing. The girl must understand that She will not get an ordinary orgasm this way. If she waits patiently She will eventually get a super orgasm which will make her forget Sex for ever. If this Mudrā is done properly She will go into Bhava-Samādhi. Her emotions will cresceade until her mind becomes totally one pointed, directed towards Śiva, and She will partly forget her Worldly existence for a while. Even Mahābhava Samādhi, which I call emotional highlights, is possible - total immersion in Śiva but with retained awareness of the Bliss, Wonderful!"

Śivalata Mudrā is meant for the expert one in Vajroli. The best carved Umā- Maheśvara or Hara-Pārvatī of Orissa with ūrdhva liṅga (penis erectus), is found at Khiching museum, in Mayurbhanj district.

A rare image of Umā-Maheśvara is found, seated on a lotus, in the Jagamohana of Megheśvara temple of Bhubaneswar, which is dated to 12th century A.D It is Sukhāsana mūrti of Hara-Parvattī, Hara-Gaurī, Śiva-Pārvatī or Umā-Maheśvara, as variously known. Maheśvara alias Śiva is having three heads and six hands. The three right hands shows varadā, japamāla and kuṭhāra, while the three left hands hold a lotus, embraces Umā by touching her left breast and the third left hand is not clearly visible. Umā is seated on the left lap of Śiva, with her right hand encircling the neck of the Lord and her left hand holds a lotus. This art shows celestial contentment in eternal sport (krida) with mascular treatment of Śiva and graceful faminine expression of Umā alias Pārvatī. Such images are meant for Tāntric worshippers of Tripurasundari, another name of Pārvatī. The Sadhakas meditate on the Śākti seated on the lap of Śiva and this helps them in Dhyānayoga.

Mostly the temples are blemished with master pieces of loving couples, lovely ladies, sura-sundaries, nāyikās, alasa-kanyās, maithunas, acrobatic maithunas, erotic scenes, fellātio scenes and amorous figures.

Oral congress or fellātio scene are plenty on temple walls. For those who can't conquest temptation and are unable to do Vajroli, Rajapana is recommended. While illustrating "The Yoni Tantra," J.A.Schoterman mentions, "The consuming of the Yonitattva, whether symbolically or actually performed, has not been accounted for in the Yonitantra. The concept which it is based, however, we can learn from other sources dealing with the same subject. The Bindu is the cause (mūla) of the human body (Gorakṣaśataka. 68), it is two-fold; pale-white (pūṇḍara) and blood red (lohita); the former being the semen virile, the latter the menstrual fluids (Gorakṣaśataka, 72). The two are identified with Śiva/ Candra and Śākti/Sūrya respectively (Gorakṣasataka 73, 74, Śivasaṁhitā IV, 58, 59). Uniting these two, the Sādhaka attains the highest state (Gorakṣaśataka 74).

Since the Bindu is the root of the body it is essential to keep it in the body (Śivasaṁhitā IV, 58), by loss of the Bindu death is inevitable, but by preserving it the Sādhaka overcomes death (Gorakṣaśataka 70, Śivasaṁhitā IV, 61, Haṭhayoga Pradipikā III, 87). In this context may be placed Yoni Tantra I, Sab : ahaṁ mṛtyuṁjayo devi tava Yoni prasādataḥ. The place of origin of the Bindu is believed to be situated above the throat, from where it comes down. To keep the Bindu in his body, the Sādhaka closes the aperture above his throat by means of the Khecarimudrā thus preventing the Bindu from going downwards (Gorakṣaśataka 69). In the Yoni tantra no mention is made of this Khecarimudrā. Here the Bindu is kept in the body by simply consuming it when discharged."

Sculptural art of Aṣṭakāmakalāpryoga (eight - phased copulation) or eight erotic composite reliefs are carved in the top sections of the vertical outer flat ribs of Vārāhi temple at Chaurasi. These Sensual figures seems to be associated with Śākta tantra ritual. These eight modes or phases of Love-making are referred to in an unedited Tāntric text in Sanskrit language, which is written in Oriya script, (vide : V.V.Mirashi Felicitation Volume, passim.), and are : (1) Vaśikaraṇa (bringing the maiden under control), (2) Sammohana (enchanting her), (3) Ākarṣaṇa and Uccāṭana (attracting and preparing her for the Sex act), (4) Vāyu-visheka (consecration of the female organ), (5) Purascaraṇa (preliminary stage of the act), (6) Rajapāna (drinking of the raja), (7) Prastāva (proposal) and (8) Nivṛiti (return to the normal state).

Tortoises are chiseled in a line, on the stone basement of Śiva temple at Mohangiri, in Kalahandi district, which was in flourishing state during 10th century A.D. At this site of the dilapidated Śiva temple of Mohangiri, two small inscriptions are found. One is of Sphita Candra who belonged to Mudgalakula and the other of Vyadha Bhairava, who was probably the presiding Deity. The reference of Vyadha Bhairava shows this site to have been a Śaiva tāntric site. The Sādhakas of this area seems to have been expert in Vajroli as Tortoises are chiseled at this site. In Vajroli Spiritual practice for Spiritual illumination, the Sādhaka should contract and draw back the penis into the abdomen, as Tortoise contracts its head, neck and legs inside its Shell. By doing this contracting Haṭha

Yoga, one can make one's semen flow upwards, when it is about to ejaculate. So, Tortoise symbolizes Vajroli.

One of the most handsome faces of Women ever sculptured in Orissa is to be found in one of the dancing figures of the second tier of Koṇārka temple. Robust erotic sculptures of Koṇārka, shows the exuding energy, which the Sun personifies, with aura of splendour and the body vibrate with tremendous zest and desire to receive greater satisfaction and deeper aesthetic pleasure, which can be achieved through Vajroli. The celerated Sun temple of Koṇārk is the noble conception which represents the crystallised and accumulated experience of several hundreds of years and expresses the fulfilment and finality of Orissan temple architecture and sculptural art.

Thus, it can be said that the erotic sculptures are the secret language, in some code doctrines and instructions and symbolic representation of high Tāntric Yoga philosophy which shows that the manifest World is merely the result of the love - play of God Śiva and the Goddess Pārvatī.

There are minor references of Haṭha Yoga in the Upaniṣhads. Therefore it can be said that the Science of Haṭhayoga was known in India, since remote past. Traces of Haṭhayoga has been found in pre-Colombian culture of America. There are large stone sculptures and images depicting Indian Haṭha Yoga practices at St. Augustine, a southern province of Colombia in South America. These show that Yogis of India had travelled abroad and had spread Indian Yoga throughout the Old World. Their influence was felt in Persia, Afghanisthan, entire Middle and Far east and all over India, Nepal and Ṣri Laṅka.

In the medieval period there was total movement of Tāntric Haṭha Yoga. The erotic sculptures give satisfaction and deeper aesthetic pleasure, for individual to rise, awake and wait not till Self - realization goal is not reached. It is not the fault of the Great Masters of Tantra that the mundane World has forgotten their teaching. Rise and Fall is the history of Mankind. Many Tantras and Śāstras of India have been lost and forgotten for thousands of years. Now the period of revival has come. Therefore an American Scholar Grace E. Cairns has realised that the erotic and maithuna arts on temple architecture are given for reintegraton and states, "The Couples in delliance represent the reunion, the reintegration of the Soul with the Divine. Such erotic imagery is common in Tāntric literature." G.E. Cairns gives the summary of Macro - Microcosmic Symbolism in the Hindu temple thus : "The Vāstupuruṣa of the Vāstupuruṣamaṇḍala, the ground plan of the building, is the Mahāpuruṣa analogous to the Agni - Prajapāti of the Vedic Fire - Altar.

As in the Fire - Altar rite, the Yajamāna identifies himself as microcosm with the Mahāpuruṣa which represets the pattern of the macrocosm that includes all the regions of space with their contents and all Time including the Kalpas. The Brahmaṣthāna in the center, points the Yogin to the ultimate Reality, just as in the microcosm the God - Consciousness in man's "Center," the heart, is source of man's desire for oneness with the Divine.

"In the Superstructure of the temple, the Garbhagṛha, the Golden Germ (Hiraṇyagarbha) is the base of the central axis directly over the Brahmāṣthāna (symbolically, if not actually). F.D.K. Bosch calls the Hiraṇyagarbha "the germ and Womb of all that lives — and it is filled with the golden exlixir of life." This golden elixir is amṛta, the nector of immortality, another symbol of the aspirant's quest. From the Golden Germ rises the entire macrocosm, the Universe with its central axis, symbol of the axis mundi, the Mt. Meru of the temple. In the individual, the microcosm, the corresponding "axis" is the Suṣammā of Tāntric Yoga. In the macrocosm, this axis rises from earth through the atmospheric heaven to the Āmalaka, then piercing it, becomes the finial that symbolically goes beyond the space - time Worlds after passing through heavenly lokas. At the point - tip of the finial is, symbolically, the one, Brāhman. In the individual, the microcosm, a similar journey is experienced in Tāntric yoga, in the ascent from the Muladhara whose tattva is "earth" through the hierarchy of the lower and higher heavens to the Sahasrāra which corresponds with the Āmalaka of the temple to culminate to the experience which pierces or transcends all time categories to attain oneness with the non - dual Brahman. This ascent of the Cakras is analogous to the similar Spiritual journey up to the finial of the temple that symbolically pierces into the eternal realm.

"Whether or not he has practised Kuṇḍalini Yoga, the devotee initiated into the meaning of the plan (the Vāstupuruṣa - maṇḍala) and super - structure of the Hindu temple can, in Pradakṣiṇa, meditate upon its significance as monumental symbol which, as representation of the macrocosmic Universe, manifests all the aspects of Man's the microcosm's, situation and ultimate destiny, i.e. Oneness with the Ultimate Reality."

## PAINTING

Orissa has a long tradition of fresco and mural paintings. Pre-historic rock shelter murals are found at Gudahandi in Kalahandi district,

Yogimath and Ghat Ghumar in Nuapada district, Manikmada; Ushakothi and several paintings in Sundargar and Ulapgarh and Vikramkhol in Jharsaguda district. Twenty-eight rock art sites are documented so far. The district of Sundargarh alone accounts for more than three-fourth of the rock art sites of Orissa province. A host of twelve rock shelters bear the name Lekhamada in Sundargarh district. It is interesting to note that the painted rock-shelters are known locally by various terms like Lekhamada, meaning (Lekha = writing and mada = rock-shelter), Ushakothi meaning (Usha = worship and Kothi = hall) and newly discovered Ushakupa ( Usha = worship and Kupa = cavity ) etc. All the Rock-shelter paintings are not yet documented. A painting of Gupta period is found on the Ceiling of a Cave at Sitābinji in Keonjhar district, which has excellence like Ajanta paintings.

There are tradition of paintings in Temples, Maṭhas, Palaces, in Paṭṭa paintings and Palm-leaf etching with painting.

The mural painting in the Jagamohana of Lakṣmī temple inside the Jagannāth temple compound at Puri, depicts the topics of art heritage of painting in Orissa. Nṛsiṁha, Pañcamukha Gaṇeśa, Rāmānuja, Hanumāna and Buddha Vijaya or Victory of Brahmaṇism over Buddhism are found there.

The topic Kāñcivijaya, where two horse riders Jagannātha and Balabhadra buy curd from Māṇika is very popular in Orissa painting and is depicted inside the Jagannāth temple of Puri. The painting of Tāntric topic is the painting of the Dasa-mahavidya or the ten aspects of Goddess Durgā in the Jagamohana of Vimalā temple, inside the compound of Jagannāth temple at Puri.

In the Patta painting of Puri; Jagannātha, Balabhadra and Subhadrā are represented in their Bhairava aspects, which is known as "Aasara Paṭṭi," different from the shape in which they are daily worshipped.

The mural paintings of Biranchi Narayan temple at Buguda in Ganjam district, depicts various episodes of the life of Rāma, Kṛṣṇa and Ten incarnations of Viṣṇu.

Orissa painting with its miniatures have a style of its own. Women are painted with full bosoms, large buttocks and slender waists like the fine chiselled sculptures of the Sun temple at Koṇark. In the earlier paintings Women were shown with bare breasts and Sari has come into use from 19th century onwards.

There are numerous illustrations of palm-leaf manuscripts in which incized with an iron stylus, pure lineworks and paintings are found.

In palm-leave manuscripts of Gītagovinda, composed by Jayadeva,

Rādhā and Kṛṣṇa in amorous love and sex play are found. More prominent palm-leave manuscripts are "Bidagha Mādhava," of Rūpa Gosvāmī, "Amaru Śataka," of Amaruka," "Uṣābhilasa," of Śiśhu Śaṅkara Dasa and "Causaṭhi Ratibandha;" of Gopāla Bhañja. The themes of these manuscripts are mostly love episodes of Rādhā and Kṛṣṇa with legendary and mythical narrations. Even in "Chitrakavya-bandhodaya," of Kavi Samrāta Upendra Bhañja plam-leave manuscripts, fine etching and painting of lovers are found. In "Pañcaśāyaka," of Kavi Samrāta Upendra Bhañja, sixty-four Sex poses are described. Gopāla Bhañja has written "Pañchaśāyaka," and "Causaṭhi - rati - bandha," where all the sixty-four Sex poses are described and depicted in etching with painting.

The Orissa artists have been able to depict the variety of emotions, romantic love, beauty of young lovers with great details in plam-leave etching. Daśa - Mahāvidyā are painted in Palm-leaves also. The most popular theme of painting is Kṛṣṇa stealing the dresses of eight Gopis, whilst they are bathing in the Yamunā river.

In a palmleave manuscript preserved in Utkal University Library, Dhyāna mantras, figures of Tāntric Deities and human figures in amorous Tāntric Sex - practices are found. God Śulāpāṇi is described as indulging in drinking. Goddess Mañjughoṣa is described as naked and sitting on Lord Śiva in reverse or viparita ratibandha. This depicts Vajroli. Gaṇeśa is also depicted here in Sexual intercourse with his Śākti.

All these sexual paintings are with Tāntric influence, which signify Vajroli i.e. Sexual transformation. In modern etching and painting of palmleaf, composite figures of Śiva and his consort Śākti as Ardhanāriśvara, Mahiṣāmardinī Durgā and traditional topics are still continuing in Orissa.

The playing of Ganjapa Cards made out of palm leaves and paṭṭas, is still continuing at Puri and Sonepur areas. Ganjapa cards have their identical stylistic art and some of them are erotic paintings. Charles Losis Fabri had remarked, "I have watched present day artisans at work and was astonished to see how these readymade formulae are employed with an almost unbelievable rapidity, the stylus running with utmost ease to form every eye - always the same every nose - always the same; every chin - all the same; and every limb - in whatever position, always identically drawn, with the same, few economic and sweeping lines."

Three Schools of paintings namely Ganjam or Dakshina, Puri and Champamal are still continuing in Orissa. Sonepur and Sambalpur are the areas where Champamal School prevails.

## WOODEN ART

There is ancient tradition of Indian buildings and temples to have been built in timber. There are always reference of wooden architectures and temples in Indian art history, but seldom Wooden works are found.

In Orissa, wooden arts are at the Maṇḍapa or open pavilion in front of Kapileśvara temple at Puruṣhottampur in Ganjam district and the timber temple of Birañchi - Nārāyaṇa at Buguda in Ganjam district. These Wooden constructions are not very old and can be dated within 19th century A.D.

The carved timber roof with Gaja - Lakṣmī, a frieze of Geese, lotus, floral decorations with peacock and details are fine wooden works in the wooden maṇḍapa of Kapileśvara temple. The entire wall, the door and the entire maṇḍapa of Viranchi - Nārāyaṇa temple at Buguda are made of carved Wood.

Wooden art can be found at Aul, in Kendrapada district. Lot of erotic figures in sex positions are carved on the wooden door of the main gate, in Varāha temple at Aul. The Varāha image was brought from Jajpur and a temple was built for the Deity, by Raja Jadunath Deb of Aul, whose ruling period was within 1887 - 1900 A.D. So, this erotic Wooden art is of 19th century A.D. The continuous making of erotic art in Temple architectures, which developed with the influence of Vajroli Sādhanā of Tāntricism, in early medieval period, still continues, but its real significance is forgotten. In moern period as revival of everything fine is continuing, it is hoped that the importance of Erotic Art is realised by every one.

Wooden relieve works are discovered by the author at Bamanpara village of Sinapali Block, Nuapada district. On 17th October 1992, the author visited Bamanpara. The Jagannāth temple of Bamanpar is of mud and teak wood construction, with local titles (Khapara) roof.

The Deity installed is single Jagannāth. The temple consists of a raised basement of mud, forming a rectangular base measuring 40 ft. by 20 ft. and height 1 meter 28 cm. Over the mud basement, there were 19 Wooden pillars of teak wood, which hold the roof. Over each wooden pillar, one relieve teak Wood Image was fixed. Many of these relieve Wooden figures have decayed, fallen from their fixation and destroyed. It is informed that an ancestor of Trilochan Majhi of Bamanpara village had built this temple by employing a Wooden art Carpenter of Ganjam district, during the period of Raja Padman Singh of Khariar, whose reigning period was within 1867 - 1889 A.D. So, the relieve wooden arts are of 19th century A.D.

Upendra Dhakul of Bamanpara - Kotamal village informed the author that among the relieve Wooden Images, one relieve work teak wood, was one female image giving birth to a baby in standing position. After it fell down from its fixation, it was floated in water of Udanti river. This shows that the idea of the creative functioning of the Mother - Goddess and mustticism of Tantra was known to the artist, who made it and the maker of this Jagannātha temple, in the interior of Western Orissa. Wooden art in small quantity are still continuing among the artists of Ganjam and Puri districts in Orissa.

Chapter V

# Tāntric Yoga of Sexual Transformation was Re-Discovered in Orissa, which is the Land of Kāmakalā

The earliest trace of Yoga can be traced at Pre-historic rock shelter painting of Yogīmath donger (hill), discovered by the author on 21st December 1970, at the left valley of Sundar river,[1] within Nuapada district of Orissa. This painting of bulls, triangles, rings and triple lines (trinity) are interesting. This painting of neolithic period,[2] speaks about prevalence of Phallism and the first trinity conception of Cosmic life, by a Yogi. Sadasiba Pradhan[3] reports about the usual depictions of the triangular female genitals at Vikramkhol rock art and the carvings of female genitals of varied shape and size with natural or carved holes and slits that predominate the engraved forms in the rock shelters baffle all interpretation, in Sundargarh district of Orissa.

Yoga is the media for becoming awakened or realised. Yoga is usually defined as union. It is the union between limited Self (Jiva) and the Cosmic Self (Atman). As separation develops because of Maya (illusion), there should be an aim or goal of Union. In fact, the separation does not exist. The aim of Yoga is to unite a human being with Cosmic consciousness, i.e. from limited Self consciousness with greater Self consciousness. So Yoga is the path to perfection.

The meaning of Yoga can also be denoted by the words unity and oneness, because the practice of Yoga aims at rooting out the ego. Once the ego is transcended, the individual realises one's inner, real nature. This definition of Yoga is a Spiritual one. Yoga therefore brings harmony between thoughts, words and deeds.

The Classical Yogic writer Rishi Patanjali in his "Yoga Sutras," defines Yoga as, "Complete control over the different patterns or modifications of consciousness."

In the words of Swami Śivananda,[4] "Yoga is for all. Yoga is Universal.

It is not a sectarian affair. It is a way to God and not a Creed.

"The practice of Yoga is not opposed to any religion or any sacred Church. It is purely Spiritual and Universal. It does not contradict any one's sincere faith.

"Yoga is not a religion, but an aid to the practice of the basic Spiritual truths in all religions. Yoga can be practised by a Christian or a Buddhist, a Parsee, a Mohammedan, a Sufi or an atheists.

"To be a Yogin, means to abide continuously in God and to live at peace with man. Yoga is union with God. Yoga is union with all. God dwells in all."

The definition of Yoga can be little different for each practitioner, because each one can relete one's Yogic experience and hence explain them in different manners or ways. But one thing is certain that Yoga is concerned with very core of human lives i.e. body, mind and consciousness.

Yoga was slowly evolved and developed by the ancient Sages, throughout the World. From Harappa and Mohenjodaro sites of Sindhu valley civilization, various statues and antiquities are discovered, which depict people practicing Yoga. The most amous among these findings is the Paśupati figure of Śiva, in Yoga posture, found at Mohenjodaro.

Yoga developed and came to be preserved in India, through Master (Guru) and disciple tradition. According to Vedic culture, Śiva is the great Gos, Mahādeva. He is the immortal Divine principle who has entered the mortal beings. He is known as the death conquering Deity, Mriṭyunjaya. He incarnates in matter and comes within the orbit of individual experience.[5] Śiva is the Lord of Yoga, Yogeśvara, who remains in eternal Samādhi or in union with his own Self, that is, a state of eternal illumination and unbroken meditation. In Yoga tradition, he is the Deity of the thousand-petalled lotus which is the mind. Therefore Śiva is the presiding Deity of the mind.

The word "Yoga," is mentioned in many places of the Rigveda. With the advent of the Brahmanas and Upanishads of the Vedas, the Yoga took shape and assumed the form, which we find today. The essential message of the Upanishads is that the Self can only be known through union (Yoga) and certainly not by mere speculation and learning. Kaṭha Upanishad says that the path is as narrow as the razor's edge. For the first time, a sitting pose, suitable for meditational practice is mentioned in Swetasvatara Upanishad of Yajurveda and the first Tāntric literature is found in "Nrisinhata-paniyopanishad," of the Atharva Veda. R.P. Mishra[6] informs that Brihadāranyaka Upanisada symbolises Woman as a medium of sacrifice, her lap as sacrificial altar, her hairs as sacrificial grass, her skin as Soma - Press and Copulation as the act of sacrifice. It proclaims a series of rules and advises its followers to observe them unmistakably for a choicible progeny. Chhāndogya Upanisad illustrates Woman as sacrificial fire and the generative organ as fuels. This proves that the Yoga of Sexual transformation was known to the Vedic Rishies. But somehow the other, this Yoga was forgotten and re-discovered in Mahāṇadi river valley. Therefore the earliest eight-handed Nataraja images with Ūrdhva-liṅga (penis erectus) of India are found at Sirpur dated to 5th century A.D. on the right bank of Mahāṇadi river[7], and at Asanapat, in Keonjhar district of Orissa, dated to 6th century A.D.

The text "Yoga Vashishtha," is regarded as the direct off-shoot and continuation of Ramayaṇa. Mahābharata has passages directly related to Yoga. "Bhagavat Gīta," is regarded as a Yogic scripture par excellence.

Rishi Patanjali wrote the text "Yoga Sutras," during 2nd century B.C.[8] and foundation of Yoga was laid thereby. The single point that has been emphasized in Yoga - is to be aware. "Be aware," and develop consciousness. Karma yoga, Jñāna yoga, Haṭha yoga, Raja yoga, Mantra yoga and Laya yoga are illustrated in the above mentioned literatures. Karma yoga is the yoga of action, Jñana yoga is the yoga of Knowledge and Wisdom. Haṭha Yoga is the yoga of attaining physical and mental purity. Raja yoga is the yoga of awakening the psychic awareness and faculties. Mantra yoga is the yoga of freeing the mind by utilizing a sound vibration and Laya yoga is the yoga of conscious dissolution of individuality. Suprabhedagama portray's God Śiva as master in various arts such as dancing, playing on musical instruments, expounding the Śāstras, as also in the practice of Yoga.[9]

Tantra had pre-historic origin, and its details are lost in mystery. From 5th century A.D. or thereabout Tantra[10] as a special religious philosophy came into use in India. With the influence of Tāntric practices, Haṭha yoga and Kriya yoga developed. Kriya yoga is interested in developing awareness than concentration. Haṭha yoga is interested in developing awareness than concentration. Haṭha yoga prescribes ASANAS (poses) for keeping the human body fit. Large number of Haṭha yoga texts were written in medieval period of Indian history. The most well known among these are "Haṭha Yoga Pradipikā," "Śiva Saṁhita" and "Gherand Saṁhitā." With this background of Yoga, it is worth knowing the use of the word "MAHA". According to Vedic etyology[11] "MAHA," means Great, exalted, wealth, the Sun, cattle, from the root "Mah," to respect, esteem and worship. According to Gopal Chandra Praharaj,[12] "Maha" means Vedic sacrifice or oblation, lusture, radiance etc. It is already mentioned that Śiva is the Great God, Mahādeva. The authorship of the Tantras, is attributed to the Lord Śiva alias Mahādeva. The main river of Orissa province in India, i.e. Bharata is Mahāṇadi. Therefore it seems that Mahāṇadi river valley is associated with Śaiva tantra and the tāntric religious eclecticism, which developed finally.

History is still unable to find out the original Siddhānta taught by Mahādeva alias Maheśvara. The Śaiva tāntric Rishis and Yogīs, from their intuitive knowledge could visualise that in Kāli age people will become SEXY, SEXY and SEXY. Therefore they laboured to discover a Yogic process to transfer the Sexual energy to Self-realization. At last the Śaiva tāntric masters alias Yogis of Mattamayūra tāntric Śaivism discovered Yogis Spiritual practice of rechannelling Sexual energy, which was named as "VAJROLI," later.[13] Vajroli mudra[14] consists of "Thunderbolt attitude," in which the muscles of the male sexual organ and lower urinary tract are contracted, redirecting Sexual energy upwards. It is a practice of Haṭha yoga and tantra. Because of Vajroli tāntric yoga and its iconographic details Śiva images with Ūrdhva-liṅga (penis erectus) were made. It seems the practice of Vajroli first developed in Vedic age and was subsequently forgotten. It was re-discovered and became methodical and systematic in Mahāṇadi river valley, i.e. Orissa province, which consists parts of Kaliṅga, Utkala and South Kōśala states of ancient and medieval periods, where Uḍḍiyāna tāntric pīṭha (site) existed, because one of the earliest inscribed Naṭāraja image of India, is Naṭāraja Śiva at Asanapat, now preserved at Orissa State Museum, Bhubaneswar, with Ūrdhvaliṅga (penis erectus) which is prominent and dated late Gupta period 6th century A.D. It is an eight-armed figure in tāṇdava dance posture. This dance posture however, does not agree with Aṃśumadbhedāgama.[15] Among the anthropomorphic representation of Śiva in whole Mahāṇadi river valley, mention may be made of an image of Śiva at Malhar in Bilaspur district of Madhya Pradesh, which is dated to 3rd century A.D. and the upper part of Śiva image wearing various ornaments dated 4th century A.D.[16]

The earliest eight-handed Naṭāraja image with Ūrdhva - liṅga (penis erectus) is found at the Sculptural shed of Sirpur on the right bank of Mahāṇadi river, Raipur district of Madhya Pradesh. C. Śivaramamūrti[17] dates this Naṭāraja in 5th century A.D. and states, "All the grace and beauty of Gupta sculpture is seen in a late example of this school from

Sirpur, Śiva dancing in lalita, eight-armed. He has a large pearl necklace, jaṭās arranged as usual in Gupta sculpture, with the crescent against it, the ūrdhvaliṅga recalls at once the tradition prevalent in this area of Central India, as at Mandasor. While the topmost pair of hands holds up the snake, the other arms carry the sūla, damaru, kapāla, while the last one fondles Devī, by caressing her chin. While the main right hand is in gajahasta, the main left, which should have been in abhaya or saṁdamsa brought nearer the ear, is broken. A drummer to the right plays the ūrdhva drum, while another beside him claps his hand to keep time. Gaṇeśa enjoys the dance, standing to Śiva's right, while Skanda, in juvenile fashion, dances exactly like his father, even while seated on the peacock. His left hand is in gajahasta and the right in pāṭāka. Devi, seated to the left, watches her husband's dance with affection and emotion and receives the caressing with joy. Between his legs peeps out a figure, dancing also in the lalita pose, exactly like Śiva. It is probably Tandu or Bharata imitating his master. This is a great master piece. The jewellery is very sparse but the carving is very effective.

Ram Prasad Mishra[18] associates the Natāraj image of Asanapat with Mattamayūra tāntric Śaivism and states that Śaṅkhamaṭhikādhipati was a disciple of Kadaṁvaguhadhivāsin. His name denotes that he was living in Śaṅkhamaṭhika and was the master of this religious establishment. This Śaṇkhanaṭinika may be identified with the famous Śaṅkhākara-maṭha of Asanapat stone inscription of the King Satrubhañja of Nāga ruling dynasty who ruled over the Kingdom of Vindhyātari as early as 4th century A.D. This Saṅkhakaramaṭha was located in Ahichhatraka which is generally identified with the modern Ramnagar of Bareily district of Uttar Pradesh. The Asanapat stone inscription displays a character of 4th century A.D. from the palaeographical standpoint and in this inscription Satrubhañja is eulogised as a donor of several lavish charities, a different religious establishment. This shows that by the 4th century A.D. the Śaṅkhamaṭhika or Śaṅkhakāramaṭha had already been a religious establishment of Indian fame. If there were any literatures on Yogic Sexual transformation, produced by the Yogis of Mattamayūra Śaivism, they have not come to light so far. The sublime ideology underlying this very characteristic dancing type of Śiva images (Naṭāraja) has been elaborately expounded by A.K. Coomaraswamy.[19]

No definite period of composition of the Tāntric Yogic works are known, however, the systematic form of Tāntric yoga and Haṭha yoga began to emerge in India sometime in the 6th century A.D. It was the period of religious eclecticism. For survival probably Buddhism developed Tāntric Buddhism. According to R.C. Majumdar[20] the earliest works dealing with Tāntric Buddhism are the Mañjuśrimūlakalpa and the Guhyasamāja. The composition of both of these works took place sometime after the Kāraṇḍavyuha and before the Mahāpratyaṅgira - dhārani i.e. about the fifth or sixth century A.D.

R.C. Majumdar[21] further informs Mañjuśrīmūlakalpa gives an exposition of endless mudrās (finger poses), maṇḍalas (mystical diagrams), mantras (mystical spells), kriyās (rites) and charyas (duties of an officiating priest in worship). - - - Even the deities like Śiva with a trident seated on a bull, the well-adorned Umā, the ever young Kārttikeya seated on a peacock are included in the paintings. This text contains mantras for both Hindu and Buddhist deities. This proves that the Buddhists learned and developed Tāntric Buddhism from Hindu Tantra.

It is known from Tāntric texts and Haṭha Yoga Pradipikā[22] that for Vajroli practice "Uḍḍiyāna bandha," which means abdominal retraction lock, drawing in of the abdomen and stomack towards the backbone after exhaling, and "Khechari mudra," i.e. folding the tongue back so that the tip touches the soft palate at the back of the mouth, are required.

"Uḍḍiyāna bandha," seems to have developed in Uḍḍiyāna pīṭha (site), which was located in Mahāṇadi valley of present Orissa province. Ram Prasad Mishra[23] states : "In Chandamarichi Tantra-ratnavali Sambalaka is described to have been located on the bank of the river Mahāṇadi. It was according to the text, the richest place of diamond (Vajrashri Kelipuri) and located in the Kingdom of Indrabhuti. Such a place located on the bank of Mahāṇadi can never be other than the present Sambalpur. Chandamarichi Tantraratnavali (M.S.D.L.N. 14343) pp. 1-2 has been quoted thus:-

> "*Eshasambalakah Visuddhayashabhuk Vajrashri Kelipuri*
> *ruchchairambarachumbi charususama susmeirasaudhavali*
> *Ya Nirghoshamishabhibadanadhiya shri Indrabhutter Yashah*
> *stutva rajate mugdhoduttaninadai Mahanadin Nirmala.*"

This literature definitely proves that Sambalaka, was situated on the bank of Mahāṇadi river, which was a part of great tāntric site Uḍḍiyāna. So, accurately it can be claimed that Uḍḍiyāna pīṭha was situated in modern province of Orissa, where Mahāṇadi river, which had association with growth of Tāntricism from early days, forms the main river.

With this background, as it is known, that for Vajroli alias Sexual transformation Yoga, "Uḍḍiyāna bandha," is most essential, it can be claimed that Uḍḍiyāna bandha developed in Uḍḍiyāna pīṭha, which was in Mahāṇadi river valley and therefore it can be claimed that the Yoga for sexual transformation, which came to be known as Vajroli, was re-discovered and developed fully in Mahāṇadi valley of present day Orissa province.

According to N.K. Sahu,[24] "It is known from the tradition embodied in the Pāg-Sām-Jon-Zāng that Tāntric Buddhism first developed in a place called Uḍḍiyāna, which is by far the most important among the four pīṭhas frequently mentioned both by the Hindu and the Buddhist Tantras.[25] A good number of Tāntric Buddhist Scholars who are connected with the introduction of many original Tantras are also believed to have hailed from this particular territory. We know from the Tibetan sources that Saraha, who introduced the Buddha Kapāla Tantra, Kaṁbala and Padmavajra, the expounders of the Hevajra Tantra, Luipā; the originator of the Samputatilaka, Lalita Vajra that of the three divisions of the Kṛṣṇayāmari Tantra, Gyambhiravajra, that of the Vajrāmṛta; Kukkuri, that of the Mahāmaya; and Pito that of the Kalachakra; are all more or less associated with the place known as Uḍḍiyāna. We further know that Indrabhūti, who was a king of Uḍḍiyāna in the 8th century A.D. organised the Mantrayāna Buddhism into what is called Vajrayāna, while his sister Lakṣminkarā is believed to have been connected with the initial development of Sahajayāna."

King Indrabhuti of Sambalaka in Uḍḍiyāna was the founder of Tāntric Buddhism Vajrayāna and Kalāchakrayana, which was developed by Pito. Lakṣmīnkarā was the sister of King Indrabhūti, who married Prince Sevola, the son of King Jalendra of Laṅkāpuri,[26] identified with modern Sonepur, situated on the right bank of Mahāṇadi river, near its confluence with the tributary Tel river. Lakṣminakarā popularised Sahajayāna. As a whole, all the branches of Tāntric Buddhism deals with the Yoga of Sexual transformation. With emphasis Ram Prasad Mishra[27] states that with all these evidences and illustrations it is logical to believe that Kalācakrayāna was a development within Vajrayāna and was of Indian origin in clear contrast in the misconception of Prof. A. Bharati who advocate it as of non-Indian origin. Indeed Kalācakrayāna is not a blind imitation of Vajrayāna for it differs from its parent vehicle in its Yogic aspect and adjusts the elements accultured from Vajrayāna with its Yogic philosophy. With the acculturations of elements from Indian astrology, Yoga and Vajrayāna, it first flourished in Sambhala, the present Sambalpur region of Orissa which is also the cradle of its Tāntric School, Vajrayāna and from there spread to Ratnagiri the monastic University of Orissa. Dhānyakaṭaka in Kaliṅga and to many other places of Orissa.

From Orissa it travelled to other parts of India and foreign countries like Tibet and Nepal.

Āli alias Aul is a prominent place in Kendrapada district of Orissa. The word Āli alias Aul is connected with Sexual transformation Yoga of Sahajayāna and therefore it is necessary to know about it. R.P. Mishra[28] informs, "Kānhupāda describes Sahajayoga through series of similies in his Charyā poems. Somewhere he analogizes himself as an elephant who having uprooted the materials of illusive confinement constituted by Āli and Kali enters into Lotus-tank of Sahaja and remains sportive in Mahāsukha with the She-elephant of Śūnyata; somewhere he portrays himself as a Kāpālika adorned with the peculiarities of dresses and ornaments which are constituted by Āli, Kāli, Sun and Moon and requests the Ḍombi alias Avadhuti for an amorous union on the fascinating bed of Lotus, blossomed with sixty-four petals, and in some other where-else he similizes himself as a bridegroom and Avadhuti as bride and he proceeds to marry this bride in a pompous procession where Saṁsāra and Nirvāṇa figure as the musical instruments, mind and vital air become the wedding baskets which contain the materials of matrimony, Anuttara Yoga-Dharma symbolises the dowry and the perfection of Sahajānanda resembles the joy of amorous Copulation."

In the Sekanirṇaya or Sekanideśha section of Advayavajra Saṁgraha very clear reference of Śiva and Śākti of the Hindu Śāktaism is cited and the copulation of Śiva and Śākti is described as the Supreme state of Bliss. Śiva accompanied with Śākti is considered Superior to Śiva alone and Śākti is defined as the vision of Śunyata and the destruction of all illusive mentations.[29]

The Yogatattvopaniṣad, which is a later Upanisad describes one of its Yogic Bandhas as Oḍḍiyana.[30] So it is definite that Oḍḍiyana bandha alias Uḍḍiyāna bandha which originated in Orissa, played an important role in Sexual transformation Yoga, which came to be named Vajroli later. There is existence of "UḌḌĪSH TANTRAM," also, composed by Lankesh Ravan.

Matsyendranāth the founder of Nāthism and Yogini cult rescued the text of the sacred knowledge from the belly of a fish was most probably the Cāmdavali-Dhārma regions in Badrak district of Orissa, which is even at present a popular citadel of the Cult of Śaivism and the Nāthas.[31] Elsewhere R.P. Mishra clearly states that Matsyendranāth was the Nātha Siddha and was born in Chandradvipa, Chāndavali Dharma region of Balasore (now Bhadrak district) in Orissa.[32] Matsyendranāth in view of popularity of the Yogini cult gained over the period, systematised and expounded it in his famous work Kaulayānanirṇaya which has become the authoritative text of the Cult. Nine Yogini temples have been discovered so far; distributed in India, belonging to the period from the eighth to twelfth century A.D.[33] This shows that Matsyendranāth existed or survived within 5th-7th century A.D. so that the principals of Yogini Cult, could be spread and temples of Yoginī cult, could be built throughout India and abroad.

The famous disciple of Matsyendranāth was Gorakhnāth, who developed to greater Yogic sadhanas, than his Master. Swami Śivananda[34] informs, "Śrī Gorakhnāth was a great Yogi like Śrī Anana Dev of Alandi. In Chandragiri village on the banks of the Godavari, there was a Brāhmin named Suraj. His wife's name was Saraswati. They had no children, Yogi Matsyendranāth went for Bhiksha in the house of Suraj. Saraswati entertained the Yogi with good food, with sraddha. She wept before him for not having a child. Yogi Matsyendranāth gave her a pinch of holy ash with blessings for a child. Some time later, She had a son. Matsyendranāth came back to Saraswati and took the boy with him when he was twelve years of age. He sent the boy to Badrinarayan for doing Tapas. Apsaras and other Devatas came to molest him. He stood firm and tided over all temptations. He got tremendous Siddhis. Matsyendranāth also imported all his powers and Vidyas to the boy, his disciple Gorakhnāth.

"Śrī Gorakhnāth in his 12th year went to Badrinarayan and performed Tapas for 12 long years, living on air alone. Gorakhnāth had tremendous Yogic powers. When his Guru Matsyendranāth entered the dead body of a Raja (Parakaya Pravesh) to obey the orders of Śrī Hanuman to produce offspring for a certain Rani. Gorakhnāth assumed the form of a lady through his Yogic powers and entered the inner apartments of the palace (Kamaroopasiddhi). At some other instance he made a toy child out of clay and gave this as a play-mate for the children of a certain village. He converted a portion of a mountain into gold and reconverted it to its former condition. He passed urine on a rock. It became Gold. Once in a Kumbhamela on the banks of the Godavari, he gave food to all by spreading only leaves but offered different rich meals to the liking of everyone. In the same Mela he slowly reduced himself in bulk and assumed the form of a mosquito (Anima siddhi). Through his own Yogic power he burnt himself to ashes and again assumed his original form. He did Akasagamanam (Walking in the Sky). In this way he performed many Siddhis. Raja Bhartrihari was his disciple."

As Matsyendranāth was born in Orissa and therefore his disciple

Gorakhnāth was associated with Orissa. In the Tantramahārnava quoted in the "Gorakṣa-Siddhānta Saṁgraha," Gorakhnāth is described as residing in the forest of Jagannāth (Orissa), and in the "Śūnya Saṁhitā," of Achyutānanda it is stated that a young Vaiṣṇava Madhurādasa, who visited the forest of the Prāchi valley (in Puri district) was led by an ascetic of the forest to the Cave of Gorakha, where the great Siddha had practised the Yoga of Nirādhāva (supportless Yoga).[35]

"Haṭha Yoga Pradipikā," was composed by Yogi Swatmarama, a disciple of Yogi Gorakhnāth and it is a very well known work on Hatta Yoga. Vajroli and Sahajoli are dealt in details, in this work. The classical descriptions of redirecting the Sexual energy upwards; through the practice of Haṭha yoga and tantra is found here. Tortoise contracts its head and neck inside its shell. In verse 10, chapter 1, of Haṭha yoga Pradipika,[36] it is mentioned, "For those continuously tempered by the heat of tapa (the three types of pain - Spiritual, environmental and physical) hatha is like the hermitage giving protection from the heat. For those always united in Yoga, hatha is the basis acting like a tortoise."

On the stone pavement of the Śiva temple at Mohangiri of Kalahandi district, Orissa, to the north-west of the temple, four tortoises are chisled on the stone pavement, in a line. Te author had witnessed and seen these four tortoises of the basement of Śiva temple there, during the archaeological field survey work in 1992. On 25th May 1996, the author visited Mohangiri site to take photograph of the four tortoises, when the reconstruction of the Maṇḍapa alias jagamohana was taking place. Because of reconstruction work, debris were scattered and the tortoises were covered by earth. Clearance was made and it was possible to take photograph of two tortoises only, while the other two tortoises still remain buried on earth. Clearance should be done and preservation of these four tortoises should be taken up, because they are of much archaeological and yogic spiritual importance. According to "Tantra-raja-Tantra,"[37] which is literature of Nātha Cult, there are four types of tortoises, known as Para, Deshagata, Gramaga and Grihaga. Para Korma (tortoise) is that which supports the earth, Deshagata supports Countries, Gramaga villages and Grihaga individual householders. Verse 88 of "Tantra-raja Tantra," says, "He who does japa without knowing Koormasthiti (the position of Koorma) not only fails to get the fruit thereof but he meets with destruction." These prove that vigorous Vajroli practice which was discovered in Orissa was continuing throughout the length and breadth of Mahāṇadi river valley. Woodroffe gives a short analysis of "Tantra - raja Tantra," and mentions thus, "He who does Japa without knowing Kurmasthiti not only fails to get the fruit thereof but he meets with destruction (V.88). Therefore should Kurma be first known. Kurma is of four kinds namely firstly Para Kurma. This which is steady (Sthira) and extends to 50 kotis (500,000,000) of Yojanas (between 8 and 9 miles) supports Prithivi. The others are Desagata, Gramaja and Grhaga. This is just as the Supre Tortoise supports the whole Universe, the others support particular Countries, Villages and Dwellings."

The discoveries of so much associations, with the Yoga of Sexual transformation, definitely proves that this Yoga, whose classical name for Male is Vajroli and for Female is Sahajoli, was re-discovered in the great Mahāṇadi river valley, i.e. present Orissa province and its adjoining area of Upper Mahāṇadi valley, from where it starts, in eastern Madhya Pradesh province, popularly called Chhattisgarh area.

Finally Swami Satyananda Saraswati[38] may be quoted, when he mentions, "Tantra aims to transform every action in life into a ritual, so that the individual performs every action and thought with a feeling of worship and awareness. The action of bathing, dressing, sitting for worship, offering various symbolic sacrifices, sexual relations, stages of development from inception in the womb, birth to marriage, etc. are transformed into worship.

"The aim of Tantra is to unleash the Cosmic energy in man, so that he rises to higher levels of awareness."

With this background, it can be claimed that all Sculptural arts on temple architectures are Tāntric.

An important text of Nāthim as "KĀMA -KALĀ -VILĀSA," which is a work on Śrīvidyā by Puṇyānandanātha. Woodroffe had translated this work with the commentary of Natanānandanātha and about verse 51 states[39]: "Śiva the Guru who abides in the Uḍḍiyāṇapīṭha did in the Kṛtayuga impart the Vidya to Her, His own Śākti the Vimarśa - rupiṇi Kāmeśvari."

This passage shows the importance of Uḍḍiyānapīṭha, which was situated in present day Orissa province, where Mahāṇadi river flows.

Woodroffe[40] states, "The Kāma - Kalā - Vilāsa is an important work in Śrīvidya by Puṇyānanda, an adherent of the Hādimata, who is also the commentator on the Yogini - hydaya, a section called Uttaracatuḥśati of the great Vāmakeśvara Tantra. The same Catuḥśati as also the Pūrvacatuḥśati hae commentaries by Bhāskararāya. The Kāma-Kalā-Vilāsa which means the spreading or emanation or evolution of the Kāmakalā that is the Supreme Triangle formed of the Bindu and Visarga, of Prakāśa and Vimarśa, of Śiva and Śākti, of the "I" (Ahaṁ) and "This"

(Idaṁ) or Universe is, in the Supreme sense; the Śiva - Svarupa and Śākti-Svarupa. To put it quite shortly Kāma - Kalā - Vilāsa is the evolution of the one in its twin aspect as changeless Consciousness (Cit or Samvit) and changing Power (Cit -Śākti and Māya - Śākti) into the multiple Universe."

The three Tāntric Śiva temples of Boud, which borrowed their plans from "Kōśali Style," of Rekha temples in Upper Mahānadi valley are placed in triangle formation, which is Kāmakalā. These three Tāntric Śiva temples of Boud influenced the development of the full fledged temples in coastal Orissa. Even Rajendra Prasad Das,[41] mentions," That 'basic conception' of a Spiritual reality were governing not only the subject matter of sacred Sculptures and that these basic conceptions were manifested in plastic form through geometrical patterns is revealed in the application of the Kāmakalā Yantra to specific Kāmabandha sculptures.

"Without Śiva and Śākti, creation would be nothing but imagination. Without the action of Kāma there would be no birth and death.

"Śiva himself is visibly manifested as the Mahāliṅga and Śākti in the form of the Bhaga (womb). By their union the whole Universe comes into being. This is called the work of desire (Śilpa Prakaśa, v.v. 498-501).

"Proceeding from the basic conception, the Śilpa Prakaśa lays down that a place (temple) without love images is known as a 'place to be shunned" (Tyakta Maṇḍala). Continuing it further says that according to Kaulacaras, which is shunned like the den of death and that without offering Puja to Kāmakalā Yantra, the Śākti puja and the Sadhana become useless as the bath of an elephant. Having said this the Śilpa Prakaśa proceeds to explain the construction of the Kāmakalā Yantra its presiding Deity, her associates and attendants and the dhyanas of Mahākāma-kaleśvari and Śiva Kāma Kuleśvara.

"This Yantra is extolled as the giver of protection to all (including obviously the temple), as the giver of power (Pratyaksa Śāktidah) and as the manifest bestower of all perfections (Siddhis). Placed in a temple it ensures the movement to stand for ever. Though this not only all obstacles and fears are destroyed, but even the ghosts (Bhutas), departed Spirits (Pretas), goblins (Pisacas), fearful demons (Kaunapas) and other hideous creatures (Vikatas) flee away at its mere sight.

"This utterly *SECRET YANTRA* is to be placed in temples dedicated to Śākti and Rudra. Since this is utterly secret, it is not be shown to every one. For this reason a love (Mithuna murti) is to be carved on the lines of the Yantra. The Kāmabandha is placed there to give delight to the people.

"That such a practice of carving Mithuna sculptures along the lines of the Kāmakalā Yantra was not confined to Orissa but was also followed elsewhere in India has been revealed by the renowned and dedicated Scholar Devangana Desai's study "Religious Imagery of Khajuraho." She found that the famous "head-down" mithuna sculpture at the juncture of the Vimana and Sala of the Kandariya Mahādeva and Viswanātha temples there has been carved along the lines of the Kāmakalā Yantra of Śilpa Prakaśa." So, Orissa province is the land of Kāmakalā, i.e. erotic Spiritual Science, where Tāntric Yoga of Sexual transformation was re-discovered and not "KAMADEVA'S PLEASURE GARDEN : ORISSA," as deemed by Thomas E. Donaldson.[42]

## REFERENCES

1. Singh Deo, J.P. *Cultural Profile of South Kōśala*, Gyan Publishing House, New Delhi, 1987, p. 20.
2. Singh Deo, J.P. "Pre-historic Cave Painting of Yogimath Donger," O.H.R.J. Vol. XXII, No. 2, pp. 21-22.
3. Pradhan, Sadasiba, "Rock Art Heritage of Orissa," *The Journal of Orissan History*, Vol. XIII-XIV, November 1995, Orissa History Congress, pp. 7-10.
4. Swami Sivananda, *BLISS DIVINE*, The Divine Life Society, Shivananda nagar, Rishikesh, Uttar Pradesh, 1974, pp. 633.
5. Agarwal, V.S. *Śiva Mahādeva—The Great God*, Prithivi Prakashan, Varanasi, 1984, p. 1.
6. Mishra, R.P. *SAHAJAYĀNA - A Study of Tantric Buddhism*. Punthi-Pustak, Calcutta, 1991, p. 4.
7. Śivaramamūrti, C. *NATARAJA IN ART. THOUGH AND LITERATURE*, Publication Division, Government of India, New Delhi, 1994, p. 159 and Fig. 9 on p. 160.
8. Puri, B.N. *India in the time of Patañjali*, Bharatiya Vidya Bhavan, Bombay, 1968, p. 15.
9. Banerjea, J.N. "Iconography," *The History and Culture of the Indian People, Vol. IV, The Age of Imperial Kanauj*, ed. Majumdar R.C. Bharatiya Vidya Bhavan, Bombay, 1964, p. 305.
10. Bhattacharyya, H.D. "Tāntrik Religion," *The History and Culture of the Indian People, Vol. IV, The Age of Imperial Kanauj*, ed. Majumdar, R.C. Bharatiya Vidya Bhavan, Bombay, 1964, p. 315.
11. Singh Fatah - *The Vedic Etymology*, National Publishing House, Delhi, (?), p. 182.

12. Purnnachandra Orḍiā Bhāshākosha (A lexicon of the Oriya language), Vol. V (Consonats, Pha-Ma), compiled by Gopal Chandra Praharaj, Cuttack, 1936, p. 6339.
13. Chela Buddhananda, "*MOOLA BANDHA THE MASTER KEY*, Bihar School of Yoga, Munger, Bihar, 1984, passim.
14. Swami Muktibodhananda Saraswati, *HATHA YOGA PRADIPIKA*, Bihar School of Yoga, Munger, 1993, p. 564.
15. Panda, L.K. *ŚAIVISM IN ORISSA*, Sundeep Prakashan, Delhi, 1985, p. 121.
16. (i) Bajpai, K.D. and Pandey, S.K. *Malhar (1975-77)*, University of Sagar, Sagar 1977, plate - XI.
    (ii) Patel, G.S. *History and Culture of India : A study of Orissa*, Amar Prakashan, Delhi, 1992, p. 129.
17. Sivaramamurti, C. *op. cit.* Publication Division, Government of India, New Delhi, 1994, pp. 159-160.
18. Mishra, R.P. *Fragments of Indian Culture*, Punthi-Pustak, Calcutta, 1995, p. 136.
19. Coomaraswamy, A.K. *The Dance of Shiva*, Munshiram Manoharlal, New Delhi, 1991, passim.
20. Majumdar, R.C. "Early Tāntrik Texts," *The History and Culture of the Indian People*, Vol. IV, *The Age of Imperial Kanauj*, ed. Majumdar, R.C. Bharatiya Vidya Bhavan, Bombay, 1964, p. 263.
21. *Ibid.*, 1964, p. 264.
22. *Haṭha Yoga Pradipika*, Bihar School of Yoga, Munger, 1993, passim.
23. Mishra, R.P. *SAHAJAYĀNA - A Study of Tāntric Buddhism*, Punthi-Pustak, Calcutta, 1991, p. 46 and p. 96.
24. Sahu, N.K. *Buddhism in Orissa*, Utkal University, Cuttack, 1958, p. 142.
25. The four Piṭhas are Uḍḍiyāna, Purāṇagiri, Kāmāksa and Sirihaṭṭa. For the analytical description of the Pithas, vide (i) *Journal of the Royal Asiatic Society of Bengal*, Vol. XIV, No. 1, 1948, (ii) Sarkar, D.C. *The Śākta Pithas.*
26. Mishra, R.P. *Advayasiddhi, the Tāntric view of Lakṣminkara*, Kant Publications, Delhi, 1995, p. 17.
27. Mishra, R.P. *SAHAJAYĀNA - A Study of Tāntric Buddhism*, Punthi - Pustak, Calcutta, 1991, p. 83.
28. *Ibid.*, 1991, p. 157.
29. *Ibid.*, 1991, pp. 262-263 (Sastri, H.P. (ed.). Advaya Vajra Saṁgraha, p. 29. Nirnada Tantra quoted in this work, "Śiva Śākti Samāyogad Jāyate Chidbhutaṁ Sukhaṁ x x x."
30. *Ibid.*, 1991, p. 266.
31. *Ibid.*, 1991, p. 281.
32. *Ibid.*, 1991, p. 125, reference of Chapter - III.
33. Das, H.C. *TĀNTRICISM: A STUDY OF YOGINI CULT*. Sterling Publishers, New Delhi, 1981, p. 3.

34. Swami Śivānanda, *KUNDALINI YOGA*, The Divine Life Society, Śivanandanagar, 1971, pp. 166-167.
35. Sahu, N.K. *Buddhism in Orissa*, Utkal University, 1958, p. 175.
36. *Haṭha Yoga Pradipika (Light on Haṭha Yoga)*, Bihar School of Yoga, Munger, Bihar, second edition, 1993, p. 31.
37. Woodroffe, Sir John - *Tantraraja Tantra and Kāma-Kalā-Vilāsa*, Ganesh & Co., Madras, 1971, p. 33.
38. Swami Satyananda Saraswati, *A Systematic Course in the Ancient Tāntric Techniques of Yoga and Kriya*. Bihar School of Yoga, Munger, Bihar, 1989, p. 335.
39. Woodroffe, Sir, John - *Tantraraja Tantra and Kāma-Kalā-Vilāsa*, Ganesh & Co., Madras, 1971, p. 234.
40. *Ibid.*, 1971, Preface, p. 133.
41. Das, R.P. "The Study of Śilpa Śāstras," *REFERENCE ORISSA*, ed. Tiwari, A.N. Enterprising Publishers, Bhubaneswar, 1999. p. 178.
42. Donaldson, T.E. *KĀMADEVA'S PLEASURE GARDEN: ORISSA*, B.R. Publishing Corporation, Delhi, 1987, passim.

APPENDIX I

# Knowledge and Reality

The knowledge which is acquired from teachers and from books are imitative, repetitive, derivative and educative. Another knowledge which is above these types of Knowledge is Intuitive. Only Intuitive knowledge reaches to the Reality.

Intuition means the power of the mind by which it immediately perceives the Truth of things without reasoning or analysis : a truth so perceived, immediate knowledge in contrast with mediate.

The realised Souls, otherwise known as Ṛṣis and Yogis in India, i.e., Bharat are Individuals of Intuitive Knowledge in Human creation. The knowledge of Intuition can't be expressed in words fully, because it is the practical physical experience. All the Holy books or Scriptures of the World therefore indicate but have failed to express the full Truth, the full Consciousness or the full realisation.

With this information, lets know the view of Swami Śivananda on the four sources of Knowledge. Swami Śivananda[1] has written that Inspiration, revelation, insight, intuition, ecstasy, Divine sight and Paramananda state are the seven plans of Knowledge. There are four sources of Knowledge, viz. instinct, reason, intuition and Super-intuition or Brahma Jñāna.

## Instinct

When an ant crawls in your right arm, the left arm automatically moves towards the right arm to drive away the ant. The mind does not reason there. When you see a Scorpion in front of your leg, you withdraw your leg automatically. This is termed instinctive or automatic movement. As you cross a street, how instinctively you move your body to save yourself from the Cars. There is no Vritti in such mechanical movement.

Instinct is found in animals and birds. In birds, the ego doesn't interfere with the free Divine flow and Divine play. Hence the work done by them through their instincts is more perfect than that done by human beings. Have you not noticed the excellent work done by birds in their building of wonderful nests?

## Reason

Reason is higher than instinct and is found only in Human beings. It collects facts, generalises, reasons out from cause to effect, from effect to cause (a priori and a posteriori methods of reasoning), from premises to conclusions, from propositions to proofs. It concluded, decides and comes to judgement. It takes you safely to the door of intuition and leaves you there.

Belief, reasoning, knowledge and faith are the four important psychic processes. First you have belief in a doctor. You go to him for diagnosis and treatment. He makes a thorough examination and then prescribes certain medicine. You take them. You reason out: "Such and such is the disease. The doctor has given me Iron and Iodine. Iron will improve my blood. The Iodine will stimulate the lymphatics and absorb the exudation and growth in the liver. So, I should take it." Then the disease is cured of these drugs, in a month. Then you get knowledge of and perfect faith in the efficacy of the medicine and the proficiency of the doctor. Then you recommend to your friends this doctor and his drugs.

## Intuition

Intuition is Spiritual Anubhava, knowledge through functioning of Karana-Śarīra is intuition. Śrī Aurobindo calls it Supermind or Supramental Consciousness. There is direct perception of Truth (Pratyakaṣa) or immediate knowledge through Samādhi. You know things by a flash. Professor Bergson preached about Intuition in France to make the people understand that there is another higher source of knowledge than intellect. In intuition, there is no reasoning process at all. It is Pratyakṣa. Intuition transcends reason, but does not contradict it. Intellect takes a man to the door of Intuition and returns back. Intuition is Divyadṛṣṭi. It is Jñāna Cakṣu. Spiritual flashes and glimpses of Truth come through Intuition, Inspiration, Revelation, Spiritual insight come through Intuition.

## Ātma-Jñāna

Ātma-Jñāna is above Intuition. It transcends the Karana Śarīra. It is the highest form of Knowledge. It is the only Reality.

In Intuitive knowledge, one individual attains Samādhi or Self-absorption. Samādhi starts with the absorption of Self in the duality of structure in consciousness and ends in the absorption of Self in identification with secondless unique Self. Self-absorption with duality of structure in consciousness is called Sabikalpa Samādhi (when Kuṇḍalini rises to Mooladhara, Swadhishthana, Manipura and Anahata chakras). Self-absorption without any sense of duality is called Nirvikalpa Samādhi (when Kuṇḍalini rises to Vishuddhi and Ajña Chakras). Sabikalpa Samādhi is of four types and Nirvikala Samādhi is of two types,[2] having sub-divisions.

In Sabikalpa Samādhi the devotee has attained realization of his oneness with Spirit but can't maintain his Cosmic consciousness except in the immobile trance state. By continuous meditation he reaches the Suprerior state of Nirbikalpa Samādhi, in which one moves freely in the World without any loss of God-perception.

In Nirbikalpa Samādhi the Yogi dissolves the last vestiges of his material or earthly Karma. Nevertheless, he still has certain astral and causal Karma to work out and there one takes astral and then causal re-embodiments on high-vibrational spheres.[3]

With this much information, let us peep into the types of Samādhi's definition of Sudhir Ranjan Sengupta[4] on Sabikalpa Samādhi and Nirvikalpa Samādhi.

These are briefly described below:-

## Sabikalpa Samādhi

(i) *Sabitarka Samādhi*—Self-absorption in the duality of structure in consciousness with latent sense of controversy in the consciousness is called Sabitarka Samādhi.

(ii) *Sabichar Samādhi*—Self-absorption in the duality of structure in consciousness with a latent sense of discretion in the consciousness is called Sabichar Samādhi.

(iii) *Sānanda Samādhi*—Self-absorption in the duality of structure in consciousness with an all-absorbing Bliss is called Sānanda Samādhi.

(iv) *Sasmita Samādhi*—Self-absorption in the duality of structure in consciousness with a latest sense of Self-existence is called Sasmita Samādhi.

**Nirvikalpa Samādhi**

(i) *Bhaba - pratyaya Videha Samādhi*—Consists in Self-absorption without the least trace of duality in consciousness with complete Self-identification with Nature of God, without the light of consciousness. Bhaba Pratyaya Videha Samādhi has three sub-divisions viz. Prakṛti Pratyaya, Ahaṁ Pratyaya and Mahat Pratyaya, i.e. Self-Consciousness lost in nature and Self-Consciousness lost in egotism and lost in Buddhisattva.

(ii) *Pūrṇa Pratyaya Samādhi*—Self-absorption in the secondless unique conscious Absolute Self of the Supreme Self without the least trace of duality is called Pūrṇa Pratyaya Nirvikalpa Samādhi. The Pūrṇa Pratyaya Nirvikalpa Samādhi is possible when the five waves of mind cease to function and the Sādhaka transcends the basic evolution. Pūrṇa Samādhi attained as a result of the realisation of the identity of Self with the Absolute Self of God without the least trace of duality in the Self-revealed Consciousness liberates an individual Soul from the ills of the World and World series as he knows no other existence except the Supreme Being. The Sages say that of these eight varieties of Samādhi, Pūrṇa Prayyaya Samādhi alone can liberate an individual Soul.

With the help of the referred three Books, mentioned in the reference, the author has tried to focus information to the seekers of knowledge, because through educative knowledge mankind has gone till the finer findings of Atom and Plotone. Many Scientists are working on the root of intuitive knowledge. In recent period Doctor Hiroshi Motoyama of Japan has developed a unit by which the waves and currents of energy which accompany the awakening of Kuṇḍalini Śākti can be recorded and measured.

Among spectacular achievements of Mankind, the greatest achievement has been the widespread development of Global thinking and such related ideas as internationalism, cosmopolitanism, World Culture, World Government, Universal Man, One World etc. In spite of all these, there is no peace. Only through Intuitive knowledge Mankind can achieve peace, contentment etc.

## REFERENCES

1. Swami Śivānanda, *MIND ITS MYSTERIES AND CONTROL*, The Divine Life Society, Shivanandanagar, 1974, pp. 27-29.

2. Sengupta, S.R. *MOTHER CULT*, Firma K.L.M. Private Limited, Calcutta, 1977, p. 106.
3. Paramahansa Yogananda, *Autobiography of a Yogi*, Jaico Publishing, Bombay, 1971, p. 427.
4. Sengupta, S.R., op. cit., 1977, pp. 106-107.

# APPENDIX II

# Śākta Pīṭhas

From remote early days, when Human being developed facundity, there was accedence of Śākti worship. Śākti is worhipped in any form or the other in every human settlement in India. According to "Tantra Cuḍāmaṇi," which is a later medieval work, there are 52 Śākta Pīṭhas, while Purāṇas say that these are 108 in number. A complete list of 108 Śākti Pīṭhas with the names of the Goddesses is found in Matsya purāṇa. The same text has been quoted in the Revākhaṇḍa sub-section of the Avanti khaṇḍa in the Skanda purāṇa, in the Sṛṣṭikhaṇḍa section of Padma purāṇa and in Devī Bhāgavata purāṇa. These purāṇas except Devī Bhāgavata do not mention the name Śākti Pīṭha or Siddha Pīṭha and use the word "Tirṭha" only. From Bṛhaddharma purāṇa (I. 14. 33) and Padma purāṇa (I. 17. 199-203) it is known that attempt was made to trace Śākti influence in Śaiva and Vaiṣṇava holy places also.

With this background, an attempt is made here to give the list of the names of places and Goddess, as found in Devī Bhāgavata, Padma purāṇa, Skanda purāṇa, Matsya purāṇa and Tāntra Cuḍāmaṇi.

| | *Pīṭha* | *Goddess* |
|---|---|---|
| 1. | Ambara | Viśvakāmā |
| 2. | Amarakantaka | Caṇḍikā |
| 3. | Acchoda | Śāktidhāriṇi |
| 4. | Aśvattha | Vandaniyā |
| 5. | Among the Mothers | Vaiṣṇavī |
| 6. | Among the beautiful Girls | Tilottamā |
| 7. | Among the Gods | Indrāṇi |
| 8. | Andhra Pradesh | Godāvari pīṭha |
| 9. | Annapurṇā | Kāncipura |
| 10. | Bhadreśvara or Madreśvara | Bhadrā or Bhadreśvarī |
| 11. | Bharat āśrama | Aṉganā |
| 12. | Badari | Urvaśi |
| 13. | Bhavāni | Tulajāpura in Mahārāṣtra |

| | | |
|---|---|---|
| 14. | Maghad pīṭh - Patna (Bihar) | |
| 15. | Beluchistān (Pakistan) | Hingula |
| 16. | Bihar (Aṭṭahāsa pīṭha) | |
| 17. | Bihar (Vaidyānath pīṭha) | |
| 18. | Banglādesh (Sugandha pīṭha) | |
| 19. | Banglādesh (Chattāl pīṭha) | |
| 20. | Banglādesh (Yashor pīṭha) | |
| 21. | Banglādesh (Kartoya-Tat pīṭha) | |
| 22. | Brindāvan pīṭha | |
| 23. | Bhairav pīṭha (Madhya Pradesh) | |
| 24. | Bahulā pīṭha (near Katwā, West Bengal) | |
| 25. | Caitraratha | Madotkaṭā |
| 26. | Citrakuṭa | Sītā |
| 27. | Chāgalaṇḍa Vegala | Pracaṇḍā |
| 28. | Candrabhāgā | Kalā |
| 29. | Citrakuta (Uttar Pradesh) Rāma Giri pīṭha | |
| 30. | Calcutta | Kāli |
| 31. | Cape Comorin, Śākti pīṭha | Kanyā Kumarī |
| 32. | Cina | Nila Sarasvatī |
| 33. | Cape Comorin, Kanya Kūshram pīṭha | Kanyā Kumarī |
| 34. | Dvāravati | Rukmiṇī |
| 35. | Devadāra vana | Puṣṭī |
| 36. | Ekāmra | Kirtmati |
| 37. | Guṇḍaki pīṭha, Nepal | |
| 38. | Gandhamadana | Kārnāksi |
| 39. | Gomanta | Gomati |
| 40. | Gokarṇa | Bhadra Kālikā or Bhadra Karṇikā |
| 41. | Gayā | Mangalā |
| 42. | Godāvari | Trisandhyā |
| 43. | Gaṅgādvāra | Ratipriyā or Haripriyā |
| 44. | Gaurī tīrtha (on the southern bank of the river Narmadā) | |
| 45. | Guhya Kāli in Nepal | |
| 46. | Gāyatri in Puṣkara | |
| 47. | Girnar Range, Gujarat, Prabhās pīṭha | |
| 48. | Gohāti Assam | |
| 49. | Gaja mountain | Durgā |

| | | |
|---|---|---|
| 50. | Hastinapura | Jayanti |
| 51. | Hiraṇyākṣa | Mahotpalā |
| 52. | Hariścandra | Caṇḍikā |
| 53. | Himālayas | Bhīmā |
| 54. | Hemakūṭa | Manmathā |
| 55. | Himachal Pradesh | Jvalamukhi |
| 56. | In the mouths of Brāhmins | Sarasvatī |
| 57. | In the Solar orb | Prabhā |
| 58. | In the hearts of men | Bhrahmakalā |
| 59. | In the living beings | Śākti |
| 60. | Jālandhara (Punjab) | Viśvamukhi |
| 61. | Jaipur, Rajasthan, Virata pīṭha | |
| 62. | Jammu | Jambunadeśvarī |
| 63. | Jawālāmukhi pīṭha (Himānchal Pradesh) | |
| 64. | Janasthān pīṭha (Nasik, Mahārāṣṭra) | |
| 65. | Jayanti pīṭha (Shillong) | |
| 66. | Kamalālayā | Kamalā |
| 67. | Kamgiri pītha | |
| 68. | Kumuda | Satyavādinī |
| 69. | Kālañjara | Kāli |
| 70. | Koṭa or Karkoṭa | Mukuteśvarī<br>Mangaleśvarī |
| 71. | Kotitirṭha | Kotavi |
| 72. | Karavira | Mahālakṣmī |
| 73. | Krtasauca | Simhika |
| 74. | Kārtikeya | Śaṅkari |
| 75. | Kiskindha hill | Tārā |
| 76. | Kāshmira | Meḍhā |
| 77. | Kapāla Mocana | Śuddhi or Śuddhā |
| 78. | Kāyavarohana | Mātā |
| 79. | Kuśadwipa | Kuśodakā |
| 80. | Kāshmira | Devī in Śrīnagara |
| 81. | Kedāra | Māryadāyini |
| 82. | Kāshmir pīṭha | |
| 83. | Karnat pīṭha (Karṇāṭaka) | |
| 84. | Kalmadhav pīṭha (?) | |
| 85. | Karveer pīṭha (Kolhāpur, Mahārāsṭra) | |
| 86. | Kānci pīṭha (Śiva Kānci) | |
| 87. | Kuṛukṣetra pīṭha (Haryana) | |
| 88. | Kalmadhav pīṭha (?) | |

| | |
|---|---|
| 89. Kireet pīṭha (West Bengal) | |
| 90. Kānyakubja | Gaurī |
| 91. Laṅkā pīṭha (?) | |
| 92. Mātṛ tīrṭha (?) | |
| 93. Mīnākṣi (?) | |
| 94. Mānasa | Kumudā |
| 95. Mandara | Kāmācārini |
| 96. Malaya | Rambhā |
| 97. Mahāliṅga | Kapilā |
| 98. Māyāpūri | Kumāri |
| 99. Mānaschala | Kalyāṇī |
| 100. Mādhavavana | Sugandhā |
| 101. Mathurā | Devaki |
| 102. Mahākāla | Maheśvarī |
| 103. Mandava | Māṇḍavi |
| 104. Maheśvaripura | Svāhā |
| 105. Mahālayā | Mahābhāgā |
| 106. Mithilā pīṭha (Uttar Pradesh) | |
| 107. Mānas pīṭha (Tibet China) | |
| 108. Manivedikā pīṭha (near Puṣkar, Rajasthan) | |
| 109. Maghad pīṭha (Patna, Bihar) | |
| 110. Naimisa | Liṅgadhāriṇi |
| 111. Nilāmbā (on the top of the Nila mount) | |
| 112. Nepāl pīṭha (Nepāl) | |
| 113. Nandipur pīṭha (West Bengal) | |
| 114. Nalhāti pīṭha (West Bengal) | |
| 115. Prayāga pīṭha | Lalitā |
| 116. Puṣkara | Puruhūtā |
| 117. Puruṣottama (Orissa) | Vimalā |
| 118. Pundra Vardhana | Pātalā |
| 119. Pātāla | Parameśvarī |
| 120. Prabhāsa | Puṣkarāvati |
| 121. Payaṣni | Pingaleśvarī |
| 122. Piṇḍāraka | Dhṛti |
| 123. Panchsag pīṭha (?) | |
| 124. Pārijāta Parvata | Mahālakṣmi |
| 125. Rudrakoti | Rudrāṇi |
| 126. Rāma tirṭha | Ramaṇā |
| 127. Ratnāvāli pīṭha (West Bengal) | |
| 128. Sthāneśvara | Bhavānī |

| | |
|---|---|
| 129. Śrīśaila | Mādhavī |
| 130. Śālagrāma | Mahādevī |
| 131. Śivaliṅga | Jalapriyā |
| 132. Śantana | Lalitā |
| 133. Sahasrākṣa | Utpalākṣi |
| 134. Supārśva | Narāyaṇī |
| 135. Śiva Kuṇḍa | Śivanandō, Sunandā |
| 136. Sahyādri (Western Ghat) | Ekavirā |
| 137. Someśvara | Varāroha |
| 138. Sarasvatī | Devamātā |
| 139. Shore of the Sea | Mātā or Parā |
| 140. Śoṇa Saṅgama or Sindhu Saṅgama | Subhadrā |
| 141. Siddhapura | Mātā Lakṣmi or Umā Lakṣmi |
| 142. Śaṅkhoddhāra | Dhārā |
| 143. Śiva | Pārvatī |
| 144. Śākambhari | |
| 145. Śitalā Tirṭha | |
| 146. Śrī Parvath pīṭha (?) | |
| 147. The Himālayas | Nandā |
| 148. Trikūṭa | Bhadra Sundarī or Rudra Sundarī |
| 149. The bank of the Devīka | Nandinī |
| 150. The Vindhyas | Vindhyeśvarī |
| 151. The Yamunā | Mṛgāvatī |
| 152. The Vindhyan Cave | Amṛtā |
| 153. The Bena | Amṛtā |
| 154. Tristrola pīṭha (West Bengal) | |
| 155. Tripurā pīṭha (Tripurā) | |
| 156. Utpalavartaka | Lolā |
| 157. Uttarakuru | Oṣadhi |
| 158. Umāvana | |
| 159. Umā Kuṇḍa in the Lohāryala region | |
| 160. Ujjaini pīṭha (Madhya Pradesh) | |
| 161. Uṣṇatirṭha | Abhayā |
| 162. Vārāṇasi | Visālākṣi |
| 163. Viśveśvara | Viśvā or Vilvā |
| 164. Vilvaka | Vilvapatrikā |
| 165. Varāha Śaila | Jayā |

| | |
|---|---|
| 166. Vipāśa | Amoghākṣi |
| 167. Vipula | Vipulā |
| 168. Vināyaka | Umā or Rūpā |
| 169. Vaidyanātha | Arogā |
| 170. Viśveśvara | Tuṣṭi |
| 171. Viśravana | Nidhi |
| 172. Vṛndāvana | Rādhā |
| 173. Varānasi pīṭha (Uttar Pradesh) | |
| 174. Vīrajā pīṭha (Jajpur in Orissa) | Vīrajā |
| 175. Vaktreśvara pīṭha (West Bengal) | |
| 176. Vibhāsh pīṭha (Midnapur in West Bengal) | |
| 177. Yugadhā pīṭha (West Bengal) | |

Sacred places of Devī (Śākti) in Mountains, Rivers, Lakes, Regions and Cities are also included in the list of the Pīṭhas thus:-

1. MOUNTAINS—The Himālayas, Hemakūṭa, Vindhyācala, Mahendra, Mahāsena, Citrakūṭa, Gopagiri and Veda Parvata.
2. RIVERS—Banks of the Ocean, Gaṅgā Sāgar, Saṁgama, banks of the rivers Gaṅges, Sarasvatī, Godāvarī, Kauśika, Triveni, Brāhmanāda, Yamunā, Mahāṇadi, Narmadā, Gaṇḍaki, Gomati, Candrabhāgā, Vetravati, Tāpti, etc.
3. LAKES—Mānasa, Bindusāra and Acchoda.
4. REGIONS—Puṣkara, Kurukṣetra, Dharmāraṇya Prayāga and Arbudāraṇya.
5. CITIES—Ayodhyā, Kāshi, Ujjayini, Hardwāra, Dvārkā, Mathurā, Śrīnagara, Kāncipuram, Kāmarūpa, Jālandhara etc.

Śākti Goddess is worshipped in various forms at every human settlements in India, with great devotion and this shows the popularity of Śākti Cult.

# Glossary

| | |
|---|---|
| Acāras | Classes. |
| Avaya | Absence of fear. |
| Āliḍha attitude | An attitude of an arch shooting with the right knee extended and the left leg retraced. |
| Bhāvas | Attitudes. |
| Bindu | Knowing, wise (Apte), bestowing, ununificent, liberal, circular mark, a point, that has no magnitude but has only position, semen. |
| Bhava | Natural disposition. |
| Chhatra | Umbrella. |
| Guna | Quality, virtue, inherent quality of a sentiment. |
| Garbhagriha | Main temple where God resides. |
| Gandi | Human body portion. |
| Jāngha | Human thigh. |
| Kāli | Goddess Chaṇḍi or Kālikā. |
| Kali | The 4th age of the World, according to the Hindu mythology, the present age of vice. |
| Khetra | Site. |
| Kula | Family or lineage. |
| Karman | An act, work, action, deed, function, fate, luck, fortune, duty, worldly duties and affairs, religious performance or observance, religious rite, one's own action. |
| Khatvāñga | Dagger. |
| Lotus | Lotus like female organ. |
| Mokṣa | Liberation. |

| | |
|---|---|
| Manṭras | A sacred mystic text, mystic syllable in the Vedic worship of different Deities, incantation and mystic formula. |
| Mahābhāva | Great disposition. |
| Mahā | Great. |
| Mastaka | Human head. |
| Marg | Path |
| Oṁkāṛa | The sound of "OM" is also called "Pranava," meaning that it is something that pervades life, or runs through prana (life) or breath. |
| Puruṣha | Cosmic body. |
| Paśu | Animal. |
| Pañca | Five. |
| Raja | The principal of Prakṛit (nature) which leads to activity and desires. |
| Rishi | Adorned holy individual who has broken the bondage of materialistic World. |
| Ratibandha | Sex pose. |
| Śākti | Power, ability, primal energy, strength, the prime energy of matter from which the World was created, the nature, potency, the female aspect of the Cosmos. |
| Shāstras | Books of revelations, scriptures, sacred lore, books of Divine authority. |
| Siddha | Accomplished in mystic formulae, success inYoga or penance. |
| Sādhanā | Accomplishment, attainment or fruition. |
| Saibites | Attaining priests. |
| Satwa | The principle of goodness in Prakrit (nature) which tends towards attainment of virtue. |
| Triśūla | Trident. |
| Tama | The principle of dullness which |

| | |
|---|---|
| | induces indolence, sleep etc. |
| Vajra | Liṅga (male penis). |
| Vara | Wished for blessing, boon, blessing or promise for the fulfilment of one's wishes. |
| Yogi | Individual who does Yoga. |
| Yoga | State of union between two opposite poles, viz.: Śiva and Śākti, body and mind, individual and universal awareness, process of uniting, opposing forces in the body and mind in order to realize the Spiritual essence of Being and existence. |
| Yantra | Symbolic diagram utilised in Tantra, geometrical symbol representing specific conformations of forces of Śākti and Consciousness. A process of concentration upon specific forms employed in Tantra to liberate potential energy and consciousness within an individual. |

# Bibliography

1. Agrawala, V.S. *Śiva Mahādeva the Great God*, Prithivi Prakashan, Varanasi, 1984.
2. Aryan, K.C. *The Little Goddesses (Mātrikās)*, Rekha Prakashan, New Delhi, 1980.
3. *Art Traditions of Orissa*, Orissa Sahitya Akademi, Bhubaneswar, 1983.
4. Bandyopadhyay, Pranab - *The Goddess of Tantra*, Punthi Pustak, Calcutta, 1987.
5. Bhattacharyya, N.N. *History of the Tāntric Religion*, Manohar Publications, New Delhi, 1982.
6. Behera, S.C. *Rise and Fall of the Śailodbhāvas*, Punthi Pustak, Calcutta, 1982.
7. Biswal, Bansidhar - *Cult of Śiva*, Punthi Pustak, Calcutta, 1988.
8. Boulton, J.V. *Phakirmohana Senapati and His Times*, Orissa Sahitya Akademi, Bhubaneswar, 1976.
9. Bhattacharyya, H.D. "Tāntric Religion," *The History and Culture of the Indian People*, Vol. IV, *The Age of Imperial Kanauj*, ed. Majumdar, R.C. Bharatiya Vidya Bhavan, Bombay, 1964.
10. Bag, A.K. "The Knowledge of Geometrical Figures, Instruments and Units in the Sulbasūtras, "*East and West*, XXI, (?), 1971.
11. Bose, D.M., Sen, S.N. Subbrayappa, S.V. (eds.), *A. Concise History of Science in India*, New Delhi, (?), 1971.
12. Bose, N.K. *Indian Temple Designs*, Private Publication, Calcutta, 1981.
13. *Bilaspur District Gazetteer*, Bhopal, Madhya Pradesh, 1978.
14. Chanda, R.P. *Memoirs of Archaeological Survey of India*, No. 44.
15. Cairns, Grace E. *Man as Microcosm in Tāntric Hinduism*, Manohar Publications, New Delhi, 1992.
16. Chela Buddhananda - *Moola Bandha the Master Key*, Bihar School of Yoga, Munger, 1984.

17. Chowdhri, L.R. *Practicals of Yantras*, Sagar Publications, New Delhi, 1984.
18. Cunningham's *Archaeological Survey of India*, Vol. XIII.
19. Das, M.N. (ed.), *Sidelights on History and Culture of Orissa*, Vidyapuri, Cuttack, 1977.
20. Deo, Prafulla Chandra Bhanja - *The Mysticism of the Tantras*, Unpublished Manuscript, now in private possession of the author.
21. De, S.K. *Ancient Indian Erotics and Erotic Literature*, Firma K.L. Mukhopadhayay, Calcutta, 1969.
22. Das, H.C. "Brahmaṇical Tāntric Art of Orissa," *The Orissa Historical Research Journal*, Vol. XXIX, No. 1.
23. Das, H.C. *Cultural Development in Orissa*, Punthi Pustak, Calcutta, 1985.
24. Das, H.C. *TĀNTRICISM: A Study of the Yogini Cult*, Sterling Publishers, New Delhi, 1981.
25. Das, H.C. "Religious History of Balasore," *The Orissa Historical Research Journal*, Vol. XXVIII, Nos. 1 and 2.
26. Dash, M.P. "Worship of Sapta Mātṛkās and their representation in Orissan Temples," *The Orissa Historical Research Journal*, Vol. XI, No. 2.
27. Dash, M.P. (Compiler), *A Descriptive Catalogue of Sanskrit Manuscripts of Orissa*, Vol. V, *(Tantra Manuscripts)*, Orissa State Museum, Bhubaneswar, 1965.
28. *Descriptive Catalogue of Sanskrit Manuscripts of Orissa*. Vol. II, Orissa Sahitya Akademi, 1960.
29. Das, D.R. "Ratnagiri School : Its Origin," *Journal of the Oriental Institute*, Vol. XXVI, No. 4, June 1977. (Calcutta).
30. Das, Anirudha - "The Mādalā pāñji," *The Orissa Historical Research Journal*,Vol. XIV, Nos. 3 and 4.
31. Das, Chittaranjan - *A Glimpse into Oriya Literature*, Orissa Sahitya Akademi, Bhubaneswar, 1982.
32. Dhatta, B. *The Science of Śulba*, Calcutta, 1932.
33. Desai, Devangana - *Erotic Sculpture of India*, Tata McGraw - Hill Publishing Co., New Delhi, 1975.
34. Dutt, M.N. *A prose English Translation of MAHANIRVANA TĀNTRAM*, Chowkhamba Sanskrit Series Office, Varanasi, 1979.
35. Dei, Santilata - *Vaiṣṇavism in Orissa*, Punthi Pustak, Calcutta, 1988.
36. Fergusson, J. *History of Indian and Eastern Architecture*, second edition, revised by J. Burgoss and R.P. Spiers, London, 1910.

37. Fabri, C.L. *History of the Art of Orissa*, Orient Longman Ltd., New Delhi, 1974.
38. *Hāṭha yoga Pradipikā - Light on Hāṭha Yoga*, commentary by Swami Muktibodhānanda Saraswati under the guidence of Swami Satyananda Saraswati Paramahansa, Bihar School of Yoga, Munger, Bihar, 1993.
39. *Inscriptions of Orissa*, Vol. II, Bhubaneswar.
40. *Inscriptions of Orissa*, Vol. III, Part-I, Bhubaneswar.
41. *Inscriptions of Orissa*, Vol. VI, Bhubaneswar.
42. *Journal of the Royal Asiatic Society of Bengal, Letters*, Vol. XIV, No. 1, 1948 and Vol. VIII.
43. Joshi, Arjun - *History and Culture of Khijjingakotta*, Vikas Publishing House, New Delhi, 1983.
44. Joshi, Lalmani - *Studies in the Buddhistic Culture of India*, Motilal Banarsidass, Delhi, 1987.
45. Kumar, Pushpendra - *Śakti Cult in Ancient India*. Bharatiya Publishing House, Varanasi, 1974.
46. Kulkarni, S.D. (ed.) - *Bhishma's Study of Indian History and Culture*, Vol. IV, *Glorious Epoch*, 1993 introduction and Vol. XI, *Adi Śaṅkaracārya - The Saviour of Mankind*, 1987, Shri Bhagvan Vedavyasa Itihas Samshodhana Mandira, Bombay, (Thane).
47. Lal, Kanwar - *SEX AND SALVATION (A Study of Koṇārk's Erotic Sculpture)*, Kayenkay Agencies, Delhi, 1971.
48. Mishra, R.P. *SAHAJAYĀNA - A Study of Tāntric Buddhism*. Punthi Pustak, Calcutta, 1991.
49. Mishra, R.P. "Humanism in Ancient Culture of Titilagarh," *SRISTI - SOUVENIR (Silver Jubilee Special issue)*. D.A.V. College, Titilagarh, 1993.
50. Mishra R.P. *ADVAYASIDDHI : The Tāntric view of Lakṣmīṅkarā*, Kant Publications, Delhi, 1995.
51. Mishra, R.P. *Fragments of Indian Culture*, Punthi Pustak, Calcutta, 1995.
52. Mahātab, H.K. "Culture of Orissa," and othe research papers, *THE ORISSA HISTORICAL RESEARCH JOURNAL (Golden Jubilee Volume)*, Vol. XXX, Nos. 2, 3 and 4, 1984.
53. Majumdar, R.C. "Kāpāla and Kālāmukha Sects," *The History and Culture of the Indian People*, Vol. V, *The Struggle for Empire*, Bharatiya Vidya Bhavan, Bombay, 1966.
54. Mirashi, V.V. *Corpus Inscriptionum Indicarum*, Vol. IV, Part-I,

Archaeological Survey of India, New Delhi, 1955.

55. Madhava - Vidyaranya, *Sankara - Digvijaya (The Traditional Life of Śrī Śaṅkaracharya)*, Śrī Rāmakrishna Math, Madras, (?), (Translated by Swami Tapasyananda).
56. Mukherjee, Prabhat - "The Missing Bhairava Image of the Jagannāth Temple," *ORISSA REVIEW*, Public Relation Department, Government of Orissa, Bhubaneswar, July, 1970, Vol. XXXVI, No. 12.
57. *MĀDALĀPĀÑJI*, ed. A.B. Mohanty, Utkal University, Bhubaneswar, 1969.
58. Majumdar, R.C. (ed.) - *The History and Culture of the Indian People*, Vol. II, *The Age of Imperial Unity*, Bharatiya Vidya Bhavan, Bombay, 1968.
59. Nema, S.R. *Political History of the Somavaṁśī Kings of South Kōśala and Orissa*, Oriental Publishers, New Delhi, 1978.
60. Panigrahi, K.C. *Archaeological Remains at Bhubaneswar*, Orient Longman, New Delhi, 1961.
61. Panigrahi, K.C. *History of Orissa*, Kitab Mahal, Cuttack, 1981.
62. Patel, C.B. *Dynastic History of Nalas*, Punthi Pustak, Calcutta, 1990.
63. Panda, Lakshman Kumar - *Śaivism in Orissa*, Sundeep Prakashan, Delhi, 1985.
64. Pradhan, B.C. "Śākta Kṣetra Puruṣottama," *The Journal of Orissan History*, Vol. IX, June 1989, The Orissa History Congress.
65. Prabhat Mukherjee, *The Buddhist Remains of Orissa*, Public Relation Department, Government of Orissa, (?), Bhubaneswar.
66. Rao, S.K. Ramachandra, *THE YANTRAS*, Śrī Satguru Publications, Delhi, 1988.
67. Rajaguru, S.N. *INSCRIPTIONS OF ORISSA*, Vol. IV, Bhubaneswar, 1966.
68. Raghavan, Smt. Kausalyarani - *Guide to Indian Culture and Spirituality*, 4th edition, United Printer Syndicate, Madras, 1987.
69. Ray, P.K. (ed.), *ARCHAEOLOGICAL SURVEY REPORT (1974-75)-PRACHI VALLEY*, Orissa State Archaeology, Bhubaneswar, 1975.
70. Svobada, Robert E. *AGHORA - At the left hand of God*, Rupa & Co. New Delhi, 1993.
71. Satpathy, Sarbeswar - *ŚĀKTI ICONOGRAPHY IN TĀNTRIC MAHAVIDYAS*, Punthi Pustak, Calcutta, 1991.
72. Staal, J.F. *AGNI: The Vedic Ritual of the Fire Altar*, 2 Vols., Berkeley, The Asian Humanities Press, U.S.A. 1983.

73. Saraswati, Swami Muktānanda - *NAWA YOGINI TANTRA*, Bihar School of Yoga, Munger, Bihar, 1983.
74. Swami Chinmayānanda - *VEDANTA THE SCIENCE OF LIFE*, Parts I, II and III, Central Chinmaya Mission Trust, Bombay, (?).
75. Sahu, N.K. *BUDDHISM IN ORISSA*, Utkal University, Bhubaneswar, 1958.
76. Subuddhi, U. *THE BHAUMA - KARAS OF ORISSA*, Punthi Pustak, Calcutta, 1978.
77. Sahu, N.K., Mishra, P.K., Sahu, J.K. *History of Orissa*, Nalanda, Cuttack, 1980.
78. Singh Deo, J.P. *CULTURAL PROFILE OF SOUTH KŌŚALA*, Gyan Publishing House, New Delhi, 1987.
79. Singh Deo, J.P. *ORIGIN OF JAGANNĀTH DEITY*, Gyan Publishing House, New Delhi, 1991.
80. Singh Deo, J.P. "Socio-Culture History of Orissa - A Case Study of Khariar Estate", *GLIMPSES OF ORISSA*, ed. Das, B.S. Punthi Pustak, Calcutta, 1986.
81. Sircar, Dines Chandra - "The Śākta Pīṭhas," *Journal of the Royal Asiatic Society of Bengal, Letters*, Vol. XIV, No. 1, 1948.
82. Schoterman, J.A. *THE YONI TANTRA*, Manohar Publications, New Delhi, 1977.
83. Tripathi, R. *HISTORY OF ANCIENT INDIA*, Motilal Banarsidass, Delhi, 1977.
84. *THE BṚHADĀRAṆYAKA UPANIṢAD*, Śrī Rāmakrishna Math Mylapore, Madras, 1968.
85. *The Orissa Historical Research Journal*, Vol. I, No.2, and Vol. II, No.2.
86. Upadhyaya, R.K. *THE CONCEPT OF GOD IN ŚAIVA TANTRA*, Jñananidhi Prakashan, Muzaffarpur, 1984.
87. V.V. Mirashi Felicitation Volume.
88. Woodroffe, Sir John - *ŚĀKTI AND ŚĀKTA*, Ganesh & Company, Madras, 1975.
89. Woodroffe, Sir John - *TANTRARĀJA TANTRA - A Short Analysis*, Ganesh & Company, Madras, 1971.
90. Williams, J.C. (ed.) *KALĀDARŚANA*, American Studies in the Art of India, Oxford & I.B.H. Publishing Co. New Delhi, 1981.

# Index